Shakespeare and Gesture in Practice

Shakespeare in Practice

Series Editors:

Stuart Hampton-Reeves, Professor of Research-informed Teaching, University of Central Lancashire, UK, and Head of the British Shakespeare Association

Bridget Escolme, Reader in Drama and Head of the School of English and Drama, Queen Mary, University of London, UK

Published:

Shakespeare and Audience in Practice
Stephen Purcell

Shakespeare and Political Theatre in Practice
Andrew Hartley

Shakespeare and Gender in Practice
Terri Power

Shakespeare and Gesture in Practice
Darren Tunstall

Forthcoming:

Shakespeare and Original Practices
Don Weingust

Shakespeare and Space in Practice
Kathryn Prince

Shakespeare and Costume in Practice
Bridget Escolme

Shakespeare and Directing in Practice
Kevin Ewert

Shakespeare and Diaspora in Practice
Alexander Huang

Shakespeare and Reviewing Performance in Practice
Paul Prescott

Shakespeare and Digital Performance in Practice
Erin Sullivan

Shakespeare and Gesture in Practice

Darren Tunstall

 palgrave

First published 2016 by
PALGRAVE

Palgrave in the UK is an imprint of Macmillan Publishers Limited, registered in England, company number 785998, of 4 Crinan Street, London, N1 9XW.

Palgrave Macmillan in the US is a division of St Martin's Press LLC, 175 Fifth Avenue, New York, NY 10010.

Palgrave is a global imprint of the above companies and is represented throughout the world.

Palgrave® and Macmillan® are registered trademarks in the United States, the United Kingdom, Europe and other countries.

ISBN 978-0-230-27641-3 hardback
ISBN 978-0-230-27642-0   ISBN 978-1-349-92988-7 (eBook)
DOI 10.1007/978-1-349-92988-7

A catalogue record for this book is available from the British Library.

A catalog record for this book is available from the Library of Congress.

Contents

Acknowledgements

My warm gratitude goes to the series editors Professor Stuart Hampton-Reeves and Dr Bridget Escolme; their friendship, their efforts, their good sense and their encouragement have been invaluable. Thanks also to the superbly professional teams at Palgrave and Integra Software Services, Pondicherry.

I am especially grateful to Professor David McNeill and to Siân Williams for granting me interviews. This book is greatly enriched by their involvement.

Too many people to mention have contributed in different ways to the writing of the book. In particular I'd like to thank my colleagues at GSA and the University of Surrey, and former colleagues at the University of Central Lancashire; all of the enthusiastic and talented students of Shakespeare and of acting that I have been privileged to teach; Dr Matthew Wagner, Dr Christian Billing, Dr Stephen Purcell, Dr Jami Rogers, Professor John Joughin and Professor Peter Holland. My thanks go to all those friends and colleagues in the theatre profession who have shown such wit, warmth and wisdom over the years. I must also acknowledge my debt to the late Professor John Russell Brown, whose guidance was inspirational, and two extraordinary men who taught me about acting, the late Nat Brenner and the late Rudi Shelley of the Bristol Old Vic Theatre School.

I would like to thank Dr Paul Hartle, my undergraduate tutor at St Catharine's College, Cambridge; I have never forgotten his words of encouragement. Heartfelt thanks also to Jennifer Tindall and David Prosser, both selfless teachers who befriended me in my salad days. And, lastly, boundless gratitude is due to my sisters Michelle and Karen.

I am proud to dedicate this book to my wife Michelle and to my son William, who was born in Warwick while I was working for the Royal Shakespeare Company.

Series Editors' Preface

The books in the *Shakespeare in Practice* series chart new directions for a performance approach to Shakespeare. They represent the diverse and exciting work being undertaken by a new generation of Shakespeareans who have either come to the field from theatre practice or have developed a career that combines academic work with performing, directing or dramaturgy. Many of these authors are based in Drama departments and use practical workshops for both teaching and research. They are conversant with the fields of English Literature and Performance Studies, and they move freely between them. This series gives them an opportunity to explore both fields and to give a greater prominence to some of the key questions that occupy performance studies in the study of Shakespeare.

We intend this series to shape the way in which Shakespeare in performance is taught and researched. Our authors approach performance as a creative practice and a work of art in its own right. We want to create a new curriculum for Shakespeare in performance, which embraces the full complexity of the art of theatre and is underpinned by performance theory.

The first part of each book explores the theoretical issues at stake, often drawing on key works in performance studies as well as seminal writings by theatre practitioners. The second part of the book consists of a series of critical studies of performance in practice, drawing on theatre history but chiefly focusing on contemporary productions and practitioners. Finally, we have asked all of our authors to engage in a debate with another scholar or practitioner so that each book ends with an engaging and unresolved debate.

All of our books draw on a wide range of plays so that teachers can choose which plays they want to focus on. There will be no volume on *Hamlet, A Midsummer Night's Dream or Romeo and Juliet* – every volume can be used as a model for every play in the canon. Similarly, none of the books exhaust the research possibilities that they open: there is more, much more, work to be done on every topic in this series.

Studies of Shakespeare in performance often leave aside the audience. Either the critic's own response is used to voice the audience, or the audience is effaced altogether. Questions about the role of the audience in constructing the theatrical event are often posed, but rarely answered, at conferences and seminars. Leaving the audience out of theatrical analysis is problematic, but including them is, if anything, even more problematic. How does one give voice to an audience? Is an audience exterior to the performance, or is it part of it – in which case, it is possible to 'read' the audience in a critical way? What research tools do we need to conduct such work? Or is the audience an illusion? Stephen Purcell addresses how notions of audience, audience configuration, audience expectation and audiences as they figure in play texts all produce meaning in the theatre. His work is the ideal book with which to begin this series.

The development of political theatre in the twentieth century has had a profound influence on the performance of Shakespeare's work. In a sense, Shakespeare's theatre has always been a political one which is keenly aware of its context. His earliest plays vividly dramatize the power games at the heart of England's bloody civil wars in the fifteenth century, and throughout his career, Shakespeare returned again and again to critical questions of authority, identity and transgression. This is one of the reasons why Bertolt Brecht studied the Elizabethan theatre, among other forms, when developing the "alienation" effect for his own highly politicized theatre. One of the consequences of Brecht's work, together with many other innovators from the last century, is that we can no longer approach Shakespeare performance in a neutral way. Andrew James Hartley's study is an important contribution to the series which demonstrates the potency (and the danger) of politicizing Shakespeare in performance.

The performance of gender in Shakespeare's plays has been a richly studied topic in Theatre studies, English literary studies and Early Modern scholarship. However, despite Shakespeare's diverse narrative profile of multiculturalism and his inclusive 'humanist' appeal, when it comes to gender in casting and playing, Shakespeare production often follows familiar, normative patterns. Terri Power's study of Shakespeare and gender challenges 'traditional' notions of casting and character through an intersectional feminist study of current Shakespeare in practice. The book explores questions of gender construction and performance arising from all-male 'original practices' productions of Shakespeare and all-female versions; challenges the stigma still attached to transvestism and cross-gender performance; offers new perspectives on how early modern attitudes to gender are dealt with in contemporary production; and considers broader issues around the terminologies, documentation and resources that might enable artists and scholars to archive and develop new challenges for Shakespeare audiences in the performance of gender.

How does the actor's body make meaning in collaboration with Shakespeare? It is perhaps easy to assume that there is a paucity of evidence about the kinds of gestures actors might have used in Shakespeare's theatre – and to assume that what actors do now might be comparably less 'formal', more 'natural'. Darren Tunstall's book offers the reader a history of gesture in rhetoric and performance: a history that sheds new light on what the acting of Shakespeare's plays might have looked at in the past. Through accounts of recent performance and interviews with practitioners, the book then explores how actors both find and use gestural language in Shakespeare performance today. The book historicizes Shakespeare's gestural languages and explores the ways in which theatre practices have imposed their own gestural languages upon them. Thus the reader is prepared for an exciting new approach to contemporary theatre's approaches to Shakespeare, asking how we make meaning from Shakespeare through the body.

Stuart Hampton-Reeves
Bridget Escolme

Introduction

What this book is about

Gesture is a kind of speaking with the body. The body makes pictures, and these pictures seem to speak. What the pictures say, though, is not always quite what they show. For example, if I want to sew a button on a shirt, I will put my hand into a particular shape to hold the needle. If I make the same hand shape while talking to you, I will create an idea about myself that I hope will be planted in your mind. Exactly what idea, though, would depend on the way in which I perform the gesture – in other words, upon my behavioural style. It may be that I try to create the idea that I have a precise grasp of the subject under discussion; in this case, my intention may be to show you that I am a precise, i.e. conscientious, competent person. Or perhaps the gesture says that in my opinion things are OK between us, so by performing it I may be trying to show you that my intentions towards you are warm – that I am a sociable, agreeable kind of person. In this book, then, I am less interested in how gesture adds information to a person's speech – which is a common belief about gesture – and more in how gesture may be used to create an idea about the speaker in another person's mind.

This transformation of an action into a gesture is a metaphoric procedure. In my example, the physical act of holding a needle between the index finger and the thumb is translated into an idea that exists only in the imagination – in this case, a belief about competence or warmth. The idea is communicated via a metaphor that makes use of our sensory knowledge of the real object (in this case, a needle), including how it can be used; in this way sensory metaphor helps to get the idea out of one person's head into the head of another. Poets like Shakespeare have always understood that metaphors emerging from sensory experience are sticky: that is, they are memorable. One of my beliefs about gesture is that, as a tool for sharing thought and feeling, it aspires to that same social stickiness by appealing to shared physical experience. The sense that cognition is embodied underpins the philosopher Henri Lefebvre's contention that metaphor and metonymy 'are not figures of speech – at least not at the outset. They *become* figures of speech. In principle, they are acts' (Lefebvre 1991: 139). Metaphor is, as Lefebvre claims, a

1

process whose 'point of departure' is 'the body metamorphosed' (ibid.). Recent evidence from cognitive psychology has helped advance this insight regarding embodied cognition – the view that, at a basic level, our thought processes make use of metaphors arising from bodily experience (see Gibbs 2005). To put it simply: *we think with our bodies*.

This book is about how actors think Shakespeare with their bodies. More broadly, it is about how gesture offers a metaphoric window into thought and feeling, and thus into personality. There is nothing particularly new about this notion as far as contemporary scholarship is concerned. What is perhaps new is that I connect the premise that gestures are embodiments of cognitive acts with *morality*. I consider cognition not as an individual act but as a social one, subject to shared understandings about what is right and wrong. I believe that shared moral understandings expressed in gesture do not originate in some abstract symbolic realm: they emerge from bodily perceptions and experiences. Thus, to reflect upon gesture in Shakespearean practice is to engage with the way that people form moral judgements. This deployment of gesture in the service of moral beliefs is also part of how a person tries to create an impression of her- or himself in the mind of another.

The book also tries to answer the question of *how* a performance achieves its effect – as opposed to *what* it might mean, or *why* it is the way it is. By narrowing the focus down to gesture in Shakespearean performance, I hope to engage with a relatively unexplored subject, as well as offer a range of case studies and examples. Inevitably, the discussion will at times venture out of the immediate zone of gesture into related fields involving the body, psychology and cultural history. That said, the subject is vast and the book cannot be an exhaustive study.

Formal versus naturalistic Shakespeare

Gesture is a difficult area for scholarship to deal with, since it would seem to require for evidence what has either already vanished into the past, or what is always fleeting and intangible – that is to say, acts of non-verbal communication. The lack of a complete and reliable visual archive of gesture (certainly before the year 1700) could be seen as the Achilles heel of the enterprise. It necessitates a degree of speculation that may seem to contradict the motive for writing. At the same time, if we fail to take account of gesture, we are in danger of missing a crucial ingredient in Shakespeare's practice. And if we fail to account for the gestures we see in our own encounters with Shakespearean performance, we may as well close our eyes.

To begin, I would like to give a flavour of some of the issues that arise from looking into the current state of scholarship. Discussion of gesture in Shakespearean performance has often been annexed to the debate on *formal* versus *naturalistic* acting. This debate has been around since at least Alfred Harbage's essay on 'Elizabethan Acting' in 1939. In support of him were Waldo McNeir (1941), Robert H. Bowers (1948), A.G.H. Bachrach (1949) and Bertram Joseph (1960). The reaction against their formalistic approach was spearheaded by John Russell Brown (1953), and gained support from Marvin Rosenberg (1954).

Since then, a middle ground has been articulated by Peter Thomson (1992) and John Astington (2010) among others. Bernard Beckerman summarized the debate: 'The formalists describe the means at the actor's disposal, the techniques of voice and gesture; the naturalists, the effect at which he aimed, the imitation of life' (Beckerman 1962: 111). This would seem to place someone like myself, who is concerned with the *how* of gesture in performance, in the camp of the formalists – except that I consider the distinction between means and effect to be false, as did many Elizabethans, who were fond of remarking that eloquence and wisdom were the same thing (Enterline 2012: 3).

David Bevington, in his book *Action is Eloquence* (1984), approached the subject by noting actions assumed to be called for in the playtext: kissing, kneeling, handshaking and so on. Bevington gives an edge to what would otherwise seem self-evident by arguing these actions have a contradictory aspect. While they appear to be displays of Shakespeare's commitment to Tudor hierarchy, in performance some gestures take on subversive resonances in instances of what he calls 'violated ceremony' – as when Cordelia spoils the ritual set up by her father in the second scene of *King Lear*. The notion that a gesture can have contradictory aspects in performance is interesting, and I will elaborate upon a related point in my exploration of competing social moralities in Elizabethan culture below.

There have been no book-length studies of Shakespearean gesture apart from Bevington's (at the time of writing Farah Karim-Cooper's *The Hand on the Shakespearean Stage* is in press). Existing articles range from those of Steven Urkowitz (1986), who deploys gesture to support a theory about Shakespeare's authorship of 'bad' quartos, to Harold Frisch's 1987 attempt to classify functions of gesture (he doesn't make use of existing classifications from gesture studies). In a book on staging (2000), Andrew Gurr and Mariko Ichikawa discuss the meanings of clutching one's head with both hands, a gesture they think Hamlet makes when he says 'Remember thee? Ay, thou poor ghost, while memory holds a seat/In this distracted globe' (1.5.95–7). This is encouraging material to read, but it doesn't lead the authors into the subject any further. Finally, Ros King's article on 'Sound and Gesture in *The Winter's Tale*' (2007) contains much I find myself in sympathy with. Yet having promised in her title that she will consider the subject of gesture she leaves it alone, focusing instead on sound patterns in the text. She suggests that the actor playing Hermione would indicate pregnancy in the character's opening scene 'perhaps by the physical stance' (ibid.: 395). Two references to a posture as opposed to a gesture, plus a mention of Leontes wiping his son's dirty nose – King's article is representative of a general reluctance to tackle the specifics of the subject.

There are two main reasons for this. One is, as I hinted above, the paucity of visual evidence, especially where one would most want to find it – in Shakespeare's own context. But that is not to say that there is no evidence at all. There is some visual material, such as paintings and woodcuts, as well as some written description, and some thoughts can be extrapolated from this material. After the revolution in mass publishing around 1700 the situation improves considerably. And of course with the arrival of cinema in the late nineteenth century, things really begin to look up. Best of all, modern video technologies have made it possible to access recordings of live performances that can be paused, replayed and analysed for the study of gesture. So, while it is necessary to recognize gaps in the evidence, that is no reason to stay silent on the subject. The other issue is that acting technique as such is not an area of expertise for many Shakespeare scholars. They are sometimes more comfortable with textual analysis than with talking about how actors use their bodies. However, this is changing, in part due to the efforts of a new generation of academics who are able to draw upon practical experience of theatre-making.

Contemporary approaches

Some recent approaches have made use of paradigms and concepts from *cognitive semantics*. A basic premise of this work is the continuity principle: the idea that human behaviour, since it is founded upon biology, must be continuous with the behaviour of those higher-order mammals from which humans evolved. As Bruce McConachie has argued, the distinctions that we make between our thoughts, feelings and actions and those of, say, chimpanzees (with whom we share at least 97 per cent of our DNA) are not ontological. They are not differences of *kind*; they are differences of *degree*. For writers like McConachie, performance is a pattern of behaviour that evolved from animal play. As well, the continuity hypothesis insists that even the most abstract cognitive reasoning processes are grounded in biology (see McConachie and Hart 2006 for a representative anthology).

A lot of recent work attempting to find synergies between cognitive science and performance has fastened upon the theory that there may exist *mirror neurons* in an area of the human brain called Broca's Area. This area is implicated in both speech and hand gestures. The theory holds that these neurons activate not only when the individual carries out an action but when the individual observes another carrying out an action. This discovery has been used to support a conception of 'simulation' as the basis for empathy – motor mimicry, it seems, affords you the capacity to read the intentions of another person. It is a seductive theory, but it must be treated with caution. These neurons were originally found in macaques, not a species known for imitative behaviour; to extrapolate their functions to the brains of higher-order primates is something of a leap in the dark. In addition, you may observe me performing an action, and your mirror system may fire up in response – but that does not mean you *feel* what I feel. Mirror neurons (if they exist in humans) may play a role in the perception of a person's actions and intentions in relation to a physical object, but empathy is rather more than action perception. At least as important is the effect upon social behaviour of hormones such as oxytocin, which is strongly associated with feelings of warmth and trust (see Churchland 2011). Mirror neuron theory cannot as yet account for human interaction in all its complexity. That said, the theory has influenced the work of scholars like Evelyn Tribble (2011) and Amy Cook, who treat gestures as evidence for embodied cognition in Shakespearean text and performance. In *Shakespearean Neuroplay* (2010) Cook introduces some concepts drawn from gesture studies (in particular, from the seminal work of psycholinguist David McNeill) but, coming then to *Hamlet*, she fails to find a way to deploy them, reverting instead to a more conventional literary criticism of the text that avoids talking directly about bodies. That said, and while there have been voices urging caution regarding some of the larger claims of neuroscience with respect to performance, this is nevertheless an exciting field of research which is already building promising bridges between 'the two cultures' of the humanities and sciences. At its heart is a strong call for the centrality of embodiment to all cognitive acts, and this book is in part a reply to that call. In these pages I try to expand the field of debate by connecting performance practice to paradigms of social morality that have both a foundation in embodied cognition and specific historical manifestations.

The thesis of the book: gesture, cognition and morality

A central thesis of this book is that gesture offers a window not only into the mind of the actor but also into the wider socio-moral background in which the actor operates; in fact I do not separate the two. In the book I will refer to something called *social cognition*. This is most simply described, in the words of the neuroscientist Matthew D. Lieberman, as 'thinking about other people, oneself, and the relation of oneself to other people' (Lieberman 2013: 18). Thinking about your relationships to others is not something you choose to do when you feel in the mood (although of course you can); it is what your brain automatically does when it is not doing anything else, because of a 'default network' that turns on like a reflex when your attention is not fixed upon a task. It is 'the brain's preferred state of being, one that it returns to literally the second it has a chance' (ibid.: 21). The default network directs you to consider people not only as physical things in the world but as creatures with minds, feelings, intentions and plans. It is present at birth, before babies can even focus their eyes properly, and thus 'precedes any conscious interest in the social world, suggesting it might be instrumental in creating those interests' (ibid.: 20). Quite simply, whenever you are not doing something specific, your brain immediately engages in social cognition.

Morality is basic to social cognition because it influences the process by which people form impressions of others and build their own reputations. My view is that it is fundamental to behaviour that people try to manage 'how they come across' to others, although much of the time this management happens below the level of immediate awareness: people do not always know they are doing it or why they are doing it. Nonetheless, it is inherent in almost every social context, and this was just as true in Shakespeare's day as it is in ours. As the social historian Keith Thomas says: 'In early modern England, the desire to secure the favourable opinion of other people was a primary determinant of human behaviour' (Thomas 2009: 147). What has changed over time are the specific ways in which people go about securing that favourable opinion. In early modern England, according to Lord Burghley, honour was 'the greatest possession that any man can have' (quoted in ibid.: 148); nowadays, you may well be more concerned about the number of 'likes' you can get for a comment on Facebook. Yet both activities are tied into the same process of what is called *social morality*.

In the words of the legal and political scholar Edward L. Rubin in *Soul, Self and Society: The New Morality and the Modern State* (2015), social morality is 'a body of beliefs by which people organize their lives and form their judgments' (Rubin 2015: 3). Thus, by morality I mean the structure of values and beliefs that lead people to act, and that work to secure a person's social reputation. Morality tells you whether a person you encounter is honest, sincere or trustworthy. Some recent work in social psychology suggests it is the primary driver of social judgement. In this view, when you encounter another person, the first thing you need to know is whether or not that person constitutes a threat to your safety – and, if not, whether instead that person represents an opportunity (see Brambilla and Leach 2014). In the field of social psychology, this aspect of judgement goes under the name of *warmth*; its primary component is a sense of morality defined as a person's basic honesty, sincerity or trustworthiness, while its secondary component is a sense of the person's sociability – their aspect of openness, friendliness or kindness. The next thing you need to know in your encounter is whether the other person is actually capable of carrying out their intention with regard to you. This component is often called *competence*, and signals whether the person's behaviour seems efficient, intelligent, strong or otherwise capable of expressing their power to carry out actions designed to influence you.

Morality is not simply a private matter or even a matter of micro-interactions between individuals. It has a two-way causal relationship to political governance – 'the particular way by which the government controls and manages the behavior of the people who lie within its jurisdiction' (Rubin 2015: 5). The notion that social morality has a dialectical aspect resonates with the central argument of Stephen Greenblatt's seminal work of new historicism *Renaissance Self-Fashioning*: that there was in the early modern period 'an increased self-consciousness about the fashioning of human identity as a manipulable, artful process' (Greenblatt 1980: 1) which led to attempts to control behaviour from the institutions of the state and church as well as from within the individual. This for Greenblatt is linked to 'manners or demeanor, particularly that of the elite … hypocrisy or deception, an adherence to mere outward ceremony; it suggests representation of one's nature or intention in speech and actions' (ibid.: 3). As influential as his work was in its time, Greenblatt's study should be placed within a context stretching back at least to Norbert Elias's monumental 1939 work on *The Civilizing Process*. Behind both works is a key assumption that identity is constituted in large part by acts of repression – whether ideological, as with Greenblatt, or psychological, as with Elias. That assumption is in my view open to debate, but the belief that people are driven to create an idea or impression of their own personality (their 'self') in others, and that this process is subject to environmental and cultural influences, is one I share.

Morality in the sense I am using the word, then, has a large-scale social and cultural dimension. Of course, to be culturally influential, there needs to be embedded in any moral framework some claim to a shared referent. In Elizabethan culture, the large-scale sociocultural dimension of morality was reflected in a well-known metaphor. In the case of Shakespeare's theatre, the basic metaphor that served as a shared referent was made quite explicit to the spectators – in fact it was written on a sign outside the Globe: 'Totus mundus agit histrionem'. Everyone is an actor. It was a commonplace metaphor in his day as it is now. Yet at root it expresses a contradiction. On the one hand, it seems to say that you have a fixed role allotted to you in life. On the other, it suggests that you are not identical with your role, but rather you *perform* it, which means that in principle you could adopt a different role, or switch between roles if you prefer.

Higher purposes and self-fulfilment

The notion that you had a fixed role was very much in keeping with the official morality of Tudor England promulgated by the preachers, philosophers, teachers and writers who allied themselves to their elite patrons. Here is a typical example from a pamphlet entitled *Certain Sermons or Homilies* published in 1547:

> Every degree of people in their vocation, calling, and office hath appointed to them their duty and order. Some are in high degree, some in low; some kings and princes, some inferiors and subjects; priests and laymen, masters and servants, fathers and children, husbands and wives, rich and poor; and every one hath need of other so that in all things is to be lauded and praised the goodly order of God without the which no house, no city, no commonwealth, can continue and endure. (in Joseph 1971: 34)

Here is how the Archbishop of Canterbury expresses it in *Henry V*:

> Therefore doth heaven divide
> The state of man in diverse functions,
> Setting endeavour in continual motion,
> To which is fixed, as an aim or butt,
> Obedience. (*Henry V* 1.2.184–8)

In this moral framework, what mattered was not your pursuit of personal happiness, but rather a *higher purpose*: the salvation of your soul. You achieved salvation by serving God and your monarch. You served God by keeping the Ten Commandments and going to church. You served the monarch by performing your allotted role in life in an appropriate manner. You did not choose your role: God chose it for you; it was your calling, and you served the community by heeding it. Your reputation – called, variously, 'honour', 'credit', 'good name', 'respectability' and, a particular favourite of Shakespeare's, 'honesty' – was held to rest upon your sticking to the calling that God had meant for you. In this way, it was believed, a stable social order would be maintained. If you did not stick to your calling, say by aspiring to better yourself, you could be accused of 'ambition', a word with mostly negative connotations in Tudor England.

Such concerns with honour or reputation were not merely the preserve of the nobility and their apologists, as Keith Thomas states: 'In the early modern period, the aristocracy was unique in managing to pass off its particular ethic as synonymous with honour itself. But every sector of society had its own values; and its members gained reputation by conforming to them' (Thomas 2009: 174). The economy, for one thing, was built almost entirely upon personal trust: there was no proper banking system, trade agreements were not formalized in written contracts, and there was a crisis in the supply of money. Worse still, there was no properly functioning welfare system. Without a good name, you simply could not find the means to live beyond bare subsistence level (ibid.: 176).

Yet, for all the official talk, there was social mobility in Shakespeare's England – as long as you had the income or occupation to avoid manual labour, to keep yourself in the manner of a gentleman, and to pay a fee to the College of Heralds, then you could cross that fundamental dividing line between 'base' and 'gentle'. Shakespeare was himself an example of such mobility. The alternative reading of the metaphor that everyone is an actor, with its suggestion of fluidity of role, can be seen to indicate a new social morality, one that in Shakespeare's lifetime was coming into being and that later came to dominate the Western world. The new social morality insists upon *self-fulfilment* as of paramount importance. Your life is, in this view, a journey full of experiences, not leading towards a higher purpose such as salvation, but more or less meaningful in itself. The new morality is largely conditional upon your seeing yourself as free and equal to all other humans, with as much right to choose how you live as anyone else – provided you do not trample on other people's equivalent rights. And anything that gets in the way of personal fulfilment is increasingly regarded as immoral. Your reputation now is premised upon how successful you are in achieving your individual goals, such as getting a higher-paid or more rewarding job. Of course, people have always wanted a fulfilling life. The matter is how you define what that is, and how you go about getting it, particularly when the opportunities available to you are limited, as they were for almost everyone in early modern England (see Thomas 2009: chapter 1).

One of the reasons for writing this book is to explore how gesture could provide evidence for this historical seismic shift from what Edward Rubin calls the *morality of higher purposes* – the moral framework that dominated English culture in Shakespeare's time – and the new *morality of self-fulfilment* – whose time had not yet fully arrived but whose outline Shakespeare was able to perceive. The situation was (and is) complex, since moral codes do not simply efface each other but tend to co-exist and overlap in time. In addition, the early feudal honour code, understood for centuries as the recognition of the superior worth of high-status people, had not withered away, but was increasingly being reconfigured as 'honesty' and applied to all walks of life. 'In the early modern period,' writes Thomas, 'when social mobility was upsetting traditional hierarchies, the need to assert one's superiority was felt intensely, by the old-established and the parvenu alike' (Thomas 2009: 151). Such complex moral layering would be reflected in the uses of the body. One of the interesting things about gesture is that while its forms – the hand shapes that people use when gesturing – follow recurring patterns through time and across cultures, these forms are then filled with shades of meaning determined by particular contexts. In other words, the metamorphoses of gesture reflect the metamorphoses of social morality.

Structure of the book

In the next chapter, I consider the changing meanings of the word 'gesture' through history, and how they can be seen to reflect changes in social morality, before giving an outline of how contemporary gesture scholars define it.

Chapter 2 looks at the broad context of influences upon Shakespeare, making reference to the rhetorical tradition inherited from classical antiquity and to the Reformation. Out of this I define and elaborate upon a central concept of the book – 'smoothness'. This is essentially a quality of movement that aims to create an impression of self-posses-sion. Movement that displays such a quality has a conspicuously precise feel to it; indeed, its precision is amplified in order to plant an idea about status in the mind of the observer. I move on to outline how gesture theory flowered in the eighteenth century through a reconfiguration of the classical tradition. I then indicate how the practice of gesture was, and still is, influenced by Darwin. This gives a context for the examples of Henry Irving and Stanislavski that I will examine in Chapters 5 and 6. In each case, I aim to suggest how connections can be forged between my core idea of smoothness in performance and the wider background of social morality.

In Chapter 3, I describe some issues and examples relating to gesture on Shakespeare's stage. The chapter is of necessity speculative in places, since there is a paucity of hard evidence. However, some reflections are offered on what I take to have been the acting style of the company. As well, I consider the possibility that the 'chirosopher' John Bulwer may have had Shakespeare's company in mind when he created a taxonomy of gestures.

Chapter 4 offers a brief contextual background leading into some case studies from the eighteenth century. I show how gesture in Shakespearean performance was conditioned in part by space. As stages and auditoria grew larger, gesture in performance adopted a more statu-esque form modelled upon classicism. In Chapter 5 I consider Henry Irving's performances from the perspective of Darwinism.

Chapter 6 considers the arrival of the intimate spaces of realism and naturalism, when Shakespearean performance adapted by revalu-ing psychology. Stanislavski's Method of Physical Actions, created in part out of his struggle with *Othello*, outlines a gestural economy that aligns closely with my core concept of smoothness. I also briefly sug-gest how some modernist discourses of gesture have reconfigured the meaning of smoothness, partly in response to a rediscovery of Asian performance traditions like Noh theatre. A modernist alternative to the gestures of naturalism is considered through the avant-garde styliza-tions of Les Kurbas. I then look at the postmodernist Shakespeares of Robert Lepage, dreamthinkspeak and The Wooster Group. At the close of this chapter I reflect upon the impact of digital technologies such as performance capture upon Shakespearean practice. In Chapter 7, I offer an analysis of some recent examples of gesture in Shakespearean prac-tice through the figure of Iago, examples which propose a video-based methodology for the study of gesture in performance. The final chapter of the book consists of transcriptions of discussions with the influential scholar David McNeill and the choreographer Siân Williams, together with some closing thoughts on possible future directions for research into Shakespeare and gesture.

At this stage a proviso is warranted. In this book I am talking about *Shakespearean* performance, and I am dealing in the main with actors who managed to gain social status for their efforts. My agenda is in part to describe how that status was won. I am not making claims for other kinds of performances such as the popular entertainments that held sway in English suburbs and provinces. I agree with Tracy C. Davis when she writes that we must not take the behaviour of (very often white male European) elite actors as representative of all performance everywhere (see especially Davis 1991: chapter 1). Neither am I discounting the significant work of scholars, for example in the field of historical materialism, who have argued for an ideological component to the cultural construct known as 'Shakespearean performance'. My aim instead is to relate those non-verbal features of acting that often go under the name of 'technique' to a larger discursive frame that will, I hope, allow for a range of viewpoints. The next chapter concerns itself with some of the theoretical issues that underpin this frame.

Part I
Theory

1
What is a Gesture?

Historical definitions

Before we can explore non-verbal acts in a Shakespeare performance, the word 'gesture' needs to be defined. Its derivation is the Latin *gerere* meaning 'to bear, to carry, to carry on, to perform'. From the late Middle Ages up to the early nineteenth century it carried the meaning of 'deportment' – the carriage, or manner of bearing, of the body. From the mid-sixteenth to the early eighteenth century, it also meant 'a posture, or attitude of the body'. In the early twentieth century it took on a new meaning as an 'action performed as a courtesy, formality or symbol to indicate an intention or evoke a response' (all references from *The Concise Oxford English Dictionary*).

Thus, from the beginning of the Renaissance up to around 1800 the word described how an individual appeared to the world in a relatively fixed way; there was often a conflation of gesture with what we understand as posture. This fixity tallies with the concept, upheld in this book, that during this period life was less about the individual feeling entitled to self-enhancement – an idea which holds the potential for flexibility in one's choice of role as well as for a kind of equality between people – than it was about identifying the individual's place in the social order. Such an identification would be physical as well as abstract, and would extend to expectations regarding appropriate use of gestures in public. Thus it can also be seen as consistent with a social morality based on the idea of serving a higher purpose such as salvation of one's soul through unwavering adherence to one's calling. But from around 1550 to around 1700 it was also used to refer to an individual's changeable attitude. This chimes with the notion that from the early modern period there began to grow a new social morality based upon self-fulfilment, which demanded that a person be given the opportunity to make choices for determining her or his own happiness rather than live out her or his given social role. With the advent of the twentieth century, the definition of gesture came to suggest behaviour that was contingent on the demands of the moment – gesture as a temporary act was separated from posture as a held position. Not surprisingly, then, the history of the word is bound up with how Western culture viewed the individual within a social, cultural and moral frame.

A related term is 'gest', from the same Latin root. This referred to (usually heroic) exploits that were recited by performers who later came to be called jesters, and that were recorded in medieval romance literature. As attitudes towards chivalric narrative began to alter in the early modern era, the word 'jest' emerged as a term for a jokey story. In the late Middle Ages and early sixteenth century 'jest' also came to mean a gesture in the sense of a person's general deportment.

'Gesture' and 'jest' combine in a scene from *The Travels of the Three English Brothers* (written in 1607 by John Day, William Rowley and George Wilkins, in Parr 1995):

> SERVANT. Sir, here's an Italianate harlequin come to offer a play to your lordship.
> SIR ANTHONY. We willingly accept it. Hark, Kemp:
> Because I like thy jesture and thy mirth
> Let me request thee play a part with them. (9.73–6)

Sir Anthony Sherley, the real-life inspiration for the play, met 'Jesting Will' (l.64) Kemp in 1601, just after Kemp had stopped working for Shakespeare's company (see Parr 1995).

From the mid-sixteenth to the mid-eighteenth centuries, 'jest/gest' was also used to refer to 'the stages of a (royal) journey'. Shakespeare applied it as well to the actual time given over to a stay, as when Hermione speaks of 'the gest/Prefix'd' for a 'parting' in *The Winter's Tale* (1.2.99). This is Shakespeare's only use of the word in this spelling – as opposed to the word 'jest' which he used over a hundred times in the sense of 'joke', often with a connotation of disapproval or anger, as for example several times in *The Comedy of Errors*:

> ANTIPHOLUS OF SYRACUSE. Think'st thou I jest? Hold, take thou that, and that. (2.2.23)

And in relation to the behaviour of Sir John Falstaff in *Henry IV, Part 2*:

HENRY V. Reply not to me with a fool-born jest ... (5.5.55)

The contemporary definition

For modern scholars 'gesture' typically has the sense of a movement of the limbs to express a thought or feeling. This sense of the word begins in late Middle English. To summarize how it is nowadays usually understood:

1. A gesture is made predominantly by the arms and hands, while a posture involves at least the torso if not the whole body. In acting, though, bodily involvement is problematized by the conditions of the playing space and the impulse to stylize behaviour – that is, to consciously amplify and manipulate selected features. Conventional thinking may hold that the greater the degree of full-body involvement, the more authentic or sincere the feeling behind the gesture. This is the assertion of the movement theorist Warren Lamb, whose notion of Posture-Gesture Merging is partly derived from his apprenticeship under the influential choreographer Rudolf Laban (see Davies 2006: 66). While the authenticity of full-body involvement may or may not be a truism offstage, in acting it cannot be taken as read.
2. A gesture carries an intention: it helps the individual *express* a particular thought or feeling. Yet intentionality is also problematized by acting: whose intention is being carried out, on behalf of whom?
3. A gesture is brief, unlike a posture which is sustained. The question 'how long is a gesture', again, is complicated in the sphere of acting by the wish to stylize behaviour, which may well involve conscious manipulation of its timing. However, the very idea that a gesture's duration can be stylized implies that there is a 'natural', i.e. average or default, timing that would in principle be perceivable by anyone. According to the biophysicist Ernst Pöppel, intentional gestures are usually performed within a specific time window (1989: 87). They occur in the psychological present, which acts as a temporal platform for consciousness. Typically, this platform is around three seconds long. In other words, every two to three seconds we segment reality into integrated 'pictures of the present' (ibid.: 88). The three-second window of *temporal integration*, as it is known, is how everyone perceives the world around them. Evidence for temporal integration

was gathered by Schleidt and Kien. They analysed 1,542 action units drawn from five different cultural groups. An action unit was defined as a segment of movement if its:

> beginning and end could be clearly seen, if it had an observable goal, and thus the individual movements are functionally related (e.g. wiping the nose with the finger). The consecutive movements do not belong to the same action unit if they are not functionally related (e.g. wiping the nose and then scratching it). (Schleidt and Kien 1997: 79)

They found that 93 per cent of the action units they analysed took between two and three seconds. This principle applies to both voluntary gestures and involuntary movements like fidgeting. Some people, of course, move more quickly or slowly than others in their everyday life. In this case, they will usually still try to incorporate their movements within a given action unit, thereby confirming the three-second principle (Schleidt 1988). This contrasts with a posture, which is held for anything up to two minutes or more. Changes of posture often operate like large motion boundaries signalling a shift in the topic of a conversation (see Scheflen 1974). To summarize: *intentionally expressive gestures are two to three seconds long*. That includes gestures-for-speaking, since they are timed to synchronize with speech and speaking itself 'is embedded in temporal windows of up to 3 seconds' duration giving speech its rhythmic structure' (Pöppel 2004: 300). Pöppel found that the rule even applied to the vocal delivery of a line of iambic pentameter: subjects preferred the speaker to complete the line in about three seconds. So, if the average length of an Elizabethan play was about 3,000 lines, then it would have taken on average 150 minutes to speak the play's dialogue. Of course, that excludes any variables such as textual edits or non-verbal stage business, and we can only be really comfortable making such statements with respect to performances for which we have concrete evidence of duration.

4. A gesture comes in three parts: the *preparation* phase, during which the hand(s) come into play; the *stroke*, which is the key moment of the gesture, and the *recovery* phase, when the hand(s) return to their resting position. Some scholars also identify a pre-stroke and a post-stroke hold, but these are not essential for the labelling of a gesture. Marr and Vaina (1982) showed that a movement sequence can

be decomposed into motion segments. These motion segments are bounded by more or less static states, producing a *tripartite structure* ('state-motion-state').

Newtson and Engquist (1976) demonstrated that perceived event boundaries (known as 'breakpoints') coincide with sudden changes of behaviour. People are remarkably consistent in segmenting observed motion events, and in viewing breakpoints as the most intelligible or salient aspect of the movement. Consistency of segmentation happens regardless of the specific interpretation people give to the motion event; that is, we perceive the boundaries of units of action in the same way whether or not we agree about the goal of the action. What this means is that people focus on the breakpoints – the boundaries – when they are making sense of gestures. Newtson and Engquist argued that the breakpoint serves not only as a demarcation point but as a kind of summary of the *meaning* of the segment. What matters are the specific motion properties of the breakpoint – in other words, how the movement is begun and (even more important) how it is completed. In terms of gesture, the 'completion breakpoint' corresponds to the execution of the stroke – the key part of the gesture.

Rubin and Richards (1985) extended this work on motion segments. They viewed visible motion boundaries as marked by a brief application of force constituting a start, a stop or a discontinuity such as a change of speed and/or direction. To summarize: *gestures have a tripartite structure* – they are like a mini-story, with a beginning, middle and end.

5. Gestures can be studied in isolation, but the total meaning of a segment of movement involves *clusters* of behaviour in a given context. To pluck a gesture out of its context for analysis can thus be a mistake; it should be considered within a larger pattern of movement. This causes potential difficulties if we are dealing with a visual archive that relies exclusively on still images, such as eighteenth-century illustrations of actors.

These general labelling constraints tend to rule out the idea that 'gesture' can refer to any action that is carried out on stage, such as fighting, eating, drinking, reading, writing, dressing, undressing and so on. Fighting may be an *action* or an *activity*, but in the strict sense under discussion here it would not constitute a gesture. Actions are instrumental, directed to a specific purpose. This purpose is not as a rule 'to generate a metaphor in order to communicate an idea'. Gestures may or may not be instrumental, but they are always, as I stressed at the outset of the Introduction, metaphorical. Again, though, this may be problematic in the special context of the stage, where actions like physical fighting might be seen as symbolic of some other conflict. However, as far as I am able I intend to stick within the narrow definition.

2
Ideas of Gesture: Before and After Shakespeare

Having outlined an etymology of the word 'gesture' along with some labelling constraints, I now wish to relate gesture theory to a history of acting. Since this book deals principally with Shakespeare within a European tradition – and draws in large part upon English cultural contexts – my focus is of necessity limited to, firstly, possible influences upon his own practice and, secondly, what might be called posthumous threads of influence that can be traced from him.

It is hardly original to claim that early modern culture was dominated by two seemingly competitive discourses: the classical and the Christian. Shakespeare's own work constantly reveals tensions, collisions and negotiations between the worlds revealed in the texts and imagery of classical and Biblical traditions. It is inevitable, then, that his under-standing of gesture in performance would have been contaminated by these discourses and traditions; it is necessary to tease out in some detail what they may have meant to him. I begin with the classical world.

The classical background: the open palm of rhetoric

In *The Advancement of Learning* (1605) Francis Bacon wrote: 'It appeareth also that logic differeth from rhetoric, not only as the fist from the palm, the one close, the other at large; but much more in this, that logic handleth reason exact and in truth, and rhetoric handleth it as it is planted in popular opinions and manners' (in Plett 2004: 59). In this widely used gestural analogy, taken from the classical philosopher Zeno, logic was like a clenched fist: tight, compressed and spare. By contrast, rhetoric was like an open palm: discursive, generous and relaxed.

From an early stage within the context of the city-states of Greece and Rome, acting was linked to the rhetorical tradition. The word 'actor', derived from *actio*, which was at first a legal term denoting a procedure in a civil court. Later, *actio* began to refer to the legal speech in itself, and then later to include other aspects of delivery such as voice and gesture (Fantham 2002: 362–3). The worlds of oratory and acting are connected through the meaning of *actio* as 'skill in performance' (Fantham 2006: 84). Shakespeare would most likely have discovered this connection at school.

The Roman politician and orator Cicero probably underwent some of his training in rhetoric with the great actor Roscius. Elaine Fantham notes:

> Cicero repeatedly presents Roscius in *De Oratore* as the model for physical performance ... The great actor stands for the aesthetic component in public speaking: for beauty (*venustas*) and consummate gesture, achieved by practice until something is impeccable. Roscius is made the embodiment of *decere*, grace and elegance. For Roscius, grace was the essence of art, and the one thing that could not be created by art itself ... (ibid.)

Thus, from the beginning of the discourse relating acting to rhetoric, an emphasis is placed upon the need for physical grace. This emphasis is not merely aesthetic, it is moral: 'Isn't it true,' Cicero wrote in *On the Limits of Good and Evil*, 'that we consider many people worthy of our contempt when they seem, through a certain kind of movement or posture, to have scorned the law and limit of nature?' (quoted and discussed in Corbeill 2004: 108). Cicero argued that both the gods and his fellow Roman citizens could and should 'recognize deviance in a human being's movement in the same way that [they] can judge an art object', and that the same basic assumptions about what is natural lay behind the judging of an artwork and the judging of virtue and vice in a person (ibid.: 109). We will see that Cicero's assumptions were adopted by Italian humanists and widely promulgated in England in the Renaissance.

There is a contradictory agenda at work in the *De Oratore*. While the performance skills of Roscius are acknowledged as a resource for imitation by orators in training, the relationship between actor and orator is at the same time disavowed. This is because manuals like Cicero's were written for the education of privileged Roman males, and it was essential that they felt keenly the responsibilities of their future roles as public figures. An orator was supposed to be truthful; Cicero argues that the speaker should genuinely feel the emotions of his speech as he delivers it (2.189). Actors, by contrast, were mere imitators (2.34; 2.193; 3.214), even if there are times when they appear to be on fire with emotion (2.193). The orator was also supposed to show dignity and authority. His behaviour should not be tainted with suggestions of womanish effeminacy or slave-like vulgarity (Fögen 2009: 28–9).

Cicero does not spend a lot of time discussing physical gestures. He does, though, offer the budding orator a set of vocal attitudes. These correspond to basic emotions: anger, lamentation, fear, passion (really an intense form of masculine assertiveness), joy or pleasure and distress. He goes on to say that these emotions should be accompanied by gestures, but he does not give specific details. Instead, he states that the orator should not make obvious pictures with the hands but should use gesture suggestively to indicate the underlying idea of the speech (*De Oratore* 3.220). In Elaine Fantham's gloss: 'the orator should avoid theatricality and indicate rather than demonstrate the idea, with virile movements closer to those of combat than of drama, inhibiting the expressiveness of the hand and fingers, and extending the arm like a kind of weapon' (Fantham 2006: 295).

These gestures call upon the hand and arm's capacity to imply decisiveness and dominance by suggesting the speaker is not afraid to solve problems using force. The primatologist John Napier distinguished between two basic prehensile movements: the *Power Grip* and the *Precision Grip*. You use a Power Grip to hold a hammer and a Precision Grip to hold a needle. Most grips are a variation on these two basic grips (Napier 1993: 62). Cicero is identifying the Power Grip with masculinity and the Precision Grip with femininity. He expressed irritation at *argutiae digitorum* ('finger-twiddling': *Orator* 59). He advocated a masculine idea of self-restraint as an essential aspect of delivery. In the *Brutus* (203) he praised the *gestus venustus* – the elegant gesturing – of Sulpicius, a tribune of the people. By contrast, he criticized orators such as the elder Curio (*Brutus* 216–17) and Sextus Titius (*Brutus* 225) for an effeminate lack of restraint in their hand and arm movements. The elite male class were being taught to display a physical behaviour that signalled their superiority. It is ironic that the best example that Cicero can find for this behaviour is a low-status actor – although Roscius was an exception in Cicero's eyes since he had 'more trustworthiness than artful skill, more truth than training. The Roman people judge him a better man than actor – his talent makes him as worthy of the stage as his restraint makes him worthy of the senate house' (in Corbeill 2004: 115). Cicero plays elsewhere on the double meaning of *agere* – to act – as 'the natural actions of the body as well as its self-conscious performance' (ibid.: 116). In the forthcoming section on smoothness in this chapter, I will show how Ciceronian aristocratic confidence in being able to distinguish (restrained) authentic behaviour from (emotionally excessive) hypocritical displays was put to new purposes in Shakespeare's theatre.

Turning from the Republic to the Empire in which Quintilian (c.35–c.100 CE) worked, the field begins to open up somewhat. Quintilian's manual *Institutio Oratoria* (c.95 CE), written in part for younger students of the rhetorical art (Fantham 1982: 244), provided practical advice on gesture. In recent years classical scholars have argued that the 'non-verbal vocabulary available to orators became much more elaborate' between the periods of Cicero and Quintilian (Aldrete 1999: 166), and the *Insitutio Oratoria* reflects this elaboration. We can see some of this elaboration in the letters of the philosopher Seneca, as when he wrote:

> Everything has its own indicator, if you pay attention, and even the smallest details offer an indication of a person's character. An effeminate man (*impudicus*) is revealed by his walk, from [the way] he brings his finger up to his head, and from his eye-movement … For those qualities come into the open through signs. (Quoted in Corbeill 2004: 114)

The morally charged word 'impudent' arrived into English through this Latin root in 'effeminacy'.

Quintilian believed that gestures can reveal the inner life of the speaker and can at times affect the audience even more than verbal language (1920: 11.3.67). The idea of delivery as *mentis index* involved 'the principle that rhetorical delivery to be effective must be sustained by impulses of "natural" emotion' and that 'the art of delivery is to perfect the natural ability to express these signals' (Sonkowsky 1959: 256). In this Quintilian followed Cicero, whose influence is acknowledged throughout Book Eleven which deals with performance. But here arises the problem of truthfulness, of the relation between spontaneity and technique, which has dogged Western discourses on acting since Plato. Quintilian's solution to the problem can be seen to connect with the idea of gesture as 'visible thought'. He proposes in Book Six (2.29–33) that the orator can call forth emotions by accessing *phantasia* (imagination or visions). In Book Eleven (3.62), he advises the orator to work with these visualization techniques if he is unable to summon up the feelings.

Quintilian divides up the expressive parts of the body and treats them separately. Thus we find sentences on the head, the eyes and brows, the nostrils, the lips, the neck, the arms, the hands and the fingers. In contrast to Cicero, specific finger gestures are given considerable detail (11.3.92–106). If the text seems overly fussy, the finger positions he describes are nonetheless 'closely related to those regularly used in conversational contexts' (Hall 2004: 149). A number of them are variations of the Precision Grip family. Quintilian also refers to pointing movements. The gestures he describes create an impression of a mind working with fine detail, seeking an intellectual subtlety and an orderliness that avoids aggression.

Quintilian was centrally concerned with the impression of decorum: 'Gesture and movement are productive of grace' (*Institutio Oratoria* 11.68). What decorum meant in practice was that the fingers should not be extended too much, and that the movements of the hand, as with the whole body, should be measured in order to convey self-control without strain. At the same time, as the orator heats up, gestures will naturally become more rapid and more frequent (11.111). However, for parts of the speech requiring great impact, it is best to adhere to the principle set by tragic actors of slowing down one's movements (11.111–12). In addition, there are larger movements of posture and gait that Quintilian warns against on grounds of inelegance. Most of these are understandable as what modern theorists call *adaptors* – nervous mannerisms made by young orators suffering from lack of confidence. Common faults include splaying the feet, swaying from side to side, meaningless pacing up and down, and pulling up the folds of the toga to thigh-level with the right hand while walking and gesturing with the left during the speech (11.3.121–31).

Summary of the classical precepts

From the prescriptions of Cicero and Quintilian some general principles can be inferred:

1. The overall stance must be upright.
2. The repertoire of gestures should be drawn from everyday usage.
3. The orator should be economical in his movements.
4. Hand and arm gestures should not seem isolated from the position or motion of the rest of the upper body, including the head.
5. Movements should be slightly slower than in everyday use.
6. Movements should be slightly more articulated than in everyday use.
7. Movements should convey an impression of masculine power combined with ease and intellectual subtlety.

8. The orator should not use pantomimic illustration.
9. Movements should be connected to the thoughts behind the speech.
10. Movements should demonstrate *enargeia*, a vivid, expressive clarity which comes from making the subject appear present to the mind's eye of the spectator. In service to this, the orator should where possible actually feel the emotion he is displaying, using visualization techniques if necessary. The concept of *enargeia* – in which something from the past is made to seem vividly present – became crucial in the early modern period, as Heinrich Plett has shown in a brilliant study (Plett 2012). In this book I speak of a new degree, or a new intensity, of realism in art at this time; the 'enargetic' technique of creating a vivid visual impression through detailed description was a key aesthetic procedure for achieving this.

These simple precepts would go on to define a Western European acting style for many centuries, and in some respects have yet to be superseded. The difference between Cicero and Quintilian is summed up by Edwin Ramage in an essay on *urbanitas*. For Cicero, this was a quality of wittiness belonging to privileged Romans. It was non-transferable: uneducated rustics could not learn it. Quintilian, a product of the first-century Empire, took a different view, seeing *urbanitas* as the 'whole aim of education as it is outlined in the *Institutio Oratoria*' (Ramage 1963: 410). For him it was a kind of cultured speaking achievable in principle by anyone:

> The exclusiveness of former times has all but disappeared. It [*urbanitas*] used to be inherited from the past and bestowed only upon the most Roman of the Romans. But according to Quintilian anyone can attain it now by combining a natural ability and alertness with a well-balanced education. As such it is a sure sign of times far different from the later years of the Republic. (ibid.: 414)

The idea that rhetoric was able to provide anyone who could learn to read with the tools to advance in life spurred many young men and women in Tudor England to climb the social ladder – Shakespeare being one of them. In his instructions to the Players, Hamlet says:

> Nor do not saw the air too much with your hand, thus, but use all gently; for in the very torrent, tempest, and, as I may say, whirlwind of your passion, you must acquire and beget a temperance that may give it smoothness. (3.2.4–8)

When Hamlet says 'you must acquire and beget a temperance that may give [your passion] smoothness' (3.2.7–8), the suggestion is that decorous behaviour ('temperance', 'smoothness') is not the birthright of the elite. It can be acquired and passed on: say, from the master to the apprentice actor. If Shakespeare took his cue from Cicero and Quintilian, then he would have felt keenly the tensions between Cicero's conception of decorum as innate, and a training in *pronunciatio* which bestowed the individual with the qualities needed to become a professional actor in a new marketplace: *decere, enargeia* and a good memory.

Shakespeare's use of classical rhetoric

Did Shakespeare know these Roman works? There is considerable agreement among scholars that he would have gone to his local grammar school at about 14. At school, Shakespeare's day would have been spent translating, parsing and imitating classical Latin texts. Textbooks such as *Rhetorica Ad Herennium*, thought to have been by Cicero, were used as a basis for catalogues of 'tropes' (devices for altering the usual meaning of a word or phrase) and 'schemes' (devices for altering the usual order or pattern of words). The pupils would identify the figures of speech and then construct their own versions of them. They would learn how to compose and present stories, sayings, descriptions, speeches, arguments and conversations in prose and verse.

A significant part of the curriculum was devoted to what was called delivery or pronunciation (*actio/pronunciatio*). This refers to the vocal and physical techniques needed for performance. It may well have required the boys (the schools were boys-only) to recite passages from Roman authors such as Horace, Virgil, Cicero, Ovid, Seneca, Plautus, Terence, Caesar, Sallust and Livy in front of the schoolmaster. The capacity to remember a speech fell under the separate rubric of *memoria*.

Looking through the plays as a whole, one can locate from the beginning traces of *progymnasmata* – rhetorical composition exercises. They are, not surprisingly, very noticeable in his Roman plays. Here is the opening of *Titus Andronicus*, in which Saturninus lays out his claim to be made emperor:

> Noble patricians, patrons of my right,
> Defend the justice of my cause with arms.
> And countrymen, my loving followers,
> Plead my successive title with your swords. (1.1.1–4)

The verbs 'defend' and 'plead' key us in to the rhetorical impulse that motivates this speech. Its method is taken from deliberative oratory – the art of political persuasion, designed to get someone to take a course of action. It invites an emotional response in the listener: it asks for righteous anger. It is followed by another rhetorical plea for support from Saturninus's political opponent, his younger brother Bassianus. Then the tribune Marcus makes another, lengthy rhetorical entreaty, urging the opposing brothers to plead their respective cases in a civilized fashion. Marcus's own brother Titus is about to return to Rome in triumph from the war against the Goths. When Titus enters 20 lines later, he begins with a lengthy encomium. An encomium is a type of *epideictic* (or demonstrative) oratory – a speech of praise or blame. In the third or fourth century CE text known as the *Peri Epideiktikon* – a manual which was widely read in the Renaissance (Vickers 1988: 61) – there is a list of functions of encomium. This includes consolatory speeches that may be delivered at funerals and speeches given on arrival in a city. Titus's opening speech encompasses both, since he is bringing back to his beloved Rome the bodies of his sons who died in combat:

> Hail, Rome, victorious in thy mourning weeds!
> Lo, as the bark that hath discharged his freight
> Returns with precious lading to the bay
> From whence at first she weighed her anchorage,
> Cometh Andronicus, bound with laurel boughs,
> To resalute his country with his tears,
> Tears of true joy for his return to Rome. (1.1.73–9)

Thus, when he came to writing plays, Shakespeare did not abandon his rhetorical training. This goes further than the use of tropes and schemes, as Brian Vickers suggests: 'Medieval and Renaissance writers seldom regard their subject-matter neutrally, but usually express a clearly positive or negative evaluation which attempts to change the reader's views' (Vickers 1988: 61). Shakespeare's writing constantly reveals this strategic eliciting of affiliation. It is achieved not through the 'clenched fist' of logic but through the 'open palm' of rhetorical appeal. Shakespeare's characters attempt to persuade each other, themselves or the spectator to think, feel, believe, say or do things using emotionally charged arguments. One of the problems for the modern audience (and perhaps a Tudor one also) is that we can easily take something said by one of his characters to be representative of Shakespeare's views. That is partly because it is often hard for people to grasp a viewpoint they do not already share; when asked to argue the opposite of their own morality in a recent study, participants failed to show the most basic understanding of values different to their own, resorting instead to arguments based on their own beliefs (Feinberg and Willer 2015). Rhetoric was partly instituted to help public figures overcome such difficulties. The dialogic features of Shakespeare's writing prevent us from reading it as didactic. The real danger of propaganda is that we might believe it to be reasonable. Reasonableness, though, is not easily attributed to many of Shakespeare's characters, least of all his political representatives, as *Titus Andronicus* abundantly reveals. Far more often we are shown how *passion* leads a character towards a distorted judgement.

Passions and humours

As Hamlet's instructions show, the actor was expected to deliver a 'whirlwind of passion' in the performance – and yet to do it 'gently'. The word 'passion' is derived from the Latin *passio* and is linked to Aristotle's term *pathos*. It connotes a body that is being acted upon rather than an agent that is intentionally acting. The individual is being *affected*. He is behaving under the influence of either external forces or internal imbalances. Reason is the default mode of being; passion is a deviation from it.

There is a small set of primary passions identified by Plato and further developed by the Stoic philosophers and by Cicero in the *Tusculan Disputations*. These four are (on the positive side) joy and desire and (on the negative) grief or sorrow and fear. Joy and grief were held to relate to the present, whereas desire and fear refer to an anticipated future. While this fourfold classification system was upheld by St Augustine, Thomas Aquinas divided it into two essential appetites, known as concupiscible and irascible. The concupiscible passions are those that relate to relatively easy things to obtain, and include love, desire, joy, hatred, aversion (i.e. disgust or contempt) and grief. The irascible passions are those that relate to things more difficult to obtain, and include hope, courage, anger, despair and fear.

In Shakespeare's England, these two ways of classifying the passions – the Graeco-Roman and the Thomist – were largely followed. The four passions identified by the Stoics form the basis of the theories of Timothy Bright's *Treatise of Melancholy* (1586), La Primaudaye's *The French Academy* (translated into English in 1586), John Davies' *Nosce Teipsum* (1599) and John Davies of Hereford's *Microcosmos* (1603). Thomas Wright in *The Passions of the Mind* (1601/1986) defines six primary passions, which correspond to the concupiscible passions in the

Thomist catalogue. In addition, Wright follows the Stoics in separating present passions from anticipated ones. Shakespeare probably read at least some of these English texts.

Interlinked with this attempt to label the passions, many writers of the era made use of Galen's theory of *humours* to describe patterns of behaviour. People were described as having an affinity with certain temperaments due to an excess of particular substances in the body, which then were held to correspond to the seasons of the year, the matter out of which everything was made – and so on. In *Wits Trenchmour* (1597) Nicholas Breton wrote:

> I find by my reading that man was compounded of the four Elements of Fire, Water, Earth and Air. I thus understand the four Elements, choler, phlegm, blood and melancholy. (In Joseph 1971: 250)

This interlocking system of correspondences for patterns of human behaviour within the cosmic order was so all-embracing, and had been promoted by scholars for so many hundreds of years, it was difficult for early modern thinkers to imagine what could be put in its place.

Did Shakespeare conceive of human personality along the lines of this theory? Gail Kern Paster (1993) has argued for the influence of humoral theory, with its insistence on the fluidity and leakiness of the human body, over the drama of this period. As well, there is an argument to be made for the use of humours by Shakespeare's actors at times. One example would be Hamlet, where gestures that represent the melancholic humour might be applied. The archetypal gesture of melancholy (really a posture), sitting with the chin resting on one hand, was portrayed by Albrecht Dürer in his woodcut *Melancholia*. This was of course later redefined as a gesture for thinking, most famously by the sculptor Auguste Rodin. Again, what is evident is how a physical position signalling a fixed temperament (in this case, melancholy) could then be reconceptualized from the perspective of social morality as a more general figure for an individual's private thought processes. In fact this reading is already available in *Hamlet*, as when the hero defines his own problem as 'thinking too precisely on th'event' (4.4.41). In the play, the word 'conscience' has at least two meanings – the conventional moral one and, more generally, 'consciousness' itself. The very fact that the two could be separated at all is revealing of a shift in social morality.

Shakespeare could be flexible in his attitude towards the theory of humours. Some recent scholars, such as Lynn Enterline, remind us that he had a way of dramatizing a character's self-conscious reflection upon their own emotional experience, a self-consciousness which was partly a result of his rhetorical training in *imitatio*, where emotional experiences were a matter of experimenting with feelings by performing different identities in the schoolroom (for example, experimenting with grief by writing and acting out speeches for tragic heroines of classical mythology). There were times when he treated humoral theory as a joke, such as in the character of Corporal Nim, whose riffing on the word 'humour' in *Henry V* and *The Merry Wives of Windsor* is extended ad nauseam:

> NIM. And this is true, I like not the humour of lying. He hath wronged me in some humours. I should have borne the humoured letter to her, but I have a sword, and it shall bite upon my necessity ... Adieu. I love not the humour of bread and cheese. Adieu.
> PAGE. The humour of it, quoth 'a! Here's a fellow frights English out of his wits. (2.1.116–25)

In *Twelfth Night* Sir Andrew Aguecheek's misunderstanding affords Shakespeare an opportunity for a sly dig at the theory:

> SIR TOBY: Does not our life consist of the four elements?
> SIR ANDREW: Faith, so they say, but I think it rather consists of eating and drinking.
> SIR TOBY: Th'art a scholar; let us therefore eat and drink. (2.3.9–13)

Whatever he made of it, it is clear that the battle to get control over the passions was played out on Shakespeare's stage. And behind much of the argument within his culture there was a moral assumption that people should not succumb to the temptations of the body. Raymond Gibbs puts it succinctly: 'Separation of the mind and body and the hierarchical ordering of mind over body haunt the history of Western philosophical accounts of knowledge from Plato, Aristotle and Augustine through to Descartes and Kant' (Gibbs 2005: 3).

Hamlet cautions the Players that they must apply to their passion 'a temperance' (3.2.4). Shakespeare relates passion to uncontrollable forces like the weather. The idea of a temperate climate is used for instance in 'Shall I compare thee to a summer's day?/Thou art more lovely and more temperate' ('Sonnet 18'). Its opposite, 'intemperate', is related to the concupiscible passions by Isabella (Angelo's 'concupiscible intemperate lust', *Measure for Measure* 5.1.101). The related 'temperament', meaning 'temperature', brings us back to the theory of humours, since that was one of the words used to describe the blend of choler, phlegm, blood and melancholy within the individual (the other word was 'complexion'). The Latin *temperare* means 'to restrain, moderate, adjust or mix'.

When Gertrude accuses Hamlet of suffering from the 'ecstasy' of madness he replies: 'My pulse as yours doth temperately keep time/And makes as healthful music' (3.4.142–3). The text here recalls the etymological connection of temperance with *tempus*, 'time'. To keep time with the body is to display health. Being out of time – missing the beat – is a symptom of mental sickness or 'distemper' – a word used four times in reference to Hamlet's own behaviour.

Christian contexts

Christian culture evolved out of a Graeco-Roman heritage. A framework for the revaluation of classicism was provided by St Augustine in *De Doctrina Christiana* (written sometime between 396 and 426 CE). Augustine made a distinction between *signa naturalia* – signs from nature, such as smoke that signals the presence of fire, or involuntary emotional expressions – and *signa data* – symbols that are created intentionally in order to communicate something. Augustine considered the sign (*signum*) as a basis for making inferences from something that is not immediately visible. He wrote that a sign was 'a thing which, in addition to what it is perceived to be by the senses also brings something else to mind' (*De Doctrina Christiana* 2.1.1, quoted in Markus 1957: 71).

This 'something else' was God's truth, a truth that was once known to Adam, and that had since the Fall been lost. Being *signa* of a corrupt human nature, gestures were hieroglyphics of the divine purpose. As Peter Harrison says, it is 'this hieroglyphic conception of nature which undergirded the medieval belief that there were two books – the book of nature and the book of scripture' (Harrison 1998: 3). The business of allegorical interpretation – ubiquitous from the time of Augustine to the Reformation – was to join the words of the Bible with natural objects. The motive, for writers such as Origen and Hugh of Saint Victor, was to produce a hermeneutics that secured the truth of scripture (ibid.: 268).

One theatrical offshoot of this motive had been ritualistic drama whose purpose was to remind the spectators of their original sin. The tableaux that characterize the drama of the later Middle Ages were thought to hold the power of salvation. Robert Scribner suggests this is due to what he calls the 'sacramental gaze' – the act of viewing *through* the image to a deeper sacred reality behind it (Scribner 1989: 459). The image – and the gesture in the image – is an Augustinian *signum*. That is why its iconography lacks individuality. It is designed to lead the viewer away from the object itself towards the spiritual meaning it contains. Only by disregarding 'the sensory images of the material world' can the postlapsarian mind 'discover within itself an image of the divine' (Harrison 2007: 38).

Another mode in which this iconography found expression is through the almost ubiquitous use of *personification*. It can come as a surprise to turn from Shakespeare's characters, who usually have proper names, to medieval dramas such as *Everyman* featuring figures called Death, Good Deeds, Beauty, Five Wits and so on. But, as Helen Cooper has shown, there are significant continuities between the allegorical drama, with its original locus in the scene of Catholic confession, and Shakespeare's work. Leaving aside such obvious examples as the occasional symbolic figure like Time in *The Winter's Tale*, there are frequent idiomatic uses of personification within the text itself that remind us of Shakespeare's debt to the medieval past. These verbal idioms often create the drama of an inner psychic conflict in which the self is a kind of warzone between apparently external influences – reason or patience versus passion or lust, the eye versus the heart, revenge versus conscience.

Seen in these terms, the subject becomes a passive victim of powerful forces rather than an active agent (note the etymological connection between 'passive' and 'passion' in the Latin *pati* 'to suffer'). Linguistically, this way of thinking produces a structure organized around nouns and verbs rather than, as is often the case in modern idiomatic speech, adjectival and adverbial phrases that flow out from the egocentric subject. Theatrically, the result is, as Cooper says, 'an intense visual and imaginative drama that requires to be taken seriously, and that occasionally steps across from the language or the imagination to actual performance' (in Morse, Cooper and Holland 2013: 141). To my mind, this suggests that actors who inherited a tendency to personify would make full use of imagistic gestures that bring out the iconic properties of the nouns and the force of the verbs felt to be acting upon them.

By contrast, the 'theological gaze' of Protestantism (Scribner 1989: 464) made use of spatial antithesis and deixis – reference to the here and now of an event. This limited the range of interpretations available to the viewer, as Glenn Ehrstine argues (Ehrstine 2001: 219). Protestants reinvigorated the Augustinian notions of the Fall and original sin. But they denied the validity of allegory. This position became more pronounced after around 1560, which saw the emergence of a Protestant defence of the Bible as being literally true (this had not been the stance of Luther or Calvin). By insisting that the scriptures were to be taken in their literal sense they gave priority to words over things, which were then stripped of their status as *signa*. One of the greatest casualties of this 'narrowing of church ceremony', as John H. Coldewey has noted, was the religious drama, now seen as 'ideologically suspect', and within a few decades doomed by political decree to become 'no more than a curious memory' (Coldewey 2004: 64–5).

It was now the duty of Christians, according to both Luther and Calvin, to pursue an earthly vocation directed towards restoring the perfection of Eden before the Fall, even if the task was impossible. For Protestants such as Francis Bacon, this legitimized the domination of nature (since originally nature had been created for the use of man) and the pursuit of natural knowledge – that is, science (for a full discussion see Harrison 2007). Thus, while Augustinian Catholicism had tended to consider nature as a sacred book in need of allegorical interpretation, from around 1500 nature in all its material manifestations had begun to be treated as an object worthy of attention and study in its own right. One clear example of this is the emergence of the practice of dissection of the human body by Andreas Vesalius. An important consequence of the shift in English culture from the Catholic allegorizing impulse to the Protestant literalizing one is that the way was paved for what would later be recognized as a new degree of realism in art. As I suggested in the section on classical rhetoric, the concept of *enargeia* was a key tool for achieving it. The essence of this realism is an attention upon the surface appearance of material life, coupled with a concern for capturing the momentary and transitional as opposed to the eternal. It was not until the mid-nineteenth century that this de-allegorizing move finally came to full fruition with the arrival of Darwinist naturalism (for a seminal account as exemplified in French painting see Nochlin 1991). But the impulse to direct one's attention away from transcendental values and towards the surface minutiae of everyday affairs was seeded in the Reformation. Catherine Belsey, in her influential book *The Subject of Tragedy*, explored how playwrights such as Shakespeare reconfigured the human self as if in response to this sociocultural shift towards what we might cautiously define as mimetic or realistic modes of representation (Belsey 1985). I would further suggest that, as with the shift from the sacramental to the theological gaze, so performance after the Reformation began to shift from ritualistic and iconographic actions towards mimetic and interactional gestures-for-speaking. Such gestures might have accompanied scenes of gossipy conversation in prose that are relatively rare in Shakespeare's early plays (there are none in *Titus*

Andronicus), but increasingly frequent in later ones including the trag-
edies (such scenes can be found, for example, in *Coriolanus* 1.3; 2.1; 2.2;
2.3; 4.3; 4.4; 5.4).

In his perceptive essay, John Coldewey reminds us that in place of
the medieval religious drama there rose up a new tradition drawn from
humanist sources – a tradition of 'interludes' that in England dates as far
as back as the 1490s. It was this drama that 'ultimately provided a professional alternative to popular communal and festive plays' (Coldewey
2004: 65). An important outcome of this, as John Parker observes, was
that the language of faith was appropriated by the apologists for the
theatre. The figure of the Prologue to *Henry VIII* says that those spectators who 'give/Their money out of hope they may believe/May here
find truth, too' (1.1.7–9). Truth here refers to the 'presence and power
of [theatre's] fictional representations' which 'had been superimposed
on a repudiated faith' (Parker 2004: 644). Successful actors like Richard
Burbage were liable to be seen as having the power to call up in the
spectator the kind of devotion previously bestowed on images of Christ
or the Saints. This is indicated by John Weever in his tribute to the
performer(s) who first acted Romeo and Richard III:

> Their sugar'd tongues and pure attractive beauty
> Say they are Saints (although that Saints they show not)
> For thousands vow to them their subjective duty.
>
> (Quoted in Parker 2004: 645)

Any spiritual authority the drama previously possessed had rested on its
power to evoke the mystery of God through iconic depictions. But in
banishing iconic imagery from the stage, Protestantism failed to diffuse
the power of theatrical representation to appeal to quasi-religious feelings in spectators. If anything, that appeal was fortified. Iconicity did
not disappear altogether – some of it was given a mimetic spin. I will
give some examples of this complex relationship between allegorical
and literal uses of gesture in Shakespeare's own practice in the next
chapter.

Smoothness

Audiences in late Tudor London craved new forms of amusement. For
this they turned to the theatre companies, run by actors or impresarios
who commissioned playwrights to produce a wide range of material
with a high turnover. Actors and playwrights had become professionals

with an obligation to provide entertainment on a daily basis to a paying public. Did this professional obligation affect performance styles? There is a passage about acting which has attracted a great deal of comment since it may have been written by John Webster:

> Whatsoever is commendable in the grave Orator, is most exquisitly perfect in him; for by a full and significant action of body, he charmes our attention: sit in a full Theater, and you will thinke you see so many lines drawne from the circumference of so many eares, whiles the *Actor* is the *Center*. (Webster 2007: 483).

The actor, says Webster, is like a sober and serious orator – except that the actor goes one better, by bringing to a form of perfection what the orator does commendably. This is achieved through the actor's focused use of his body, which draws the visual attention of the spectator in order that the spectator will listen better.

Such texts as these are indicators of a concerted effort by professional players to gain a new status for the art of acting. Actors would from this moment on begin to claim a special place in the cultural life of the nation. By the mid-eighteenth century, I suggest, this claim was substantially secured. I will furnish examples of how this claim related to gestural practice in Chapter 5, which deals with David Garrick and Sarah Siddons. But it was with Shakespeare's company of players, and their rivals under Philip Henslowe and Edward Alleyn, that the claim was first staked out.

This was partly achieved through pinning the practice of acting to classical traditions of rhetoric, partly through the transfer by audiences of feelings previously held towards icons such as saints onto actors. But another very important method by which it was achieved was through gestural displays of what was called *passing* – in the sense of 'passing yourself off as someone else'. It was symptomatic of an era in which so much wealth and power was in the hands of less than five per cent of the populace that anyone seeking to climb the ladder would have to adopt the behaviour and attitudes of the nobility. In practice, actors took things one step further: they imitated the bodily comportment and gestural behaviour of their social superiors, and did it so persuasively that they threw into question the foundation upon which this superiority was based – the notion that the status of an elite person was somehow ordained from above. If Richard Burbage, the son of a carpenter, could in a literal sense appear to be 'the man himself' when he played Prince Hamlet, how did he achieve that apparently mesmerizing effect? To answer this, we need to see how Italian humanists exported to England an idea of behaviour known as *sprezzatura*.

In 1506 the Italian diplomat Castiglione visited the court of Henry VII, where he found himself the object of much deferential attention by the king's ministers and dignitaries keen to learn more of his home Urbino, at that time considered the most cultured of Italian courts. As political power had begun to rapidly centralize around the figure of the absolutist monarch at court, the existing warrior class had to learn to adjust its behaviour (see Elias 1939/1994). Castiglione presented himself as one of a new kind of Western humanist courtier for whom the soft power of diplomacy at court was increasingly important. He set forth his approach to the problem of how the new courtier should behave in a four-volume work that was later translated by Sir Thomas Hoby as *The Book of the Courtier*. This was far from being the only conduct manual produced at that time, but it was among the most influential (Burke 1995/2007).

The model for courtly behaviour promoted by the humanists was based on a combination of self-discipline, elegant and witty politeness and a quality Castiglione calls *sprezzatura*. This translates as a sense of ease in comportment, speech and manner that is only achieved after great effort. For the humanist courtier, much of this effort was devoted to mastering pastimes such as dancing, fencing and wrestling – three activities that Shakespeare's actors would have needed competence in, and that offered opportunities for them to display their own *sprezzatura*. Castiglione did not advocate a weird set of behavioural codes. His advice often comes across as rather obvious – but that is part of his persuasive power. He did not offer a new repertoire that had to be learnt but a refinement of practices that recalled the advice of classical authorities like Cicero and Quintilian – practices centred upon the cultivation of precision, and upon an economy in the use of force. The aim was not to show off one's acquired social skills but in fact to make them transparent through a kind of studied negligence, which nonetheless revealed a sophisticated attunement to the behaviour that is appropriate in the situation.

The idea of an economy of force can be seen as the embodiment of a shift in moral values. The feudal honour code rested upon an idea that an elite person had the right to defend his superior status by violence. But for a Tudor courtier, it was no longer as necessary to show that you were willing to defend your honour quickly, and that you were committed to keeping your word, upon any threat to your status (although many English courtiers continued to behave as though that were not the case). Instead, you had to learn a behavioural style that would allow you to plan for your own preferment by the monarch. The courtier had to hold his desire for retaliation in check, to conceal his true motives and to play the new social game of soft power. Hence the need to display in posture, gesture and action an economy of force: a refined physical tact blended with bodily signs of power in potential.

A key image for understanding this economy of force is in the motto *festina lente* – 'make haste slowly'. As Edgar Wind points out, this motto, coined by the Emperor Augustus, blends 'speed with patience, daring abandon with prudent restraint', often in some curious image like a dolphin tied to a tortoise (Wind 1968: 98). Erasmus devoted no less than six folio pages of his *Adagia* to explicating this motto, while woodcuts of the *Hypnerotomachia* feature as many as 80 variations on it.

In *Love's Labour's Lost*, Moth and Armado dispute over whether lead can be quick:

> ARMADO.   I say, lead is slow.
> MOTH.   You are too swift, sir, to say so.
>   Is that lead slow which is fir'd from a gun?
> ARMADO.   Sweet smoke of rhetoric!
>   He reputes me a cannon … (3.1.60–63)

A cannon holds in potential the mysterious forces of nature, 'forces which man carries also in his own breast', then releases them to dramatically explosive effect (Wind 1968: 109). Energy-in-potential was a quality of behaviour held up for imitation – and also open to 'counterfeiting', i.e. Machiavellian deception. 'Elasticity of conduct', wrote Edgar Wind, 'was a Renaissance ideal and, what is more, a Renaissance habit, a strategy of life sustained and sanctioned by the classical motto *festina lente*' (100–1).

Festina lente is a good description of what Hamlet means when he asks for smoothness in the Players. It is a paradoxical quality of movement conveyed by the tempering of force. Force is the sum of the product of mass and acceleration. Smoothness is achieved through the control of mass (in particular, at the centre of gravity) while the body speeds up or slows down. The excursion of a smooth gesture, like the movement of a projectile from a cannon, embodies the principle of *festina lente*. It is a paradoxical quality of movement, but there is nothing inherently bizarre about it. The actors were responding to the classical ideal of decorum and the Christian idea of grace in the same way as the humanist courtiers were supposed to. The motives were different, of course; the actors' intention was not to accomplish soft diplomacy but to create a memorable impression upon the spectator. In so doing, they cemented their reputations as professionals whose unique selling point was a behavioural display that separated them from the amateur players of the medieval guilds.

After Shakespeare: the neoclassical language of gesture

In the year of Shakespeare's death (1616), Giovanni Bonifacio published in Vicenza *L'Arte de' Cenni*: 'The Art of Signs'. This was a bold attempt to describe all of the signs that could be produced by the body (as well as by other semiotic systems like clothing). His claim – there was nothing new in it – was that from the movements of the body one can read the movements of the soul.

In a strategy reminiscent of Quintilian, Bonifacio begins with the head and the face, and works his way down, body part by body part, to the feet. Not only does he detach the body as a whole from its context, he detaches the individual parts from each other. Gesture from Bonifacio's period on would increasingly become a subject of this kind of minute analysis. In effect, Bonifacio was groping towards a science of non-verbal communication.

Bonifacio's work was symptomatic of a general anxiety arising from the collapse in Western Europe of a shared religious framework. The Reformation and Counter-Reformation did not lead to the weakening of Christianity in itself – arguably the reverse. But Bonifacio lamented the loss of faith that had afflicted Europe, which he felt had led to doctrinal tribalism. Europe was failing to have a rational conversation with itself because it did not have a common language. The analogy that Bonifacio made was with the Tower of Babel. It is an understandable analogy to make given the explosion of printed material in the period, much of which was in a vernacular rather than the *lingua franca* of Latin. Bonifacio saw the answer to the problem in uncovering the categories of a *common language of gesture* which could return humanity to its prelapsarian state.

The imagined solution of a common language led to a set of principles by which non-verbal behaviour could be understood. Thus, the discourse around performance from around 1650 to 1750 became crystallized into principles that can be called neoclassical, since they ultimately derived from the traditional rhetorical sources as well as paintings and sculpture influenced by classicism. These principles were set out in manuals of oratory for the consumption of amateur speakers as well as professionals. In giving the essence of the principles here, I owe a large debt, as do all students of the subject, to the opera scholar Dene Barnett (Barnett 1987):

1. The *weight* is placed over one foot to ensure an elegant curve of the body. The feet are never set in parallel or 'ten to two'. If the weight is over the front foot, the rear leg is relaxed with a slight knee-bend, and the two feet can form right angles with the toes turned out to display the calves as in ballet. So in essence the front foot points towards the scene partner and the back foot towards the auditorium using ballet positions two and four. This opens the body out to the audience.
2. There are two basic resting *hand positions*. These are artistically elegant variations of Precision Grip (with the middle fingers touching the thumb) and Power Grip (with the index finger extended slightly) gestures and are found in Quintilian.
3. Most gestures are made with the *right hand*. Charles Gildon in his *Life of Thomas Betterton* (1710) writes, 'If an Action comes to be used by only one Hand, that must be the *Right*, it being indecent to make a Gesture with the *Left* alone' (Gildon 1710: 74). The left foot would in this case be set forward to create a curve in the body. An exception was made for aversive gestures, that is, expressive gestures of contempt, scorn, disgust, rejection, horror and repulsion. For these, the actor was permitted to use the left hand as the dominant hand. The eighteenth-century manuals all stressed the appropriate use of the right and left hand in oratory and acting. For example, Péchantrés around 1700 wrote: 'In pleasure and delight it is the right hand which must act, in anger and hatred it is the left hand – come to me, it is the right hand – go away from me, it is the left hand' (in Barnett 1987: 63). The idea that the right side (*dexter*) is good and the left (*sinister*) is evil was further translated into general practice regarding stage compositions, so that socially or morally superior characters would tend to occupy stage right (i.e. on the right from the perspective of the actor looking out at the audience) and inferior ones stage left.
4. Gestures should be made using graceful *curving lines*. Lessing (1755) argued that straight lines were only appropriate for portraying rustic characters or characters in the grip of certain violent passions. He gives the example of a gesture of proud dismissal, which he says is performed better in an oblique straight line (as if sweeping something

away). The wrist was usually turned upward (unlike the prone hand position of the ballet dancer).

5. The gesturing hands should not travel above the eyes or below the waist, since that looks unrestrained. Gilbert Austin (1806) suggested this is not true for 'epic' passages, where a sense of largeness is required. By the time Austin was writing, theatre auditoria had grown in size, and gestures needed to be scaled up.

6. The *upper arms* should be lifted slightly away from the torso, using the bend of the elbow, rather than touching it. This raises the centre of mass of the body towards the upper chest, and creates an impression that the performer is in a state of anticipation or preparation to move.

7. The performer should take care not to cross the arms over the trunk where possible, since this action blurs the outline of the performer for the audience. The hands should not be at the same height since that could also blur the picture.

The aim was to create an aesthetically pleasing body according to the neoclassical prescription – a body akin in some ways to that of a ballet dancer, with turned-out feet and calves, a feeling of lift in the torso, and elegantly curving extended arms and hands.

Dene Barnett, whose 1987 publication *The Art of Gesture* remains a crucial reference, moved beyond these general principles to outline a set of eight basic categories of gesture described in the manuals. Barnett's work can be criticized for its restrictive over-reliance on gesture as a semiotic system rather than as an adaptive tool for the revelation of individual thought and feeling. That said, it seems from the available evidence of illustrations and descriptions that during the 'long eighteenth century' (from around 1650 to around 1830), tragic actors and opera singers did at least sometimes make use of this repertoire of gestures in performance, even if their use of it was more flexible than Barnett's typology might suggest. Thus, it is helpful to consider his typology of gesture at this point. The headings are Barnett's; in each case, I offer the terminology from modern authorities on gesture like David McNeill, Adam Kendon and Ekman and Friesen.

Indicative gestures

These are gestures that point to something. David McNeill, the psycholinguist whose work informs this book and who is interviewed in Chapter 8, calls them *deictics*.

Gildon writes: 'Do they not in shewing of Places and Persons, sup-ply the Place of Adverbs and Pronouns?' (Gildon 1710: 47). Gilbert Austin (1806) offered an example from Sarah Siddons as Imogen: 'Wert thou the son of Jupiter, and no more/But what thou art besides, thou wert too base/To be his groom' (*Cymbeline* 2.3.121–4). On the words 'the son of Jupiter' Siddons is pictured raising her pointing hand up to the sky.

Imitative gestures

McNeill classifies these under the term *iconics*. These are gestures that make pictures of what is being described in the accompanying speech. They usually model some spatial or motor aspect of the topic, illustrat-ing how fast something was moving, in what direction, what size or shape it was, how one is meant to do something, etc.

Barnett's category also includes what McNeill calls *metaphorics*. These are a special class of iconics that create a referent for an abstract idea. They usually derive from basic cognitive metaphors such as the *con-tainer* metaphor – where the hand(s) forms a container shape such as a bowl; and the *conduit* metaphor – where the hand(s) models a channel such as a pipe. In the opening paragraph of this book, I gave an example of the metaphoric Precision Grip gesture of imitating the holding of a needle, where the index finger is in contact with the thumb. The great virtue of metaphoric gestures like this is that they can be used in subtle ways to communicate the idea that the speaker has about her- or him-self. The example I gave was that this gesture could be taken to mean the speaker wishes to draw attention to her or his own competence – the capacity to achieve her or his intention – by suggesting a degree of delicacy or difficulty inherent in the subject, which the speaker is none-theless capable of handling.

Given the warnings from Quintilian onward about the use of 'pantomime' – i.e. literal illustration with the hands – it was always thought necessary to proceed with caution with imitative gestures. Charles Gildon warned against putting oneself 'into the Posture of one bending a Bow, presenting a Musquet or playing on any Musical instru-ment, as if you had it in your Hands'; as well, even when the actor is speaking of 'the Debaucheries of the Age, or any thing of that Nature' he or she must not 'imitate any lewd, obscene or indecent Postures' (Gildon 1710: 78). In practice, what such strictures also meant was that only the general features of an object would be outlined, such as its overall direction of movement, speed or shape. Thus the actor John Walker in his *Elements of Elocution*:

> When anything sublime, lofty, or heavenly is expressed, the eye and the right hand may be properly elevated, and when anything low, inferior, or grovelling is referred to, the eye and hand may be directed downwards: when anything distant or extensive is mentioned, the hand may naturally describe the distance or extent. (Walker 1781: II, 266)

Very often, iconics are used by a person when they are telling a story, and want to indicate features of an object within the story. They are only used as accompaniments to speech, and reveal something of the mental image that the speaker has about the event described. The gesture shows the perspective the speaker is taking of it, which could be from the character's point of view, the object's point of view or an observer's point of view. But there is a difficulty here: in passages of narration, at times Shakespeare seems to confuse the point of view of the speech. A good example is Gertrude's passage describing the death of Ophelia, which is rich in the kind of detail that might make a spectator wonder how she remembers so much, since she was not actually there when Ophelia died (4.7.166–83). How does she know that Ophelia 'chanted snatches of old lauds' while she was floating along on the brook (1.177), for instance? If the actor made iconic gestures to lend concrete support to the material events of the narration, the spectators might well start wondering how she can be so sure of what she did not see for herself.

One result of this is that the performer may well avoid iconic gestures, and instead try to draw the spectator's attention to the speaker's attitude to the other characters (or to the spectators themselves) rather than to the logical consistency of the narration. In a recent example, Robert Hapgood tells us that 'Clare Higgins, in the Rylance/Daniels production comforted Laertes, he on his knees with his head at her breast, she stroking his head' (Hapgood 1999: 248). The stroking gesture is figured in the seventeenth-century self-styled chirosopher John Bulwer's catalogue of gestures under the name of *Foveo* (Latin for 'keep warm'): 'We use to stroke them gently with our Hand whom we make much of, cherish, humour or affectionately love ... being a kinde of indulgent declaration of the minde, used to pacifie and please others ...' (Bulwer 1644: 78). John Bulwer's work is discussed in the next chapter.

There is in *Hamlet*, though, a speech that seems to openly invite iconics. In 2.1, Ophelia describes how Hamlet came to her private closet in a dishevelled state and frightened her:

> He took me by the wrist and held me hard,
> Then goes he to the length of all his arm
> And with his other hand thus o'er his brow
> He falls to such perusal of my face
> As 'a would draw it. Long stayed he so;
> At last, a little shaking of mine arm
> And thrice his head thus waving up and down,
> He raised a sigh so piteous and profound
> As it did seem to shatter all his bulk
> And end his being. (2.1.87–96)

The word 'thus' twice invites the actor to pantomime; first, as Hamlet stepped back he placed his hand 'thus' on his forehead, and then, after scrutinizing Ophelia's face he nodded 'thus' three times before issuing forth a sigh of profound melancholy. Julia Marlowe, among the more forceful of pre-twentieth-century Ophelias, acted out this entire scenario, casting herself as Hamlet and making her father stand in for her. Even here, though, the richer content of the gesture is not found in the features of the object described but in the intention of the speaker towards the listener. That is why the advice given in the eighteenth-century manuals is that the speaker should be sparing in the use of literal representation while drawing more freely upon metaphoric gestures.

Gestures of address

These are essentially *pragmatic gestures* (this term is taken from the influential gesture theorist Adam Kendon) that are deployed to focus the audience's attention on the interaction partner on stage, to signal who is being spoken to.

In Gilbert Austin's *Chironomia* (1806), which can be taken as a summation of the eighteenth-century treatment of the subject rather than an original contribution, the equivalent term 'formal gestures' is introduced and then broken down as follows:

1. *Commencing gestures*: the speaker's hand or eyes are lifted to get the listener's attention and show that the speaker is about to begin talking.

This corresponds to what gesture scholars refer to as the preparation phase of a co-verbal gesture.

2. *Discriminating gestures*: these are the gestures of address to signal who is being spoken to.
3. *Auxiliary or alternate gestures*: these are made with the non-dominant hand. They are in essence extra gestures made in the flow of speech as the topic is parsed or complicated further.
4. *Suspended or preparatory gestures*: indicating a pause for thought or to increase feelings of anticipation in the interlocutor.
5. *Terminating gestures*: the hand or eyes lowered to signal the end of the speech. These correspond to the rest phase of the gesture in modern theory. A terminating gesture should be carried out gently, with minimum jerk, 'and then only little by little as the speech ends' as Goethe says (in Barnett 1987: 82).

Expressive gestures

This group refers to bodily movements that are symptomatic of an emotional reaction: smiling, laughter, tears, sneering, teeth chattering, goosebumps, and so on. While not strictly speaking intentionally expressive gestures, they constitute an important category for this study. They were named *affect displays* in a classic paper by Paul Ekman and Wally Friesen (1969). Affect displays are thus the gestures that show temporary emotional reactions or attitudes. Bridget Escolme has argued for the importance of affect displays (what she refers to as emotional 'excess') for the spectator of Shakespeare's theatre: 'the expression of extreme emotion was something that people came to the theatre to see and hear – to take pleasure in, in fact' (Escolme 2013: xviii).

Gestures of emphasis

These are gestures whose stroke is timed to lay stress on a particular word or syllable. They mark the accents of speech. We tend to use them to emphasize particular words. In David McNeill's terminology, these are called *beats*.

The gesture expresses 'the predominant idea' in that part of the speech (Austin 1806: 392). The word 'stroke' is used by Gilbert Austin (ibid.: 377). He writes that the 'stroke of the gesture is to the eye, what the emphasis and inflexions of the voice are to the ear' (ibid.). It is these gestures, I suspect, that Hamlet cautions the Players about when he says, 'Nor do not saw the air too much with your hand, thus, but use all gently' (3.2.4–5). Austin noted that all gestures, whatever their function, should actually coincide with the relevant part of speech, so, as Barnett comments, all gestures should in a way be seen as gestures of emphasis (Barnett 1987: 86).

There are two further categories of gesture in modern theory that are not treated in the manuals of oratory at any length, and so are not discussed by Dene Barnett. However, I refer to them elsewhere in this book so they need to be defined. They are:

1. *Emblems*. These are gestures that replace words: for example, the 'OK' gesture. They are for obvious reasons produced without accompanying speech. McNeill argues that most of these gestures are metaphors codified by culture. Since many of them are quite ancient, they often have a 'magical' aura – as when one gives someone the finger with the intention not merely to insult but to inflict damage (McNeill 2014a).
2. *Adaptors*. This is a class of involuntary movements (see Ekman and Friesen 1969). The class is subdivided into *object adaptors* – such as playing with a pen – and *self-adaptors* – such as playing with one's hair, scratching one's nose, etc. Such movements might well be made by a person who is under stress, thinking through a problem, or bored. Some scholars do not treat these movements as gestures since they are not intentionally expressive, but for the purposes of this book they are important.

The reasons why these two particular classes of gesture are not discussed in this period are open to debate, but I think in both cases they would not have been seen as beautiful, or as conducive to an artistic presentation, although they may well have been considered appropriate for vulgar comedy.

The gestures of the passions

In the eighteenth century the passions were given characteristic facial and bodily configurations. An important source of information on the forms taken by expressive gestures were the late seventeenth century and early eighteenth century manuals of painters such as Charles Le Brun, Karel Mander and Gérard Lairesse. The following passions were usually illustrated:

1. *Grief*: a weeping face, clasped hands and hanging head. Despair is indicated by the arms hanging down. Drooping hands were taken as a sign of unmanly weakness, a sign still used in English culture at

least into the 1970s for an effete or homosexual man. With either posture, as Lang notes, it was important that the actor held the hands away from the torso for the purposes of visual clarity. A hanging head also indicated shame. Austin also suggested a gesture for grief arising from suddenly hearing disastrous news: the actor 'covers the eyes with one hand, advances forwards and throws back the other hand' (Austin 1806: 489).

2. *Surprise*: the eyes and mouth open wide and the arms are held away from the body with fingers opened out, while the actor takes a step back. Gildon said that 'Nature by a sort of Mechanic Motion throws the Hands out as Guards to the Eyes on such an Occasion' (Gildon 1710: 76). The use of the word 'Mechanic' here by Gildon is interesting. In *The Players' Passion* (1985), Joseph Roach argues that discourses on acting in the West have since the Renaissance been driven by two competing models of the body, one vitalist-organicist and one mechanistic. Here, the implication is that a 'Mechanic Motion' is one that is largely involuntary. The expressive form of surprise is extended in wonder and amazement, and from thence enlarged into astonishment and terror, where the body draws back further and the legs are set further apart. Walker wrote that 'the body seems shrinking from the danger, and putting itself in a posture for flight' (Walker 1781: II, 329).

3. *Anger*: the forehead frowns, the eyelids are raised and the eyes blaze, the outer part of the eyebrows raises while the inner contracts, the teeth gnash or the jaw sets with the lower jaw protruding and the mouth firms up into a horizontal line; the fists clench and the elbows bend 'in a straining manner to the body' (ibid.: II, 364), while the neck muscles extend. In wrath, an extension of anger, the actor walks up and down, and stamps his or her feet. The hair is also supposed to rise up.

4. *Contempt*: this is somewhat similar to the anger face, but the corners of the mouth are pulled down. With respect to hand gestures, contempt resembles anger in that graceful curving lines were eschewed in favour of broken, violent movements.

5. *Jealousy*: as Le Brun's drawing indicates, the most important aspect of this is that the eyes are screwed together and look sideways. The mouth is closed and the lower lip protrudes (as if sulking), while the nostrils are turned up to create a strong line on the cheeks. The body, according to Jelgerhuis (1827), is made 'tighter, the hands into fists, now and then breaking away' (Jelgerhuis 1827: 153). The problem with this representation is that the jealous person will usually try to

mask their true feelings. As well, jealousy is not usually a temporary emotional reaction that can be visually articulated in a change of appearance.

6. *Aversion, hatred or refusal*: the body draws back from the unwanted object, the hands are thrown out like a vertical barrier against the object and the head turns away. Austin prefaced this motion with an anticipatory one, in which at first 'the hand held vertical is retracted towards the face, the eyes and head are for a moment directed eagerly towards the object, and the feet advance' (Austin 1806: 487). The preparation move – going to look at what will disgust us – serves to intensify the drama of looking away. The extension of this gesture is in horror. Following Quintilian, the general advice was to thrust the right hand to the left, turn the left shoulder towards the right and turn the head to the right.

7. *Scorn*: this is expressed by a toss of the left hand.

8. *Shame*: the head hangs down and the hands cover the face, or one hand covers the face while the other is held slightly away from the face in an elegant contrast. In extreme cases of shame, the knees sink to the ground and both hands cover the eyes. Austin said 'this is a feminine expression of it' (Austin 1806: 489).

9. *Welcome*: Barnett includes the gesture of holding the arms out in welcome as among the expressive gestures. It indicates a spontaneous display of love, affection or benevolence. The foot takes a step back in surprise at the sight of one's friend, and the body leans back a little before the person advances with spread-out arms.

There is a considerable amount of evidence from this period that these passionate gestures were a part of the visual vocabulary of an educated person. In Chapter 5 I look in more detail at how some of them were deployed by actors like David Garrick and Sarah Siddons.

Charles Darwin and the modern era

By the mid-nineteenth century, as the social morality of self-fulfilment began to take hold more fully, considerations of the appropriateness of a gesture for a 'beautiful' artistic presentation would begin to be set aside. From the point of view of affect displays and adaptors the major work of the next hundred years is Charles Darwin's *The Expression of the Emotions in Man and Animals* (1872/1998). Darwin's text should be positioned within the long history of discourse on the passions. It stands as a kind of bridge between the neoclassical account of the passions and the modern understanding of emotion. Darwin used photographs of actors performing emotional reactions, images that can be seen to relate to the attitudinizing of classical actors and to the illustrations of Le Brun and Lairesse. Essentially, the same expressions are given more of a behavioural appearance, as if situated in a real-world context. Up to a point anyway – the actors in the photographs Darwin used look to me like they are faking it. That is partly due to historical distance, of course: they are wearing Victorian clothes, and the man in the pictures has Victorian lambchop whiskers. Then again, Darwin knew they were faking it. He was well aware that people have differing capacities for control over their reflex emotionality, and that actors are able to do apparently extraordinary feats like 'bring the grief muscles freely into play' (Darwin 1872: 182). Darwin was being a touch naïve here: it is not hard to pull a believable sad face, and children who want sympathy are quite capable of it.

   At the same time, Darwin elaborated upon a rather more explosive idea: that there were analogues of human emotional displays in the behaviour of other animals. This is a logical extension of the basic 'continuity principle' of evolutionary theory (mentioned in the Introduction). Illustrations in *The Expression of the Emotions* show, for instance, an angry human face alongside an angry dog's face and an angry swan's face. Such images recall the physiognomic tradition of texts such as Giambattista Della Porta's *De humana physiognomia* (1586). The difference was that in the Renaissance and the eighteenth century the image of pantomimic 'apishness' was a moral judgement on uncivilized behaviour – it was meant to indicate what you were *not* supposed to be. Darwin's message was that you *already were* what you were not supposed to be. In that respect, evolutionary theory was analogous to the medieval conception of original sin. Yet its impact was nothing short of scandalous. The most revolutionary aspect of his theory was the idea that humans are not set apart from other species. Inevitably Darwin's challenge led to parodies in the popular media of men and women – including, of course, the great man Darwin himself – as apish. But Darwin's work on emotional reactions pushed forward the social morality of self-fulfilment because it divorced the emotions from moral judgements – they were seen instead as physiological manifestations of core instincts or as by-products of other evolved functions. And his proposition in *The Descent of Man* (1871/1981) that the moral sense in humans is derived from the social instincts at once removed it still further from the domain of higher purposes such as salvation. As I will show in the discussion of Henry Irving (Chapter 5), the influence of

Darwin's theory of the emotions on acting can be seen in the development of behavioural gestures such as adaptors, tokens of an imagined spontaneity and authenticity, both on stage and in the cinema.

Gesture theory in the twentieth century took on board a range of insights and models from other disciplines such as anthropology, dance, semiotics, cultural politics and psycholinguistics. It is impossible to tease out a master narrative that could account for the influence of these discourses upon Shakespearean performance since the advent of modernism. Suffice to say here that the shadows of a few key figures, such as Michael Chekhov and Rudolf Laban, loom large in the arena of performance. In the bibliography I offer a few indicative pointers to further reading.

How smoothness connects with social morality

In the outline given above, I drew attention to a number of concepts: decorum (in Cicero), *sprezzatura* (in Castiglione), *festina lente* (in Erasmus), the aesthetically pleasing body (in the eighteenth-century manuals) and smoothness (in *Hamlet*). There is clearly a relationship between these concepts, since they all point to the importance of control over one's bodily impulses. I want now to return to the argument I introduced at the beginning of the chapter, and connect these concepts to my central claim for gesture as a window onto social morality.

Smoothness is a quality of movement that is often felt to signal an attractive, sociable, trustworthy or competent person – and this fact is crucial to an understanding of how gesture plays into questions of social cognition. As I suggested in the Introduction, *warmth* and *competence* have been proposed in recent social psychology as core factors in the formation of social judgements. Warmth is seen as having a moral dimension in that it signifies trustworthiness and honesty, as well as associations with likeability. Signs of warmth show that the other person's intentions are beneficial not harmful. Signs of competence show that the other person is actually capable of carrying out their intentions (see Fiske, Cuddy and Glick 2006).

My proposition is that smoothness of movement tends to communicate that the other person wishes to be seen as both non-threatening (warmth dimension) and capable with respect to their intentions (competence dimension); in other words, it can cover both of the primary components in the formation of social judgements. Therein lies its power as a bodily display. I would argue that it is key to managing one's social relationships, because it constitutes a set of discreet signals that people respond to when conferring status upon others. Thus, in a performance smoothness can be seen as an expression of the actor's concern with managing the impression she or he makes on both the audience and her or his fellow actors.

To talk of *impression management* is to invoke the spectre of the sociologist Erving Goffman, who studied the subject in depth. The impulse behind his work was to treat behaviour from the perspective of *theatrum mundi* – all the world's a stage, therefore people are constantly engaged in acts of managing the *face* they show to each other. Face is an aspect of an individual's social capital: it is a positive value which, if managed well, can bring meaningful benefits to the person, such as increased access to resources. Clearly, a person's face is directly related to their social status. It is not difficult to see how his perspective can be seen to relate to the concept of 'self-fashioning' put forward by Stephen Greenblatt (see Introduction).

Goffman was uncomfortable with stage acting because, as far as he was concerned, in their daily lives people were already performing. He held a prejudice against the theatre derived from a feeling of ontological queasiness about its purpose. For Goffman, theatre cannot hold the mirror up to nature (as Hamlet proposes), because natural behaviour does not exist. The nearest thing to natural – i.e. 'authentic' – behaviour Goffman allowed were the dysphoric responses of inmates in the asylum where he worked for a while. But Goffman had failed to grasp the nature of the drama's power. Everyone knows that the drama is make-believe, yet audiences still respond, at least to some extent, as if the events on stage or on screen were actually taking place in the world. They do not respond because they think that what is being portrayed is real. They react in spite of the fact that they know it is not real – perhaps even *because* they know it is not real – so they feel safe to react. From that point of view, the widely held notion that the audience must engage in a 'suspension of disbelief' is misplaced, because in my experience most audiences are usually very willing to suspend disbelief since the trade-off for them is a pleasurable experience. Part of the pleasure, I think, is the result of the smooth gestures that actors make, which can subtly cue the audience's feelings of safety at being in a low-risk environment. The actor sends out a physical signal to the audience that the performance is under control, is not directly threatening to them, is simply engaging in a kind of playing; at the same time, this gives the actor the freedom to provide displays of amplified emotion, aggression or risk-taking behaviour if desired.

To be sure, such displays can be quite complex with respect to the maintenance of self-possession, conditioned as they are by cultural and historical contexts as well as by physiology. To argue for the importance of smoothness is not the same as simply promoting an aesthetic of restraint. Acting tends to involve displays of emotion, and all emotion necessitates the surrender of self-possession to some extent, in the sense that one is not fully able in emotional moments to get control over what one pays attention to. An extreme example would be grief at the loss of a loved one. It can be exceptionally difficult to put one's attention on anything other than the person one has lost in such a situation, even though one may be desperate to attend to other matters, so that normal functioning becomes a problem. However, while within a dramatic fiction the character may appear to lose self-control, the actor for the most part cannot afford to, and the maintenance of this dynamic balance between emotion and self-possession is critical to the actor's success.

Smooth movement is characteristic of high-status behaviour. On stage, it offers reassurance to the spectator that the actor is in control of her or his anxiety, that she or he is a trustworthy professional who will cause no harm and that she or he is a skilled artist concerned with providing a pleasurable emotional experience. In addition, an actor may attempt to convey an idea that the character she or he is playing – or the actor her- or himself – is in some way attractive, for example through a display of heroic energy directed towards overcoming a problem. The actor might undertake to perform actions that are obviously hard to accomplish, such as dancing, fencing or gymnastics. And the actor might accomplish her or his tasks with apparent effortlessness. This feeling of effortlessness is conveyed by smoothness of movement, by virtue of which it seems that nothing is extraneous to the accomplishment of that task.

Joseph Roach does a good job in his book *It* (2007) of explaining the effect that charismatic performers have upon us mere mortals. But he does not say anything about how they might achieve it. The implication is the conventional one – you either have it or you don't. I suggest, though, that actors develop charisma through modelling the behaviour of high-status people, or at least of common perceptions regarding such behaviour. Actors use charismatic display as a shield against the *anti-theatrical prejudice*: the widespread feeling, promulgated since antiquity, that acting is somehow a wrong thing to do (the word the Greeks used for actor was *hupokrates* – hypocrite), and that actors are socially untrustworthy individuals. It is through the manipulation of charismatic signals that some actors from Shakespeare's time onwards were able to claim a professional status and thus possess wealth and influence: they sold their stage presence to the public. My point is that presence – charisma – is not something one is simply born with, but is something that actors can cultivate and practise.

I agree with Joseph Roach, however, that the *effect* of smoothness in a performance is mysterious: for all the passions on display, smooth behaviour suggests there is something hidden from the spectator, a sense that the actor is always keeping a secret from you, the spectator. From the perspective of social morality, this secret is the idea of an individual self who does not exist to serve God, or the monarch, or even you, but to discover the source of their own fulfilment. Michael Clune, writing about classicism, argues that the hero of antiquity did not need an audience to confirm his significance; his immortality was built into his name, which stood for his monumental deeds. Smoothness, a bodily technique co-opted from the classical tradition, retains a vestige of that coolness in relation to the spectator. That is what Hamlet is alluding to when he says, 'You would play upon me, you would seem to know my stops, you would pluck out the heart of my mystery ... 'Sblood, do you think I am easier to be played on than a pipe?' (3.2.366–73)

In this opening part of the book I have outlined some theoretical issues regarding gesture in Shakespearean performance. I have tried to define what a gesture is and how it has been understood in Western European discourses, which I have labelled classical, medieval, early modern, neoclassical and modern. My use of these labels is largely for the sake of convenience, since my interpretation of the issues is premised upon a sense of gesture as existing in a continuum, where sociocultural shifts tend to happen slowly and quite imperceptibly rather than in distinct and separable movements. Thus, I have argued for the validity of social morality as a driver of both continuities and changes within gestural behaviour over time, and we must recognize that social morality as it is manifested in behaviour, even in a time of great upheaval such as the Reformation, does not suddenly alter overnight. Historically minded critics have worked tirelessly to dismantle the myth that Shakespeare was a singular phenomenon who somehow radically broke free from the past and invented everything from scratch; creativity such as his is less a matter of invention *ex nihilo* and more one of juxtaposition of already existing elements. I have also advanced an idea of smoothness in performance, which I am arguing has both psycho-physiological and sociocultural components, and thus can be seen as exemplifying how gestural behaviour embodies in one movement both continuity *and* difference. In what follows I will look in more detail at the practice of gesture, through an examination first of all of some of the performance conditions of Shakespeare's own context, and then beyond into exploring the work of some very influential actors.

Part II
Practice

3
Shakespeare's Practice

Uses of the word 'gesture' in Shakespeare's plays

The word 'gesture(s)' is found ten times in Shakespeare's plays. He only used it from 1599 – after his company had moved into the Globe. If there is a common thread in his deployment of the word, it is in the notion that gesture is revelatory: it presents things, yields things, imports things, it speaks, it expresses. For example, in *As You Like It* the use of the word suggests an involuntary emotional reaction:

> If you do love Rosalind so near the heart as your gesture cries it out ... (5.2.61–2)

By contrast, in *Henry V* it infers a postural attitude:

> ... and their gesture sad,
> Investing lank-lean cheeks and war-torn coats,
> Presenteth them unto the gazing moon
> So many horrid ghosts ... (4.0.25–8)

In both cases, it is assumed that gesture is expressive: it cries out, it invests, it presents things in terms of both a physical appearance ('horrid ghosts') and an abstraction (as 'the heart'). But where in *Henry V* the suggestion is of a static position, with Orlando's gesture in *As You Like It* the indication is of a quick movement betraying rapid emotional reactions and thought patterns.

The sense of gesture as a sudden betrayal of a fleeting inner life is taken up by Shakespeare in *Hamlet*. Here, the dialogue seems to describe what is sometimes called *incongruence*, where Ophelia's speech is held to be disconnected from her bodily movement:

> Her speech is nothing,
> Yet the unshaped use of it doth move
> The hearers to collection. They aim at it,
> And botch the words up fit to their own thoughts,
> Which as her winks and nods and gestures yield them,
> Indeed would make one think there might be thought
> Though nothing sure, yet much unhappily. (4.5.7–13)

That gesture could represent the 'nothing sure' of thought, a secret that cannot be fully grasped by the observer, was something quite new in English drama. It is tempting to view it as an instance of a growing crisis within Elizabethan culture, whereby the Protestant regime struggled to maintain some kind of surveillance over the religious beliefs of individuals still wedded to the old faith. In any case, at the same time that it offers a window into rapid emotional thought processes, it seems that for Shakespeare a gesture requires an act of construal, of interpretation, to be fully understood. In *Othello*, Shakespeare pursues this conception – of gesture as a clue in need of decoding – in three references within the same key scene. To begin with, by directing our attention towards bodily behaviour, Iago determines (one might say overdetermines) its significance:

> I say, but mark his gesture ... (4.1.88)

In the next example, Iago introduces the idea that gesture is subject to potentially dangerous misreading by those in thrall to their own passions:

> As he shall smile, Othello shall go mad.
> And his unbookish jealousy must construe
> Poor Cassio's smiles, gestures and light behaviour
> Quite in the wrong. (4.1.101–4)

In the third, he lays claim for his own interpretation as authoritative:

> ... his gesture imports it. (4.1.136)

Thus, a tension is perceivable between the meaning conventionally attached to a gesture by virtue of its visible shape and the hidden psychological attitude that may or may not be alluded to by the shape.

This was, broadly speaking, the situation of gesture in performance in the aftermath of the Reformation. Like the walls of Shakespeare's local church in Stratford-upon-Avon, where Protestants (administered by Shakespeare's father) had whitewashed the *Biblia pauperum* painted on the walls, in its openness to (mis)reading gesture had become a site of contest over social meanings. Here, through his manipulation of the semantics of behaviour, Iago paves the way for a shift in social morality from a concern with higher purposes to a focus on self-fulfilment. In the penultimate chapter to this book, I return to Iago as a pivotal figure in the history of gesture in performance.

From around 1609, gesture in Shakespeare's practice – so far as can be understood from his texts – seems to undergo its own further process of 'whitewashing', in the sense of a move from the specific bodily detail to the abstract concept. In the opening of *Timon of Athens*, a poet compliments a painter on a portrait shown to him. The figure in the portrait is pictured speaking, and the gesture – which could be facial – gives the impression of the thought behind the words. But Shakespeare does not say what that impression is:

> How big imagination
> Moves in this lip! To th' dumbness of the gesture
> One might interpret. (1.1.33–4)

In the later plays, Shakespeare enlarged his association of the word with dumbness, again without declaring what this dumb language of gesture is really saying:

> ... there was speech in their dumbness, language in their very gesture ... (*The Winter's Tale* 5.2.14–15)

Coming to *The Tempest*, the shift away from the specific towards the abstract is further suggested by the word 'discourse' here:

> Such shapes, such gesture and such sound, expressing
> (Although they want the use of tongue) a kind
> Of excellent dumb discourse. (3.3.38–40)

There is also a stage direction in *The Tempest*, perhaps not written by Shakespeare:

> *Here enters Ariel before; then Alonso with a frantic gesture ...* (5.1.58)

Alonso's gesture is a conventional display of guilt. The play is reminiscent of a court masque, a form that required detailed choreography of its elaborate audiovisual effects, and the gesture would have taken its place within a larger image. It is almost as though gesture in Shakespearean performance underwent a crisis of representation at the close of the 1590s, before returning by the end of the next decade with its provocative ambiguity flattened out into a new kind of formality. This formal style of gesturing – Alonso's archetypal 'frantic gesture' for instance – could be seen as presaging the cultural impulse that led to Giovanni Bonifacio's call for a universal language of gesture.

Having considered Shakespeare's deployment of the word itself, I want to look in a little more detail at an important example of what could have been a 'provocative' gesture in the context of Shakespeare's practice.

Supplication

In a *supplication* gesture, the hand was stretched out in an appeal either to the gods or to an individual who wields power. Frances A. Sullivan finds 19 examples of this gesture in Virgil's *Aeneid* as well as in Homer, Ovid, Sallust, Caesar, Livy, Ennius and Cicero (Sullivan 1968: 359–61).

Returning to *Titus Andronicus*, after Titus finishes his funeral oration to Rome and his sons, as he prepares to sacrifice the eldest born boy of his captured enemy Tamora, she seizes the moment to launch her own oratorical performance:

> Stay, Roman brethren, gracious conqueror,
> Victorious Titus, rue the tears I shed,
> A mother's tears in passion for her son!
> And if thy sons were ever dear to thee,
> O, think my son to be as dear to me. (1.1.107–11)

Here is a highly emotional speech of supplication, apparently performed while kneeling going by the evidence of her later words, 'I'll find a day to massacre them all ... And make them know what 'tis to let a queen/ Kneel in the streets and beg for grace in vain' (1.1.455–60). In Cicero's eyes, such a speech would call for physical accompaniment as well as a suitable vocal attitude for imploring pity. Shakespeare's use of the word 'passion' here is the equivalent of a director's instruction coded in the dialogue – as is the phrase 'rue the tears I shed'.

Supplication was performed with the right arm extended either at an angle towards the addressee or vertically towards heaven, and with the palm up. Palm up gestures are discussed by Adam Kendon (2004: chapter 13), who treats them as one among a number of gesture families. Kendon shows that such gestures are widely used across many cultures with the same basic range of functions: 'Open Hand Supine (or "palm up") family gestures…are used in contexts where the speaker is offering, giving or showing something or requesting the reception of something' (Kendon 2004: 248). The precise meaning of the gesture may shift in specific contexts, but the basic hand shape on the whole does not. To offer yourself up to the other person by exposing vulnerable areas of the body (the heart, the wrists) is to show acceptance of their dominance over you and – since you have no other weapon to fight with in the situation – your emotional honesty.

In extending her arm out towards the object of her pleading, Tamora would be making it obvious to Titus (and everyone else in the scene) that she expects to receive something specific from him. The gesture displays submission and request in equal measure. Scholars like John Gould (1973) have shown how, in classical culture, supplicating gestures were ignored by the powerful at their peril since they had a quasi-legal status. In Ancient Greece, failure to attend to the supplicant's plea could bring on the wrath of Zeus. Shakespeare's audience would have recognized the status relationship here as a representation of both the classical Roman conqueror and slave and the medieval Christian lord and vassal. Thus the gesture promotes a strong association between the legal and religious procedures of Ancient Rome, as far as Shakespeare would have understood them, and the feudal concept of *noblesse oblige*.

Jan Bremmer gives another interpretation of the supplication gesture: he argues that the upturned hand would denote a man who had symbolically abdicated his weapons. He argues that the upturned hand was seen as womanish in classical culture, and could even indicate homosexuality (Bremmer 1991: 22). He points out that 'Spartan youths, like their Athenian contemporaries, were obliged to keep their hands within their garments. In Greece, the hand was considered the organ for action and therefore could only be shown by real males' (ibid.). It is interesting from this point of view to see how Tamora's rhetorical demand is that she is looked upon not merely as a queen who is willing to acknowledge her victor's power, but as a mother who cannot bear to see her son killed merely for acting honourably on the battlefield.

Prayer

The association between the classical and the feudal in supplication is clarified further by considering the related gesture of *praying*. For one thing, it was quite common in early modern England for Protestant commentators to divide the act of prayer into different parts, among which was sometimes 'supplication', which tended to mean petitions for mercy and for the remission of sins (see Ryrie 2013: 108). There is, though, a larger point to be made regarding the idea of sacrifice, among the most fiercely contested points of debate in the Reformation conflicts. Luther believed that to think of the Mass as a kind of sacrifice offered to God was to deny the real sacrifice of Christ (see Cavanaugh 2001). If the Mass is not something we can offer to God, then neither can we offer it to others – such as the dead souls in purgatory. We can pray for them, but we cannot have a direct impact upon them through our participation in the Mass. Prayer is allowed as an action offered up to others, but the Mass is for the individual alone.

The prayer gesture (known as *Orans*) in antiquity had two basic forms: with hands raised upwards to heaven, as described in *1 Timothy 2:8*, and with hands spread out in an open palm shape, as mentioned in *Isaiah 1:15*. During the twelfth-century Carolingian Renaissance, a new configuration of the gesture developed – the *junctis manibus*, or folded hands. By the thirteenth century, this had become the dominant form of the gesture in Europe. Its shape relates it to a gesture in the feudal ritual of 'commendation', where the vassal put his joined hands in those of his lord to connote a surrendering of power (as if the vassal is stretching out his hands to be bound), as well as trust, fidelity and dependence (see Barasch 1987/1990: 60). There are representations of the gesture in this form in the *Sachsenspiegel* manuscripts, the key legal codebook of the German Middle Ages dating from around 1220.

Because Protestantism was capable of conceiving of prayer as an act that serves the living not the dead, there was a place for it on Shakespeare's stage. Besides, it would have been difficult to avoid representing it since, as Alec Ryrie demonstrates, private prayer was a ubiquitous feature of the lives of English Protestants; it was 'the most fundamental and most mysterious feature of Protestant pious practice', and what made it of special theatrical interest was that it was seen as 'a business less of quiet contemplation than of struggle' (Ryrie 2013: 3). One thinks of Claudius's guilty failure to pray in *Hamlet*:

CLAUDIUS. My words fly up, my thoughts remain below.
Words without thoughts never to heaven go. (3.3.97–8)

Claudius's long speech is not a prayer, but a verbalized effort to find a form of prayer that will serve his turn. Ryrie reveals that there was a fascinating slippage between terms in religious texts of the period, where 'prayer' often blurred into 'meditation', a word which in turn had near-synonyms in 'musing', 'cogitation' – and, most tellingly, in 'soliloquy', a term 'applied to texts which were more affective and passionate, and less informative and didactic' (ibid.: 110–11). Thus, a Protestant audience may well have looked upon the soliloquy of Claudius as a spin on the conventions of meditation or prayer.

This gesture is also found in what may be one of the only existing illustrations of a contemporary Shakespearean performance. The *Longleat manuscript* depicts a scene, or possibly a composite of scenes, above a page of text from *Titus Andronicus*. On the left of the drawing stands a figure who is probably Titus, holding a ceremonial spear that divides the image in half. He is opening out his body in what looks like a reaction of surprise. On the right, a woman wearing a crown kneels before him in a gesture of praying with folded hands. She is, in all likelihood, Tamora, and is on her knees before Titus to plead for her son's life.

Whoever made the drawing could have seen a performance of *Titus* sometime around 1594. So it is reasonable to say that this is a representation of how an act of supplication was staged in Shakespeare's day. It is not a silent prayer moment, directed at God, or a communal act of worship. It is an intentional gesture accompanying a speech directed at a human character in a dominant position. It reveals the connection between supplication and prayer, both being social acts performed by an inferior.

At the same time, the barbarian Tamora is depicted like a lady from a medieval Book of Hours. Furthermore, her face is not remotely expressive of anguish; in fact, she looks rather serene. Underneath the drawing is written the line: 'Enter Tamora pleadinge for her sonnes going to execution' – clearly Tamora is supposed to be pleading. So why doesn't she look upset? Was the artist incompetent at facial expressions? Perhaps – the drawing hardly stands up alongside portraits made by such contemporaries as Nicholas Hilliard. But if the artist was Henry Peacham (who is named on the manuscript), then we are dealing with a man who wrote a treatise called *The Art of Drawing*. And in other respects the drawing is not incompetent but rather a cartoon. What Peacham has attempted to do is show the character's decorum. The face is held poised, because that way it suggests the performer's charisma. Furthermore, if this is an image of a performance, this Tamora was a young man.

It was not only the gesture of supplication that was subject to seman-tic shift as social morality, in its everyday expression, began very slowly to relax its ties both to the culture of honour and to the higher purposes of religion, and to move towards an ethos of self-fulfilment. A further example can be found in the gesture of *benediction*. This gesture recurs in the Bible, as when John baptizes Christ; the basic move involves lay-ing the right hand on a person's head. The Gospels of *Matthew* (19:13 ff) and *Mark* (10:16) both refer to the placing of hands on the blessed. Thus, for example, the 'well-known Byzantine images representing the emperor's right to rule through the laying of a hand on the emper-or's head by Christ or a saint are in imitation of the baptism of Christ' (Kalavrezou 1997/2004: 73).

During the medieval period, the baptism gesture became important to the liturgy, marking as it did a ceremonial transition from one state to another. But by the time Shakespeare wrote *The Merchant of Venice*, the gesture had evolved to communicate the more quotidian intention of bestowing favour upon a social inferior:

> LAUNCELOT. Well, old man, I will tell you news of your son. *(He kneels.)* Give me your blessing. Truth will come to light; murder can-not be hid long – a man's son may, but in the end truth will out.
> GOBBO. Pray you, sir, stand up. I am sure you are not Launcelot my boy.
> LAUNCELOT. Pray you let's have no more fooling about it, but give me your blessing. I am Launcelot, your boy that was, your son that is, your child that shall be.
> GOBBO. I cannot think you are my son. (2.2.74–83)

After having made fun of his blind father, Launcelot, locked in an essen-tially feudal mindset of salvation, now seems to panic at the possibility that Old Gobbo will not actually give him a benediction. He lapses into a pseudo-Biblical language – 'your boy that was, your son that is, your child that shall be' – in a scene whose physical comedy relies upon the audience's sense that a formerly sacred ritualistic act can be reduced to a family farce.

Both of these gestures have clear Christian overtones. Yet there is very little specifically Christian ritual to be found in Shakespeare's plays. John Russell Brown argues instead for 'the lesser rituals of ceremony' (Brown 1999: 53). By ceremony, he means 'the repetition of actions and forms of speech which have general rather than individual or personal meaning and acknowledge power or authority' (ibid.). Tudor social life was saturated with displays of status and of affiliation to a particular group identity. The basic displays of obedience are listed by David Bevington as kissing hands, off-capping, bowing and kneeling. By contrast, hand-clasping and embracing 'connote a harmony and reconciliation' (Bevington 1984: 162). Brown sees such ceremonies as crucial to the efficient use of minimal rehearsal time, since all of the actors would have been able to slip into the performance of them without instruction. For instance, it would have been quite obvious to the whole playing company when to enter, where to stand and how to behave in a scene involving a monarch or a noble.

Cue-taking: interaction gestures

Shakespeare's actors had 'roles' with their lines and minimal cues written on them rather than a full script. While certain scenes and actions, usually involving many characters, would have needed choreographing for reasons of safety, it seems that actors were left alone to learn their lines and the few words preceding them by way of cue, and devise their own physical movements, probably in conversation with each other. This argument has been made in detail by Tiffany Stern. Her system accounts for the phenomenal workload of Elizabethan actors.

However, even if this is how the actors worked, it does not imply there was a mishmash of acting styles on Shakespeare's stage. M. M. Mahood writes that nothing 'in the theatrical documents implies that minimal roles in Shakespeare's plays were acted otherwise than with conviction and intelligence' (Mahood 1998: 15). A leading actor such as Richard Burbage would not have tolerated performances out of line with the impression he wished the production to convey. The ethos of the company was likely modelled on the Elizabethan household, demanding loyalty and obedience to the authority figures. There was no shortage of would-be actors hungry for work in London, and Shakespeare, Burbage and their colleagues could no doubt hire and fire as they saw fit. And while the spectators may have felt they had permission to talk, eat, move about, react loudly to the play and so on, this would serve only to strengthen the need to produce a coherent group message.

For the cue-part system to work, actors would have needed to display behaviour that guaranteed the cue would be passed on as they arrived at the end of a speech. It makes sense in this system to write speeches that climax with a sense of import or a certain punch, for example in a phrase dominated by Anglo-Saxon, monosyllabic words, or with an expression that somehow sums up everything you have just said.

Shakespeare appears to have deployed such a writing strategy often. The point has been well made by Simon Palfrey:

> We can see in this how the cue-exchange, or what we can call the cue-space, has the potential equally to embody connection (sharing, coordination, continuity) and competition (rivalry, jealousy, resistance). This makes it a classically dramatic form, a hinge-point where decisions are made, relationships tested, and identities forged. (Palfrey 2011: 135)

It is likely also that *interaction gestures* would be made in the cue-spaces. It is well established among gesture scholars that spontaneous gestures are usually launched slightly in advance of the speech they relate to. We prepare the gesture so that the stroke phase times with the syllable(s) we wish to emphasize (see chapter 10 of McNeill 1992/1995). The actors could signal using their eyes or their hands and the timing of the speech to pass the cue smoothly. The actor in this way reduced the cue-space to a minimum, or filled it with a movement like the preparation phase of a gesture, to give the impression of flow. Palfrey says the cue-space 'can be conceived of as a very real space, shared or fought between two players, one that is neither owned by nor identical to either' (Palfrey 2011: 136). With experienced performers who know each other well, the opportunities for playing with timing in the cue-space were manifold.

What did an interaction gesture look like? It probably resembled what was called *adlocutio*, a gesture that originated in antiquity (Dodwell 2000: 35). Originally it referred to an emperor's address to his soldiers or the people. One of the most characteristic gestures of Roman art, it is found on many coins and statues. In the most famous depictions, such as the statue known as the Prima Porta Augustus, the right arm is raised in open hand vertical palm position. It is a familiar gesture, one that a leader would use to acknowledge a crowd or to demand their silence so that he can talk.

Richard Brilliant argues that the gesturing hand remained empty (i.e. open) in order to signal 'the intangibles of power' (Brilliant 1963: 69). Perhaps, but the idea needs unpacking a little further. With the vertical palm turned out towards the addressee, it creates a metaphoric barrier indicating the intention of the speaker: to stop, or interrupt, the addressee's action. The distance of the arm from the body is significant. Fully extended (like a traffic policeperson), the arm signals 'you stop', as opposed to the half-extended arm that means 'let us stop', and the arm closer to the body, meaning 'I stop'.

Shakespeare's actors may well have deployed interaction gestures of *adlocutio* in both their conventional, 'imperial' form – say, when a ruler spoke to the crowd – and in smaller, more sophisticated ways to indicate 'stop talking', or 'my/your turn to speak', or 'I am (or I'm not) finished'. They would serve to maintain mimetic credibility as well as interactional flow, since when people talk they tend to produce these gestures; it would also have helped to create a group style.

In a survey of the gestures depicted in medieval manuscripts of the plays of Terence, Charles Dodwell refers to a variation of the *adlocutio* – the 'two-finger point'. There are many instances of this gesture in the different manuscripts, some of which date back to the Carolingian period. Two-finger and thumb horizontal pointing (as depicted in the Terentian manuscripts) was used to suggest that the speaker is in midspeech. However, a two-finger vertical palm gesture would still have been linked to the iconographic tradition – as in countless Byzantine images of Christ Pantocrator – so its use in the theatre of Protestant England may have been circumscribed. In the tradition, the gesture also connoted teaching and blessing.

Face acting

The question of *face acting* on Shakespeare's stage leads us to an interesting philosophical problem. Hamlet tells his mother that he will show her true self in a mirror: 'You go not till I set you up a glass/Where you may see the inmost part of you' (3.4.18–19). Moments later, after uncovering the body of Polonius, instead of using a mirror Hamlet shows her two pictures, the 'counterfeit presentment of two brothers' (3.4.54). Why doesn't Hamlet show his mother her own face?

People were unable to see themselves properly in mirrors before the Venetians invented clear 'crystal' glass in 1507. Before that, one saw through brass or green glass, darkly. But the arrival of clear mirrors did not instantly alter the way that people were *represented*. The object seen in the mirror was not usually oneself (Shuger 1999: 22). Instead, the image was of an exemplary figure such as Death, or Christ, or some other paradigm for human conduct – the mirror essentially revealed the invisible behind the visible, a reflection of theological commonplaces (ibid.: 26). The word *mirror* was interchangeable with *image* – it was a device with literary or pictorial uses. This way of representing the human face – as a mask that the mirror sees through – is a product of a social morality of higher purposes: what matters is the condition of the soul beyond the face, which the mirror reveals.

Faced with a real mirror as opposed to a 'theological' one, the inward self may be eclipsed. In *Richard II* (4.1.275–91), the king smashes a mirror on the ground after looking at himself in it and finding insufficient physical evidence of his inward sorrow. Perhaps this is also why Hamlet – consciously or otherwise – does not show Gertrude her face in a mirror: there is no point, since it will reveal not her soul but only her face. And Hamlet has already learnt that 'one may smile and smile and be a villain' (1.5.108). Hamlet's conception of the face as a lying mask (commonplace in the age of Machiavellianism) is put to the test with Rosencrantz:

> HAMLET. Man delights not me – no, nor woman neither, though by your smiling you seem to say so.
> ROSENCRANTZ. My lord, there was no such stuff in my thoughts.
> HAMLET. Why did you laugh then when I said man delights not me?
> (2.2.310–15)

Like Hamlet, the spectator cannot know what is in Rosencrantz's mind from the evidence of his face, because Rosencrantz is both attempting to control the passions acting upon him and probably lying about what he was smiling about. Admit the existence of Machiavellianism, and there is no reliable art to finding the mind's construction on the face. Rosencrantz's impulse in the situation is to save or protect his *face* in the more sociological sense of the word. Hamlet may have been his chum at university, but he certainly isn't any more, and his status as a 'mad prince' is basically contradictory and therefore unsettling. The appropriate response for Rosencrantz is to put on a lying face that helps him maintain his own status.

There is good reason to think that the actors on Shakespeare's stage would have kept their faces relatively still while performing. Deceptiveness of behaviour could still be considered the territory of the Devil, but the Reformation had taught many English people the necessity to control one's behavioural output. This is forcefully expressed in 'Sonnet 94', where those who maintain control over their emotions and the temptations that assail them are praised as 'the lords and owners of their faces' (l.7). Eye movements would be more significant. If the spectator could see his eyes, the actor could suggest who or what he was interested in, or whether he was supposed to be introspecting at that moment. This was known to Cicero, who wrote that 'all depends on the countenance; and even in that the eyes bear sovereign sway' (in Cole and Chinoy 1995: 24). As well, stillness in the face offers the actor the possibility of temporary emotional reactions while maintaining an overall impression of poise, of the 'well-graced' actor (*Richard II* 5.2.24). The presentation of these involuntary reactions – smiling, laughing, bursting into tears, displaying an angry or disgusted face, widening the face in surprise or fear – is in the great majority of cases a matter of a few seconds in everyday life. This is why it can be so difficult to read a person's emotions from an unposed expression in a photo: emotional expressions are mobile. If the actor held his face in an emotional reaction for much longer, he would be accused of looking unnatural. In addition, an open face (i.e. a face that is not held in an emotional expression) is more relatable, because the spectator can project onto the actor her or his own fantasy of the character's feelings, rather than having to interpret the actor's feelings – feelings the spectator may in any case not share.

Obviously, we are unable to see for ourselves what natural behaviour on stage was supposed to look like. But there is no doubt mimetic skill was highly prized. Thomas Heywood in his *An Apology for Actors* advises the actor:

> not to use any impudent or forced motion in any part of the body, no rough or other violent gesture; nor on the contrary to stand like a stiffe starcht man, but to qualifie every thing according to the nature of the person personated. (Heywood 1612/1841: 29)

Heywood, whose advice echoes Hamlet's to the Players, stresses the need 'to keep a decorum' in the face, and not to merely 'stand in his place like a livelesse image, demurely plodding, and without any smooth and formal motion' (ibid.) in his pursuit of mimesis:

> [Without a] comely and elegant gesture, a gratious and a bewitching kinde of action, a natural and a familiar motion of the head, the hand, the body, and a moderate and fit countenance sutable to all the rest, I hold all the rest as nothing. (ibid.)

It is worth recalling that Heywood was not writing purely for the elite; he collaborated on plays for the popular theatre such as the domestic middle-class tragedy *A Woman Killed with Kindness* and the potboiler *The Late Lancashire Witches*. Yet his pamphlet, in staking a claim for the status of acting as an art, reads like Cicero seen through *Hamlet*. So: realism in the matter of 'personation', yes, but the influence of classicism was never far away from the early modern discourse on acting.

After Shakespeare: John Bulwer

In 1644, the English physician and philosopher John Bulwer (1606–56) published his *Chirologia* and *Chironomia*. Bulwer's interest in how the body communicates meaning is evident in all of his writings; he even styled himself 'The Chirosopher'. He was especially interested in the problem of a language of and for deaf people – in fact he seems to have been the first person to devise a finger alphabet as a pedagogical method, as outlined in *Philocopus: Or the Deaf and Dumb Man's Friend* (1648). Bulwer was attempting to provide a road map for communication on behalf of the deaf sons of landowners, who had an obligation to administer their estates. His fascination with bodily communication was also personally motivated as he had a deaf daughter.

In *Chirologia*, Bulwer built a map of natural hand movements. In *Chironomia*, he attempted to list what he called the canons of rhetoricians – that is, the artificial gestures deployed by orators; so this second book can be read as an elaboration of the first (see Fudge 2011). The essential distinction between *Chirologia* and *Chironomia* is that in the first Bulwer describes gestures that people make quite naturally while they are talking, and in the second he describes gestures that a person can prepare in advance and then add on to a persuasive speech. Perhaps as a consequence of this, the description of gestures in *Chironomia* are more specific, often involving details of finger positions, rather as one finds in Quintilian.

Chirologia describes the gesture of wringing one's hands. Bulwer calls this gesture *Ploro* and takes it as a sign of grief. He suggests that in grief the brain is compressed, which forces tears into the eyes: 'from which compression of the Braine proceeds the HARD WRINGING OF THE HANDS, which is a Gesture of expression of moysture' (Bulwer 1644: 28). Bulwer probably derived the idea of brain compression inducing tears and hand-wringing from Francis Bacon. It seems a little odd to suggest the brain is compressed by grief. But of course a person may well experience migraine-style headaches when depressed, and that may feel as though the brain is being compressed.

Hamlet tells his mother to 'Leave wringing of your hands' (3.4.34), a conventional gesture of grief in Renaissance culture. Nowadays it would be understood not as a formal sign of grief but as an affect display (Ekman and Friesen 1969). Again, the form of the gesture has not changed, but as social morality has moved from an attention upon higher purposes to self-fulfilment, the meaning of the gesture has been reconfigured accordingly. Hand-wringing is now seen as the kind of gesture that shows a person is very anxious. Stress often leads to a feeling of sweaty palms, because when the autonomic nervous system is aroused, there is greater activity in the sweat glands. At the same time, the skin's capacity to conduct electricity goes up when one is aroused by a challenging event – this is known as the electrodermal response. Seeing such a gesture often arouses a mimetic response in the spectator. (Even *thinking* about situations in which one is aroused increases the conductivity of the skin.) The more intense and surprising the performance of the gesture, the more aroused the spectator may feel.

In the domestic context of the scene in practice, both social moralities are afforded space by Shakespeare. More than an implied stage direction to the actor – which it surely is – the line 'Leave wringing of your hands' draws attention to the moment of performance. The gesture is not just conventionally indicative of the need for salvation: it is also grounded in a bodily experience that produces the metaphor of wringing, an experience that is both intensely personal and shared – it is both Gertrude's and ours.

If you hold out your hand palm up, then you are performing a frequently used open hand supine (Kendon 2004) gesture labelled *Profero* by Bulwer. What does it mean without any speech to accompany it? Clearly it *looks like* you want to offer, present or receive something. There are actually some quite specific ways in which this gesture tends to be used. If the hand does not move and the palm is presented, then it is often used to introduce, comment, explain or clarify your words. If the palm is addressed – the hand is directed to something as if it were a flat surface – then it is more likely you are acknowledging me, offering me something with your words or showing me your readiness to receive something. In this form, it can function as an interactional turn-taking gesture.

According to Bulwer, the gesture of *Profero* was 'the first expression that ere appeared in the Hand, and was used by Eve in the fatall profer of the forbidden fruit to the first man' (Bulwer 1644: 71). It was also:

> the second gesture of any signification that is recorded to have appeared in the Hand, and the first that shewed itself in the Hand of the first man Adam, when hee accepted of that forbidden fruit ... From this unhappy gesture the Hand may be well called *Manus a manando* ['flowing hand'] because all evill proceeded from this action' (ibid.).

This assertion may strike the modern reader as surprising, but it is typical of the era, as Peter Harrison shows (Harrison 2007). For Bulwer, the primal scene, and thus the origin of all gesture, is the error committed at the Fall. Before Eve's *Profero*, Eden was a kind of communal paradise premised upon sharing resources according to basic needs rather than merit or claims to dominance, always excepting the absolute superiority of God. Afterwards, man was turned into a slave of death and nature, and woman was made subordinate to man, while beasts like the serpent had to crawl on the ground.

Where did Bulwer get his gestures from? In the 1950s, the theatre scholar Bertram Joseph published a series of books in which he speculated upon Elizabethan acting. His contention was that John Bulwer's taxonomy could be related to the acting style of tragedians that survived at least up to the closing of the Globe in 1642. He showed how certain gestures on Bulwer's list could be applied – and in his view *were* applied – by Shakespeare's actors to the text.

Joseph places Renaissance rhetoric alongside evidence of testimonies from the period that suggests audiences reacted to good actors like Burbage 'as if the personator were the man personated' (Thomas Heywood, quoted in Joseph 1960: 92). For Joseph, the only difference between the actor and the orator is that the actor speaks in the person of another rather than as himself or herself. This was also the opinion, he tells us, of Thomas Wright (ibid.: 95). It is true that Wright says 'in the substance of external action for most part orators and actors agree'. But where Wright argues that the actors 'act feignedly' whereas orators 'act really', Joseph is suggesting that 'in each case the emotion is truly felt' (ibid.). He needs to say this to shore up his belief that it was 'the orators who used the techniques of the actors' rather than the other way around, because that allows him to use texts like *Chironomia* as evidence for actors' behaviour on stage (ibid.: 94). In the absence of hard evidence he privileges the actor over the orator.

There is no way of knowing whether John Bulwer took some of his ideas from actors. He used the usual repertoire of source material – classical literature and the Bible. He was interested in developing a sign language, so he regarded gestures as being like a natural language. In this, as has been noted by scholars (Kendon 2004: 28), what has seemed from the viewpoint of historicism as a blind spot in his thinking – that he falls into an unwarranted universalism – can be seen from another angle as surprisingly astute. Bulwer, being a physician, developed an idea of a universal language that was not purely arbitrary; rather, it was psycho-physiological.

Whether or not you choose to accept that Bulwer had some kind of access to Shakespeare's practice, even if second-hand through actors such as Burbage's apprentice Joseph Taylor, it is clear that Bulwer had his own agenda. His attempt to create a taxonomy reflected a wider cultural impulse that would lead to a reconfiguration of Shakespearean performance in England over the next hundred years, and that is the subject of the next chapter.

4
Eighteenth-Century Gesture

In this chapter I will outline a number of themes that emerge from reflecting upon gesture in Shakespearean performance during the eighteenth century. I begin with the domineering figure of Thomas Betterton, whose presence threw a shadow over the theatre in England for several decades.

Thomas Betterton

The fact that it was rather difficult, as I suggested in the previous chapter, to flesh out an entire dictionary of a common language of deaf people did not stop other writers from asserting the universality of gesture – such as Charles Gildon, the author of *The Life of Mr Thomas Betterton* (1710). Borrowing at length from a translation of a French treatise by Le Faucheur, Gildon's Betterton advises against uncivilized hand and facial gestures, such as using the left arm (more of that in a moment) and licking or biting one's lips while performing, seen by Betterton (who in large part is simply a mouthpiece for Le Faucheur's plagiarized prescriptions) as 'ungenteel and unmannerly Actions' (Gildon 1710: 72). Licking or biting the lips, here during speechmaking on stage, are self-adaptors that might be seen as a symptom of anxiety in the actor, hence 'unmannerly'. To correct or prevent such lapses, Gildon's Betterton suggests the use of a mirror, or, failing that, get a friend 'who is a Master in all the Beauties of Gesture and Motion' to help out (ibid.: 55).

It is with Thomas Betterton that the myth of a Shakespearean tradition of influence gathers steam. This myth declares that actors pass on their knowledge to each succeeding generation, and that therefore a line can be traced back to Shakespeare's original intentions.

Right from the outset, though, this line is questionable. It begins with the claim of William Davenant, a key figure of the Restoration theatre. Davenant had, it was claimed, seen Joseph Taylor's Hamlet before the Interregnum, and was thus able to give Betterton instructions on playing the role, which he first did at the age of 26 in August 1661. Furthermore, Taylor probably modelled his performance upon his master Richard Burbage, and may even have received direction from Shakespeare himself. Since Taylor joined the company three years after Shakespeare's death, though, the claim that Shakespeare taught him is on shaky ground. British actors and acting companies have frequently used the idea of a tradition harking back to Shakespeare to enhance their own reputations. It ties in with the rise of the actor as celebrity, which, having begun with actors like Richard Burbage, took off in this period. The actor's interpretive self from this moment was foregrounded and tested in relation to Shakespeare's putative textual intentions. And as Shakespearean actors gained in status, so did Shakespeare.

We do not have a lot of information about Thomas Betterton's physical style. He was a well-built man, who probably did not throw himself around on stage; he was known more for his declamatory vocal skills than for his movement. However, Anthony Aston recorded his impressions of seeing the actor when the great man was 63 years old. He tells us that Betterton had 'short fat Arms, which he rarely lifted higher than his Stomach. – His left Hand frequently lodg'd in his Breast, between his Coat and Waistcoat, while, with his Right, he prepar'd his Speech'. In this posture he would declaim his speeches in a 'low and grumbling Tone' that yet could rise to 'an artful Climax'. At this late stage in his career, being 'corpulent' and thick-legged, Betterton did not move very much: 'His Actions were few, but just'. Aston suggests that his 'Aspect' in his 'latter time' was 'a little Paralytic' (Nicholson 1920: 75). He did not dance on the stage any more, and Aston rather wishes that he had resigned the role of Hamlet to a younger actor 'who might have Personated, though not have Acted, it better' (ibid.: 76) since, when Betterton's Hamlet threw himself at Ophelia's feet (which would probably have been around 3.2.114 when Hamlet chooses to sit with his head on Ophelia's lap rather than next to his mother), he came across as 'a little too grave for a young Student' (ibid.).

One gets a sense from the passage of the old veteran who does not quite cut the mustard physically anymore, but who still commands respect, borne along on a wave of nostalgia from his audience. Betterton can still 'act', in the oratorical sense of delivering a passage of text in an aurally charming manner, but he does not persuade Aston that he presents a credible image of Hamlet.

The Restoration theatres

William Davenant and his friend Thomas Killigrew were granted patents by Charles II to organize two playing companies, the Duke of York's company and the King's Men. Charles's taste had been decisively shaped by his time spent at the French court under Louis XIV. Betterton was sent on an official trip to Paris in 1662 to take a look for himself at the staging practices of the French (and the Italians). He made two more trips later, and the results of his visits and subsequent efforts were innovations in theatrical presentation. The Restoration theatres in London were indoor spaces, with basically picture frame stages, although an apron protruded from the proscenium arch into the auditorium and boxes were placed at the sides of the stage where fashionable people would sit. These spaces were lit by girandoles (chandeliers) hanging over the stage, and perhaps in the wings or at the back of the stage. The girandoles could be raised or lowered to alter the amount of light on the acting area. There were also candles on sconces in the auditorium, and these were kept lit throughout the performances. This meant the fashionable set could display themselves to each other during the entire evening. Playgoing was a social affair, a matter of being seen as well as seeing.

The Restoration theatres also introduced changeable scenery. From available visual evidence, it seems that flats were painted with perspective scenes. The actors tended to position themselves on the apron for soliloquies, and to perform dialogue scenes in a lateral corridor of space along the front of the stage near to the proscenium arch. In this way visual distortions to the perspective of the backdrop were avoided and the actors could find their best positions in the available light (Palmer 2013: 51). In effect, the actors were playing most of the time in a kind of flattened, almost two-dimensional space, separated from a backdrop that was purely decorative. At the sides of the apron were the so-called Doors of Entrance, which meant the actor did not have to appear upstage of the proscenium arch if not desired.

From the point of view of gesture, such a staging model would demand a kind of flattened silhouetting of the body into vivid shapes. The gesture would play out in width not depth and would require a strong sense of figural separation of the backdrop and darker upstage areas from the ground.

The rise of the actress

Betterton took over from William Davenant the training of young performers – especially the actresses. There had been English women performers as far back as the fifteenth century, and it seems that in 1626 Queen Henrietta Maria may have received acting instruction for a court entertainment in which she appeared from Burbage's successor Joseph Taylor. The first performance of a *professional* British actress in a female Shakespearean role was probably in Thomas Killigrew's revival of *Othello* on 8 December 1660. The occasion was marked by a prologue that declared: 'The Woman plays today, mistake me not,/No Man in Gown, or Page in Petty-Coat' (quoted by Shaughnessy in Ritchie and Sabor 2012: 181).

Overnight, a revolution in English theatre had taken place. It is impossible to give precise assessments of general influence, but the physical presence of actresses in the theatres decisively altered the playgoing public's taste. The private Caroline theatres (as the Blackfriars became) had been by no means merely an extension of court life; their principal audiences were 'drawn from those same parliamentary classes from which the political challenge to Charles in 1640 would come' – that is, the gentry, including some Puritan gentry. And this was the same audience that remained hostile to female players, such as when French actresses performed at the Blackfriars in 1629 (Howe 1992: 22). In reality, there was a marked distinction between the court entertainments that featured women performers like the queen and her ladies-in-waiting and the commercial theatres before the Civil War. When Charles II was installed on the throne, this distinction no longer pertained, because Charles took an interest in how the commercial theatres were organized.

In effect, in the early days of the Restoration the court around Charles commandeered what had been a broader, more gentry-based theatre culture. And women were accepted as a natural part of that Royalist theatre culture. A royal patent of 1662 to Thomas Killigrew made it a matter of law that women should play women, giving the reason that in former days it was considered offensive to some that men should dress up and act female roles – presumably this expression in the patent was a dig at the Puritans. The patent was a legalizing justification of the king's own preferences; once it was signed, there was no going back.

Some actresses became known for their *breeches roles*. These were popular because the men got to look at the actresses' legs. Sometimes the actresses would take young male roles, but more often would play young women disguised as men in comedies. Apart from the obvious possibilities for pleasing the audience in a play like *As You Like It*, other Shakespearean plays were altered so that breeches roles could be inserted into them, as in John Crowne's adaptation of *Henry VI, Parts 1 and 2* (1680), which provides Henry's son with a mistress who dresses up so she can follow him onto the battlefield. The sexual cynicism of these staging ploys is reflected in William Davenant and John Dryden's version of *The Tempest* (1667). In the play, Prospero, dispensing advice to Dorinda (Miranda's sister, a character thrown into the play to add females to the story – as is Caliban's sister) warns her not to touch the bare hand of Hippolito – 'It is the way to make him love you more' (3.1.136). The non-verbal teasing and flirting that must have been going on during these performances is encouraged by the dramatic representation.

The sexual appeal of beautiful actresses carried over into their tragic performances. 'Actresses were frequently required to do no more than pose, like pictures or statues, to be gazed upon and desired by male characters in the play and, presumably, by male spectators' (Howe 1992: 39). Violence performed upon the female body, sometimes carried out by themselves in a fetching state of helpless insanity, added value to the entertainment. In Nahum Tate's adaptation of *Coriolanus* (1681), the hero's wife Virgilia begs for mercy at the feet of his enemy Aufidius, which serves only to make her still more sexually appealing to him. She is later brought in wounded (presumably, raped offstage) before her husband. Thomas Durfey's version of *Cymbeline* (1682) similarly sets up the exciting prospect of a rape taking place under the loved one's eyes. The actress would have been expected to deliver an alabaster-white portrayal of chaste virtue traumatized by male lust. Her job was to supply images of masculine wish-fulfilment. The fact that the rapes were not actually staged is a sleight of hand, a trick of flattery to the rakes in the audience who would presumably ally themselves with the heroic rescuer, and thus feel more justified than ever in their pursuit of the actresses. The Crowne, Dryden and Davenant, Tate and Durfey adaptations of Shakespeare, as well as several other examples, are discussed by Howe (1992: 37–51).

As Elizabeth Howe shows, the widely held assumption at this time was that actresses were basically prostitutes. Some, like Mary Betterton, were in a position to marry a man who could, to a degree, offer some protection; otherwise, they were considered fair game to the rakes and

gallants. The word 'whore', though, may not have implied a professional sex worker: Kirsten Pullen argues that:

> Traditionally, power and privilege were the rights of those who had
> earned them by birth, rather than labor, or especially sex. Labelling
> actresses as whores and publicizing their sexual peccadilloes was an
> attempt to limit the threat to class hierarchy their position as aristo-
> cratic mistresses indicated as well as downplay their entry into the
> public sphere. (Pullen 2005: 25)

Furthermore, the audience was lit almost as brightly as the performers
on stage. It could be argued that such lighting conditions complicated
the relationship between actor and spectator, such that it is too simple
to talk of a unidirectional 'male gaze', a view articulated persuasively by
Tracy Davis. Indeed, the granting to women of the right to perform on
stage can be seen as another cultural milestone in the gradual transformation of social morality in England that underpins this book.

Whatever the (no doubt complex) reality was – and it certainly included
significant numbers of women of different social groups in the audience
as well as onstage – it is unfortunate for us that very little in the way of
serious documentation of their performances, especially in Shakespearean
roles, was undertaken compared to the influential male actors. We read
a lot about the 'charms' of individual women – and we can learn from
scholars like Howe a significant amount about the kinds of lives they led
and the influence they may have wielded – but little about what they
actually did on stage by way of gestural behaviour. As Howe says, 'Even
if an actress's life private life seemed exemplary, writers focused on her
sexuality rather than on her acting ability' (Howe 1992: 35).

It is curiously apposite then that the first recorded instance of a professional actress is in the role of Desdemona. Desdemona is usually conceived of as an innocent victim of male Machiavellianism and jealousy.
Accused of whoredom, she is insulted, slapped across the face, then
smothered to death with a pillow in her nightdress while she is in bed.
The possibility of titillating a voyeuristic male audience with this play
is already suggested in an illustration that accompanied the text of the
play in Nicholas Rowe's celebrated 1709 edition of Shakespeare's works.
Desdemona lies still asleep, the 'whiter skin of hers than snow/And
smooth as monumental alabaster' of her bosom exposed (*Othello* 5.2.4–
5), while Othello stands over her, his right hand clutching a pillow, his
left held in the air in an oratorical gesture indicating that he is speaking

his great soliloquy and that he is tragically conflicted. He wears the uniform of a British army officer, perhaps bringing back memories for some readers of the Civil War, and thus affiliating him with the Royalist cause. His blackness set against her whiteness, of course, may well also have contributed to the audience's erotic interest in the play. Rowe's images are a key moment in the history of gesture in Shakespearean performance: at last, a visual record begins to emerge, however 'staged' his illustrations were (and it is impossible to be certain on this point).

Aaron Hill and the rules of gesture

As I have indicated in Chapter 2, out of the conditions for playing there developed a number of rules. These rules were codified through repetition in a large number of manuals for orators, opera singers and actors over the course of a hundred years. The first instruction manuals, as we might call them, emerged in mid-seventeenth century France. In England, we can date a serious interest in acting considered as a set of techniques that needed to be learnt and practised from around the time of Aaron Hill. For two years from 1734 Hill published a magazine called *The Prompter*. Here, he expounded his views on the current state of acting in England, which he saw as having declined since the Restoration. He argued for the creation of a training academy for actors modelled on the Royal Academy. The Royal Academy of Arts was founded in 1768, and the Royal Academy of Music in 1822, so although Hill did not see an acting academy built in his own lifetime, he was nonetheless prescient in his wish to reform actor training in Britain.

Hill's attempted reforms centred upon the basic issue of intentionality. What he was trying to do was separate the personality of the actor from the character. For Hill what this meant in practice was that the actor needed to 'get into' the character more, since that meant the actor would 'get out of' his or her own personality in the process. Hill's argument that actors needed to stay in character recalls a remark of Richard Flecknoe's concerning Richard Burbage:

> [We] may say that he was a delightful Proteus, so wholly transforming himself into his part, and putting off himself with his clothes, as he never (not so much as in the tiring-house) assum'd himself again until the play was done … his auditors [were] never more delighted than when he spoke, nor more sorry than when he held his peace; yet even then he was an excellent actor still, never falling in his part when he had done speaking, but with his looks and gestures

maintaining it still unto the heighth, he imagining *age quod agis* only spoke to him … (in Chambers 1923: IV, 370)

The likelihood is that Flecknoe did not see Burbage in action. Flecknoe is possibly thinking of Thomas Betterton; if so, his description sits within the emerging myth of an acting tradition – as if Betterton was 'channelling' Burbage. That the actor should sustain the character while on stage became an imperative for the profession over the course of the next fifty years or so. The essence of it was that, at least to begin with, one was supposed to feel what the character feels. Aaron Hill argued for this; he said that, in order to act a passion well, 'the actor must never attempt its imitation, until his fancy has conceived so strong an image, or idea, of it, as to move the same impressive springs within his mind, which form that passion, when it is undesigned, and natural' (in Cole and Chinoy 1970/1995: 117). The idea of acting as emotional transformation is thus premised upon the preparatory work of the imagination ('fancy').

Dr. Johnson famously said that what survives in art are just representations of general nature. After the Bloodless Revolution of 1688, it was the urban middle class who eventually made up the majority of the playgoing public, not the rakes and gallants of the Restoration. What the new audiences craved were just representations of their own general nature. They wanted to see themselves as a social group depicted on stage. Aaron Hill's complaint was at root a call for a theatre that would do a better job at giving them representations of their own nature than did the existing companies who had arisen to serve the Francophone taste of Charles's court. Classicism had to be reshaped to look like the behaviour of the middle classes.

Partly, it was a matter of textual editing. Partly, it was a matter of writing new plays, or of dressing up the characters of old plays in fashionable modern clothes. And, partly, it meant acting was reformed so that the audience was invited to take an empathic position with respect to socially superior characters. As well, the increasing emphasis on visual display, related as this was to patterns of consumption fed by the importation of artistic objects from China and from the Grand Tours to Italy, spoke to the need for the newly rising class to assert its independence in the marketplace. In accord with the taste for visual tokens of this independence, the individual gestures of actors and actresses began to assume a greater prominence within public conversations about theatre, partly because a vocabulary of expressive action was taught in schools 'and so became common knowledge in the eighteenth century' (Kendon 2004: 86).

At the same time, costume created a set of physical constraints that led actors to make greater use of their hands and upper arms. For actresses, this was particularly the case, since their legs were hidden underneath petticoats, hoops and skirts, and their upper bodies were squeezed into tightly fitting corsets. Their spines were kept straight, and their pelvic movements were largely invisible. The audience's attention was drawn to the elaborate wig, the face, the décolletage and the movements of the arms and hands.

Sensibility

Gestural displays now incorporated an idea of *sensibility*. What mattered about sensibility was that it involved 'empathising with the feelings of another when one's own interests are not directly involved' (Taylor 1989: 32). This necessitated a high level of mimetic skill. If you could get the audience to feel what it must be like to be your character, which you did by calling upon a common stock of socio-moral emotional attitudes, you were an artist, and you had a better chance of accruing status as a social player. The evidence for the actor's sensibility was seen in how she or he handled the presentation of the basic passions. It was essential that, in the words of John Hill (1750), the actor displayed a 'pliantness of disposition by means of which the different passions are made easily to succeed to one another in the soul' (ibid.: 33). The actor became a kind of emotional lightning rod, and the articulation of transitions between passions was critical to the effect. As Taylor says, audiences wanted to see actors *perceiving* (ibid.: 31).

In the previous chapter I discussed the crucial function of gesture as part of the turn-taking process on Shakespeare's stage. I said that if we accept the validity of the argument for cue parts, then it becomes essential for the actors to control the flow of the dialogue with their bodies, and this control becomes a sign of their professional skill as opposed to something that could be left to chance. Turn-taking moves would need to be accomplished discreetly, without obvious signalling that one is condescending to hand over power. This could be a highly sophisticated game within a social circle involving a number of individuals playing for reputational high stakes. An elegantly curving open hand supine gesture as one transfers responsibility for maintaining the social relations to someone else in the room disguises the game better than the force implied in a straight line. It makes the handover look like an invitation rather than an obligation: in John Bulwer's terminology, a *Profero*.

It is important to note that, as part of this sophisticated social game, the actor had to address the audience as well as the interlocutor. This was done by what is still known as *cheating*: angling the face and body somewhat towards the audience, and directing the eye gaze and gestures towards the interlocutor. The main reason for cheating is to give the audience a clear vantage point on what was a relatively flat stage composition. More than that, though, the technique aimed to make the audience feel included in the social act of the performance. In a duologue, if the actor's torso is facing the audience it creates the impression that a triangular interaction is taking place. A configuration of the dialogue in which the audience is positioned as an uninvited eavesdropper would be uncivilized. The Jesuit acting teacher Franciscus Lang (1727) wrote:

> For if the Actors talk among themselves, as if no-one else were present, and listening, and so turn their faces and words reciprocally towards each other, then half the audience is deprived of the Actor's appearance, and see him only from the side or entirely from the back, and that is opposed to propriety and natural decency and especially to the honour of the Audience itself. (In Barnett 1987: 437)

Similarly, John Walker argued that if the actor does not figure the audience within his point of view with respect to the stage composition he places himself in positions 'as would be highly ungraceful and disgusting' (Walker 1789: x). As Lang and Walker revealed, the question of positioning oneself in relation to the audience was moral as much as it was practical.

The writers of the eighteenth century were concerned to represent behaviour in an artistic form. They were profoundly aware that theatre was not a transparent, ethically neutral mirror. It was, rather, a created picture. Gildon says, 'I have shewn you how Art improves these Gestures, and on what occasions they are proper, and how to make them graceful' (Gildon 1710: 138). Art, or grace, was to be seen not in marks of effort but in an elegant abstraction from natural behaviour, a complexity and abundance of detail in invention, and a self-conscious *savoir faire*.

In acting, it meant the capacity to perform actions that are physically difficult while making them look easy, along with a sense of restraint that is conveyed by the idea that one could display more emotion or force, but one is choosing not to. Georg Lichtenberg wrote of David Garrick:

> I fear that many years and much grilling went toward the exercising of his body, before it attained at length to this effortless ease, which,

enhanced by perpetual observation of handsome men, admired and envied by persons of both sexes, now looks as though it came to him naturally. (Quoted in Sechelski 1996: 371)

Here again, what Hamlet calls 'smoothness' can be seen to operate as a controlling idea over the style of the performance.

Actors believed that they were improving upon nature through stylization. Standing (according to Colley Cibber) on the apron of the stage for the most part, Thomas Betterton was able to modify his passions because he was relatively close to the audience in what were relatively small theatres. Perhaps under the influence of new developments in physiognomy, evidenced in Descartes' *Treatise on the Passions* (1649), and Charles Le Brun's artistic portraits of faces displaying these passions, it is possible that Betterton and his colleagues traced the contours of emotions in their faces (Downer 1943: 1006). But the tragic actor had to sustain the character's nobility in adversity, and nobility was identified with poise and restraint.

The same held true for gesture. Often the tragic actor's gestures were described as actions, and the comedian's gestures were called *gesticulations*. Anthony Aston, a stage comedian among many other things, wrote that Mr. Doggett is 'the best Face-player and Gesticulator' (Nicholson 1920: 88). There is the suggestion of apish behaviour in the word 'gesticulator', which links the pantomimic style of the low comedians with the fashionable satiric representations of monkeys mimicking people, as in the portraits of *The Monkey Painter* by Jean Siméon Chardin or in *A Monkey Smoking and Drinking with an Owl* by Ferdinand van Kessel. In the Middle Ages monkeys tended to be taken as symbols for concupiscent desire, which is why they were often represented either in chains (as in keeping one's desires in check) or eating an apple (as in Adam and Eve). From 1650, artists began to reimagine monkey behaviour in relation to new modes of behaviour such as the conspicuous consumption of luxury goods; again, the emerging social morality of self-fulfilment altered the parameters within which shared referents could be understood. The newly moneyed and increasingly powerful classes would not tolerate being told what they were and were not allowed to wear, what to buy, what places to visit, and how to behave in public by Parliament or the monarch. Instead, they would make their own social rules, called 'fashion', and regulate them through the systems of gossip and publishing. This was a social class that wanted to run its own system of social policing, and satirical representations of monkey-like behaviour were one way it did that.

Points and starts

Celestine Woo argues that the primary activity of Betterton's audience was listening rather than looking (Woo 2008: 35). Perhaps, but after Betterton the visual would gradually begin to assume a more equal role in performance. The period style, for example, demanded that actors developed skill in what were called *points* and *starts*. A *point* was the embodiment of a dramatic moment. As George Taylor puts it, 'by making a gesture, striking an attitude, or changing the tone of his voice, [the actor] created the impression of a new passion' (Taylor 1989: 34). A position is held in a suspended moment. It is a 'breakpoint' – a visible motion boundary (as discussed in Chapter 1) – at which the body is dynamically poised rather than merely posed. In effect, it marks the end of the motion segment, where the meaning of the segment is gathered up. It is more of a pause than a stop (see Rubin and Richards 1985) because it carries within itself the preparation for the launch of the next motion event. Poise implies readiness for action, and is related to the Renaissance adage *festina lente*. The actor is meant to look as though she or he is a kind of coiled spring.

This also implies physical imbalance, among the most important signals of spontaneity in performance. The impression that the actor is about to lose his or her balance was created by a trick borrowed from neoclassical painting and sculpture known as *contrapposto*. Hogarth, in an influential treatise on art, argued that the line of beauty was a curve. There was nothing new in this, since it underpinned the representations of human form in much Graeco-Roman and Renaissance art, and was taken to extremes in late sixteenth-century mannerism. The basic premise behind Hogarth's argument is that there are no absolutely straight lines in nature. In representations of the moving body, elegant curves along one line would be contrasted with suggested motion in an opposing direction. The upper body, the head or the hands will seem to move in one direction, the trunk and legs in another. In performance, the underlying feeling of movement in the point is related to the need for the actor to prepare for the next moment. The actor paused in order to make the *point*, as if underlining that moment with a pencil or adding a punctuation mark.

A *start* was a moment of sudden emotional reaction – in other words, an affect display. Again, it is a visible motion boundary – but, as the term indicates, it marks the beginning of a motion segment rather than the end. In the previous chapter, in discussing the closet scene in *Hamlet* I said that electrodermal conductance is increased during emotional arousal. A *start* is in essence a startle reflex due to quick activation of the sympathetic nervous system, and is also marked by a spike in electro-dermal activity. Francis Bacon's description of the phenomenon antici-pates how it would come to be understood in the eighteenth century:

> The Passions of the *Minde* work upon the Body the impressions fol-lowing. *Fear*, causeth *Paleness*, *Trembling*, the *Standing* of the *Hair* upright, Starting, and Scrieching ... Starting is both an apprehension of the thing feared, (and in that kinde it is a motion of shrinking;) and likewise an Inquisition in the beginning what the matter should be, (and in that kinde it is a motion of Erection;) and therefore when a Man would listen suddenly to anything, he starteth; for the starting is an Erection of the Spirits to attend ... (Bacon 1670: 149–50)

The body responds to a sudden noise, or a sharp movement, or some other surprising change, such as a person suddenly appearing next to you. The dorsal neck muscles stiffen, the eyes tighten and blink and the limbs and torso stiffen and bend in preparation to defend from attack. Although there are variations between individuals in the capacity to inhibit this response, it is largely involuntary, and is correlated with fear and threat anxiety.

The example of David Garrick, discussed in the next chapter, shows that the capacity to produce compelling points and starts could secure a Shakespearean actor's reputation.

5
Gestural Landmarks from Garrick to Irving

This chapter will discuss the gestural behaviour of some influential Shakespearean actors from around 1750 to around 1900. My intention is not to establish a canon of gesture – for one thing, my evidence base is too Anglocentric for that. Rather, I mean to situate the illustrations I offer within the larger framework of my argument for a historical shift in social morality. The chapter will move through some key moments when the paradigms of gesture in Shakespearean performance (and by implication, within the wider culture) were subject to redefinition. I begin with David Garrick and move, via some other influential actors, towards Henry Irving; in the process, I hope to show that there are instructive comparisons and contrasts to be made between those two influential figures with respect to the motives for gestural style. Although I pin familiar labels to my paradigms – neoclassicism, romanticism, realism, naturalism – I want to stress that the aspects of the performances I describe should be understood as existing on a continuum of non-verbal behaviour. Thus, gesture in Shakespearean performance is not a matter of 'either/or' but is rather a blend of 'more or less'.

David Garrick

On 14 November 1746 James Quin, whose fortunes were already beginning to decline, found himself out-acted by David Garrick during a performance of Nicholas Rowe's play *The Fair Penitent*. Afterwards, Richard Cumberland wrote, 'It seemed as if a whole century had been stepped over in the transition of a single scene' (quoted in Stone and Kahrl 1979: 187).

Quin's was an imposingly large physical presence. His style was described as manly and declamatory, and he accompanied his sonorities with 'a sawing kind of action, which had more of the senate than the stage in it' (ibid.). The word 'sawing' of course references Hamlet's advice to the Players, and reveals the writer's personal bias. Garrick, by contrast, 'young and light and alive in every muscle and in every feature, came bounding on the stage, and pointing at the wittol Altamont and the heavy-paced Horatio, – heavens what a transition!' (ibid.). The heavy-paced Horatio was Quin who, for all his notorious vanity, had the perceptiveness to see that if Garrick was right, 'I and the rest of the players must have been all wrong' (ibid.: 188).

Garrick's pointing gesture speaks of a desire to level the social distances between him and Quin. Garrick was a paradox: the respectable Harlequin, the artistic gesticulator, the dignified self-mocker. He wrote a self-satirizing anonymous verse pamphlet in which he features as Pug 'The Sick Monkey', chastised by his fellow animals (i.e. his envious critics) for his shameless pantomimic imitations of the styles of others (Woods 1984: 132). Not cut out for the kind of postural demonstrations of manly seriousness that characterized the titanic performances of Betterton and Quin, he chose the contrary path: he turned himself into what we now call a character actor.

His style was marked by a close attention to the psychology of the passions. He found a way of creating the impression that he was utterly absorbed by the role he was playing. In other words, he had a gift for a new mode of social behaviour that was gaining rapid currency, one that was described at the time as *sensibility* but in modern parlance would be called empathy. Sensibility was defined by John Hill as 'a disposition to be affected by the passions, which are the subjects of dramatic writing' (Downer 1943: 1027). It was not expected of an actor performing Herod in a Tudor play that he would be skilled at imaginatively stepping into the shoes of his character. It is a measure of how far the profession of acting had changed that this was exactly what Garrick was praised for. He backed up this impression of imaginative sympathy with the roles he took on by making significant changes in his relationship to his public.

The net result of these changes was manifold. First, the audience was banished into the auditorium. There would be no more fops messing around on the stage, flirting with the actors and distracting the audience from the intense emotional experience that Garrick had rehearsed for them – for Garrick did rehearse, and insisted that his acting company rehearsed along with him (Woo 2008: 40). The pictorial illusion of the stage was then enhanced by Garrick's preferred scene designer Philippe de Loutherbourg, as well as by the carefully atmospheric use of onstage and side-stage lighting in preference to girandoles hanging down from the proscenium arch. It was essential to Garrick's influence over his audience that he used every technical means available to control their emotional responses. However, there were still stage boxes at Garrick's Drury Lane theatre at the sides of the forestage, as there were in the provincial theatres modelled upon the London buildings, and the people sitting in them were close enough for the actors to touch. The developments inaugurated by Garrick had to wait until the next century before they were fully realized in the proscenium arch stage facing a darkened auditorium.

Garrick appropriated Shakespeare as an English genius who, like Garrick himself, excelled in range and variety of characterization. In claiming Shakespeare for a newly confident Britain, Garrick claimed Shakespeare as his own property, then proved it by extensive correspondence with his admirers and critics and by mounting productions of plays that included more of the actual words written by Shakespeare than anyone had bothered to include since 1642, when the Globe Theatre closed down. His apotheosis of Shakespeare in turn served his own reputation extremely well, helping to make a celebrity of the media-savvy and visually educated Garrick.

From the existing portraits of Garrick 'in character' we can get a cautious sense of his movement style. He bent his knees so that he could shift his balance quickly. He was a pioneer in this, an approach to movement on the stage that recalls the *commedia dell'arte*, and Harlequin in particular. A resultant lower centre of gravity meant he was able to effect rapid transitions between points of focus and emotional responses. Of course, it was not very manly or heroic to suddenly swerve from one attitude to the next with your knees bent. Garrick was after something else: the impression of a keen sensibility.

Garrick often gave the feeling that he was in the grip of involuntary passion, of one fleeting emotional perception after another. He would then ally this idea of emotional sensitivity to his own masculine agency as a performer by conveying an impression of decisiveness. If Garrick's Hamlet went weak at the knees, he didn't just wobble a bit: he intensified it into the 'start – the heave – the stagger – the stare' (Kelley, quoted in Hapgood 1999: 15). And he counterbalanced this with displays of adventurous heroism. In so doing, he modelled a new kind of masculine behaviour to a newly important social group: the middle class that was driving forward the wealth-creating activities of the British Empire with ever-increasing confidence. The gravitas of the Grand Manner was replaced by agility in action and flexibility in reaction.

Garrick's first major Shakespearean outing was as *Richard III* in 1741, where his performance was 'sandwiched between two portions of a musical concert' (Cole and Chinoy 1970/1995: 131). This role was perhaps well chosen to fit with his physical attributes, such as his diminutive stature. He 'played Richard the Third to the surprise of everybody', as he told his brother in a letter the next day (ibid.). It was this performance that prompted Quin's remark about the old guard perhaps having been wrong in their approach. A much-reproduced painting by Hogarth (1745) shows him having just woken up from his nightmare before the Battle of Bosworth: 'Richard starteth up out of a dream' (*Richard III* 5.3.178). The image shows the end point of a start – a sudden sitting up in bed in fright, his face a picture of fear, his right arm raised up to show shock, his left hand reaching for his sword on the bed behind. Again, it was essential to Garrick's appeal that he showed both the startle response and the decisive heroic action. He is sitting in a *contrapposto* pose, what Hogarth referred to in *The Analysis of Beauty* (1753) as the serpentine (s-shaped) line (see Paulson's introduction to that work 1971).

The picture – the first important Shakespearean painting, as well as the first in a line of publicity images of Garrick – binds Garrick's own destiny to the performance history of Shakespeare, as well as creating a new genre of the theatrical portrait. How much of the pose can be taken to represent what Garrick actually did at that moment on stage is a matter of conjecture. For one thing, Hogarth used Charles Le Brun's *Tent of Darius* (1660–1) as a compositional model, while Garrick's head was painted separately later. The attitude of Garrick in the picture is not, though, drawn from Le Brun. It is reasonable to infer that Garrick, since he approved of the portrait, felt that it was the kind of image of his acting that he wanted people to see. In his actual performance, according to Roger Pickering (in Donohue Jr. 1970/2015: 231), he grabbed the sword as he sat up in bed suddenly on 'Give me another horse', paused in the middle of the line, then rushed forward with a look of dismay on 'Bind up my wounds', before dropping to his knees on 'Have mercy, Heaven' – using Cibber's rewrite of 'Have mercy, Jesu' in the process (5.3.178–9). This seems quite characteristic of Garrick in showing his skill in the detailed creation of vivid actions and responses at the level of each phrase.

His destiny as the Shakespearean supremo was further cemented by the descriptions of his performance of *Hamlet*. In particular, it was his acting of Hamlet's start at seeing his father's ghost that provoked response. Georg Christoph Lichtenberg was a visitor to London from

Germany and, although his account is not the only one, it is the most detailed. He wrote:

> Suddenly, as Hamlet moves towards the back of the stage slightly to the left, and turns his back on the audience, Horatio starts, and saying: 'Look, my lord, it comes,' points to the right, where the ghost has already appeared and stands motionless, before any one is aware of him. At these words Garrick turns sharply and at the same moment staggers back two or three paces with his knees giving way under him; his hat falls to the ground and both his arms, especially the left, are stretched out nearly to their full length, with the hands as high as the head, the right arm more bent and the hand lower, and the fingers apart; his mouth is open: thus he stands rooted to the spot, with legs apart, but no loss of dignity, supported by his friends, who are better acquainted with the apparition and fear lest he should collapse. His whole demeanour is so expressive of terror that it made my flesh creep even before he began to speak. The almost terror-struck silence of the audience, which preceded this appearance and filled one with a sense of insecurity, probably did much to enhance this effect. At last he speaks, not at the beginning, but at the end of a breath, with a trembling voice: 'Angels and ministers of grace defend us!' (Lichtenberg 1938: 9–10)

Garrick positioned his Hamlet within a tradition. Thomas Betterton, according to his admirer Colley Cibber, in the presence of his father's ghost displayed a 'passion' that never rose 'beyond an almost breathless astonishment, or an impatience, limited by filial reverence' (in Cole and Chinoy 1995: 104). Opening with 'a pause of mute amazement' Betterton rose 'slowly to a solemn, trembling voice' in which 'he made the Ghost equally terrible to the spectator as himself ... his voice never rising into that seeming outrage, or wild defiance of what he naturally revered' (ibid.). The key note of Cibber's description is that Betterton evoked terror while maintaining his customary sense of restraint. Cibber is attentive to Betterton's vocal technique, while hardly mentioning that the man had a body (and a rather large one at that).

Garrick, by contrast, made the audience attend to his physicality. In this respect, Lichtenberg's passage rewards study. The opening word 'suddenly' keys us in to the tenor of the performance. Garrick was keenly aware of the value, in terms of both controlling the audience's attention and of creating an aura – a sense of stage presence – around oneself, of springing surprises on the audience by changes of rhythm.

Garrick at a number of moments seems to upset the audience's expectations through the defying of neoclassical conventions. He turned his back to the audience – because he knew it would get a shock reaction when he turned back sharply again and showed a dramatic change on his face at seeing the ghost. The ghost had meanwhile already entered, rather than having its entrance prepared for by Horatio's cue and the cast composing themselves in anticipation. Garrick's knees then bent in a decidedly unheroic way; his hat fell off unceremoniously; he stretched his arms right out, both of them above his head, the left higher than the right; he opened his stance; he appeared to be about to faint so that his friends must rush to support him and, after a pause whose length we can only guess at, he spoke pathetically, on an out-breath. Every one of these ten performance decisions could be read as calculated to upset the audience's sense of decorum as laid down in the acting manuals.

Garrick's brilliance lay in deviating from tradition in the details rather than in breaking with it altogether. At the same time, he nudged his audience into a new attentiveness to the visual image. As a result, the image of his reaction to the ghost lodged itself very clearly in the minds of his audience. It was a vividly different response from his predecessors, but by drawing upon a shared knowledge about how the passions could be perceived to work through the body, it remained objectively coherent. Thus, the shock of Garrick's first performances was rapidly replaced by a common belief that his acting was more realistic than that of Quin's generation.

A legend grew up around this moment of Garrick's Hamlet. It was that Garrick's dresser Perkins had created for him a hydraulically inflatable wig. Whether the story is true or not – and for Joseph Roach it is true, since it helps to bolster his argument about the influence of Cartesian mechanistic conceptions of the body on actors such as Garrick (Roach 1982: 431) – is less important than the reason why such a legend would emerge at all. In his satirical essay on acting of 1744, written to anticipate and disarm criticism of his performance of Macbeth in advance, Garrick reveals his anxiety about being the victim of the sort of pedantic and class-based snobbery that would not accept a character actor, an expert in low-status comic roles like Abel Drugger, to play a warrior like Macbeth. Garrick noted that tragedy traditionally 'fixes her empire on the passions' while comedy 'holds her rule over the less ennobled qualities and districts of human nature, which are called the humors' (Cole and Chinoy 1995: 134). But then he argued that a common haberdasher may feel passion as well as Alexander the Great, for example in his desire for revenge over a competitor in business. The object of the desire may be rather more local than in Alexander's subversion of an entire kingdom to satisfy his passion, 'yet, still it is revenge' and 'the mind of one is equally affected in proportion to the other, and all the difference lies in the different ways of satisfying their common passion' (ibid.). There's the key phrase: common passion. Abel Drugger displays his passion in a certain manner that recalls 'the completest low picture of grotesque terror that can be imagined by a Dutch painter' when he breaks a urinal; while Macbeth, horrified by the thought of having murdered Duncan, behaves like 'a moving statue, or indeed a petrified man', with 'quick and permanent' attitudes, and should seem to 'tread on air', for which the wearing of a pair of cork heels is advised (ibid.: 135).

For Joseph Roach (Roach 1982: 438), Garrick's description of Macbeth's reaction at seeing the air-drawn dagger is to be taken as evidence that the actor had at least a working knowledge of Descartes, perhaps through the letters he had received from Aaron Hill. I am much less inclined to take anything that Garrick says in this essay at face value. While I agree that it was in Garrick's professional interest to promote acting as having the status of a science, the prevailing discourse on acting was tied to rhetoric much more than to Cartesianism – which, after all, would demote the actor to the status of an automaton devoid of agency. Indeed, it was Georg Lichtenberg, whose letters are used as evidence by Roach, who said of Garrick, 'he moves to and fro among players like a man among marionettes ... where other players in the movements of their arms and legs allow themselves six inches or more scope in every direction farther than the canons of beauty would permit, he hits the mark with admirable certainty and firmness' (quoted in Bertelsen 1978: 315). That is self-possession; in other words, *sprezzatura*. Garrick may have borrowed some of the fashionable Cartesian terminology to serve his agenda of self-promotion, but he was too much of a pragmatist – and an egoist – to imagine himself as an automaton.

The originality of Garrick's approach to acting can be clarified. Natural acting was being redefined as democratic acting, i.e. as an expression of the *sameness* of humanity rather than its *difference*, and the action of the sympathetic imagination was the key to the redefinition. As was written in one of Garrick's obituaries, 'If he was angry, so was you: if he was distressed, so was you: if he was terrified, so was you: if he was merry, so was you: if he was mad, so was you' (in Taylor 1989: 33). Clearly, we should not forget that the idea of sameness didn't apply to all social groups – it applied to the middle classes. I think it was this empathic skill that fed into the legend of the wig. Garrick's hat fell off, and, coupled with the other features of his start, the result was a kind of priming effect. Because the audience's hair stood on end, they believed that Garrick's did. Then they looked for an explanation of how that could be, since a person cannot actually make their hair stand on end.

David Garrick did not want you, the audience, to be in awe of him. He wanted to be your friend, so that you would care about him as one of you. Thomas Davies records how he replaced Colley Cibber's 'bombast' with 'nature, ease, simplicity, and genuine humour' (Davies 1818: 45). Thomas Wilkes (1759) felt able to 'share in his calamities' as Lear, 'feel the dark drifting rain, and the sharp tempest, with his *Blow winds –* '*till you have burst your cheeks*' (ibid.: 234), while of his 'mad' scenes Wilkes writes:

> I never see him coming down from one corner of the Stage, with his old grey hair standing, as it were, erect upon his head, his face filled with horror and attention, his hands expanded, and his whole frame accentuated by a dreadful solemnity, but I am astounded, and share in all his distresses. (ibid.)

For Garrick, it makes sense to focus upon the character as an old man, like other old men, frail and vulnerable in the storm.

Garrick's Lear no doubt seems sentimental. If it seems that way, it is partly because Western culture has since undermined the idea of obligation to authority figures in the interests of assertions of the individual's right to freedom, and has lost its understanding of what the eighteenth century meant by sentiment. The period had asserted the human personality as 'natural character', that is, as underwritten by general principles of nature. The actor was praised for gestural behaviour that aligned the performance with the general principles – the question was not how unique your acting was, but how well you imitated the passions.

Garrick's debt to Charles Macklin

In the latter part of Garrick's essay on Macbeth, the word 'passion' is put to one side in favour of 'humour'. To perform the humours is to be a character actor. Garrick was probably thinking here about his precursor Charles Macklin. To be a great actor, suggests Garrick, it is necessary to 'be introduced to the world', to 'be conversant with humors of every kind' (Cole and Chinoy 1995: 135). Garrick put the theory into practice himself by visiting asylums as part of his preparation to play Lear. His performance, by contrast with his Hamlet, featured:

> no sudden starts, no violent gesticulations; his movements were slow and feeble, misery was depicted in his countenance; he moved his head in the most deliberate manner; his eyes were fixed; or if they turned to anyone near him, he made a pause, and fixed his look on the person after much delay; his features at the same time telling what he was going to say before he uttered a word. (Genest 1832: IV, 468)

Studying human behaviour in everyday contexts in the service of a role would seem quite a revolutionary thing to do in that period, but Garrick got the idea from Macklin, who had spent time in the Jewish quarter of London in preparation for his performance as Shylock. Macklin brought onto the stage pieces of business that he copied from his observations. Without mentioning his mentor, Garrick pays homage to Macklin here:

> Another comedian now living ... has been observed constantly to attend the exchange for weeks together, before he exhibited one of Shakespeare's most inimitable and difficult characters, and so far succeeded by his great attention and observation of the manner, dress, and behavior of a particular tribe of people, that the judgment, application, and extraordinary pains he took to divert the public rationally, was amply returned with crowded theatres, and unequalled applause. (ibid.)

Macklin's Shylock was performed at Drury Lane on 14 February 1741, a year that seems significant in the history of Shakespearean acting given that Garrick's Richard III took to the stage at Goodman's Fields on 19 October. In *The Art and Duty of an Actor*, which was copied out verbatim by his biographer James Thomas Kirkman, Macklin insisted that the actor needs to be able to distinguish, as he claimed that Shakespeare himself did in his writing, the 'habits and characteristics' of the entire range of social groups (in Cole and Chinoy 1995: 121). He focused on the behaviour of the professional middle classes – attorneys, barristers, judges, clerks, merchants and so on – as well as on the military, ecclesiastical and agricultural communities and what we might call the leisure and service industries – musicians, hairdressers and the like. He ignored ideas about inherited social status and fixed instead on occupation as the marker of affiliation.

In addition, the actor 'must restrict all his powers, and convert them to the purposes of imitating the *looks*, *tones*, and *gestures*, that can best describe the characteristic that the poet has drawn' (ibid.). The passions and humours of each individual character can be defined within this behavioural taxonomy, and the actor's job is to 'mould and suit his looks, tones, gestures, and manners to the character' rather than 'suiting the character to the powers of the actor' (ibid.: 122). The individual characteristic he refers to is the display of a specific passion or humour – a 'genus', for example of avarice (surely he was thinking of Shylock). The intention seems to be to give dignity to character acting, in this case by associating it with social groups who liked to see themselves as educated, respectable producers and consumers of British culture.

Macklin appears to have taught Garrick about 'breaking the tones' of speech, that is, disrupting the musical rhythm of utterance at unexpected places. Admitting that he never was able to speak 'in the hoity-toity tone of the Tragedy of the day' (Parry 1891: 21), he seems to have specialized instead on underplaying, as when he gave the impression of suppressing his violent feelings of rage as Shylock until the third act, where 'a forcible and terrifying ferocity' emerged as he reacted to his daughter's elopement with a Christian (ibid.: 67). Where the opportunity arose for him to display 'alternate passions' (ibid.), principally between 'joy at the merchant's losses, and grief for the elopement of Jessica' (ibid.: 64), he 'varied his countenance admirably' (ibid.: 67). The results were judged to be an advance in natural acting. Lacking in Garrick's self-conscious sense of his own physical artistry, Macklin instead worked at getting the audience to take all of his characters seriously: 'he seemed,' wrote John Taylor, 'to be more in earnest in the character [of Macbeth] than any actor I have consequently seen' (ibid.: 161), an effect enhanced in this case by his innovative adoption of (as far as was possible) historically authentic costume.

Critics have sometimes mistakenly used the word 'pantomimic' when describing David Garrick's gestural behaviour. He had played Harlequin in pantomime in Ipswich and was to play it again in a burlesque way as a celebrity. But not a single one of the 96 existing images of Garrick 'in character' show him using pantomime gestures. Stylization is not pantomime. His was not an art of mime but of physical characterization, and it involved a sense of composing himself into precise emotional attitudes. Garrick's blended physical style – emotional dynamism plus sinuous elegance – was a visual enthymeme for a sense of respectability that was coming to replace the old ideal of nobility. He taught his audience by recontextualizing smoothness.

Equally, we must be careful not to take the mezzotints of Garrick's attitudes as evidence of static posing on stage. The classical statue fixed on a pedestal was undoubtedly an inspiration for actors in their search for attitudes. What appealed about these images was not only their *contrapposto* elegance but their declaration of a heroic, defiant individualism. But their relationship to the viewer is hierarchical: they tower over you, as if they do not care you exist; your reaction is meant to be a kind of passive awe in the presence of their greatness (see Stallybrass and White 1986: 21–2). They are exceptional figures, not symbols of a socially agreed norm. By standing outside of the ethical affiliations of their audience, they claim to stand outside of time itself. That is, as Michael Clune argues, the essence of the classical – the immortal reputation of the hero does not require you to authenticate it according to your own moral valuations, merely to witness it. It embodies its own authority (Clune 2013: 7–8).

The attitudes of Garrick, by contrast, betray his orientation towards a new community driven by a morality of self-fulfilment. He mobilized statuesque postures and combined them with startling gestures in order to make his audience feel that they too could be heroes like him – bourgeois British heroes, in effect. It is the Renaissance trick of *passing* given a new, secular, mercantile, democratizing twist. In this, he had many competitors but few, if any, serious rivals – until the emergence of Sarah Siddons, who dominated the theatrical discourse of the late eighteenth century in England like no one else.

Sarah Siddons: neoclassical authority and Romantic melancholy

Siddons excelled as Lady Macbeth. Her challenge was to elicit the audience's sympathetic imagination on behalf of a character who tells her husband she would kill her own child to further his personal ambition. Her strategy was to embody two sets of behavioural signals.

The first was founded upon the neoclassical presumption of authority over the audience, which generated a feeling of the sublime – in Edmund Burke's sense, as mixed awe and dread in the face of an object against which the viewer senses his own insignificance. For this, she needed to get across that 'quality of abstraction' that she saw as 'so necessary in the art of acting' (Campbell 1834: I, 214). As with Garrick and Macklin, she was playing to her strengths, since there was about her 'a native stiffness of gesture' (Downer 1943: 1017). It seems that more than Garrick, Sarah Siddons and her brother John Philip Kemble modelled their acting style on fine art, and statuary in particular. As Shearer

West shows, the terms in which their performances were discussed were usually taken from art theory and criticism (West 1991: 112).

Siddons's biographer James Boaden wrote, 'Conspiring with the larger stage to produce some change in her *style*, was her delight in statuary, which directed her attention to the antique, and made a remarkable impression upon her, as to simplicity of attire and severity of attitude' (Boaden 1827: 334). Boaden was thinking of the period after Garrick's original Drury Lane building had been condemned in 1792, and Siddons was performing in an Italianate opera house. Bigger theatres demanded more physically expansive attitudes, and fine art provided a model for the composition of such attitudes. Thus, Siddons extended her upper arm gestures to the limit of what the twentieth-century choreographer Rudolf Laban called the kinesphere of the actor – that area beyond which the body cannot reach without taking a step. The idea of a kinesphere was not alien to the period: in Gilbert Austin's manual *Chironomia* there are diagrams (reminiscent of Leonardo da Vinci's Vitruvian Man) illustrating the circular trajectories of the actor's limb extensions.

As she entered middle age, Sarah Siddons was spoken of more and more as, in the words of Shearer West, 'an immobile piece of sculpture, the living embodiment of the tragic muse' (in Asleson 2003: 162). This was more than simply down to the enlargement of the patent theatres. Joseph Roach notes how attentive she was to the condition of her skin. Her admirers 'deferred to her as the conservator of whiteness, the visible icon of its putative timelessness' (ibid.: 197). Roach sees her cultural iconicity as quasi-religious, as here in William Hazlitt's piece for *The Examiner* in 1816: 'she was regarded less with admiration than with wonder, as if a being of a superior order had dropped from another sphere to awe the world with the majesty of her appearance' (quoted in ibid.: 202).

Boaden noted how the sculptural influence played itself out in her gestures:

> I have said that her deportment varied considerably; and I have no doubt of the fact. In a small space the turns are quick and short. Where the area is considerable the step is wider, the figure more erect, and the whole progress more grand and powerful, the action is more from the shoulder; and we now first began to hear of the perfect form of Mrs. Siddons's arm. (Boaden 1827: 334)

Siddons's appropriation of classical imagery was not unique, though, so does not fully explain her astonishing appeal. There was clearly something else going on.

The second set of behavioural signals drew upon *Romanticism*. Heather McPherson has noted how the representations of Sarah Siddons conflate tragedy and melancholy. Thomas Beach in 1782 painted her as Melancholy in the Character of Milton's 'Il Penseroso', standing beneath an archway with her hands interlaced in front of her, the conventional gesture of melancholy found in Bulwer.

Joshua Reynolds's portrait of *Mrs. Siddons as the Tragic Muse* was turned by Siddons into a *tableau vivant* as part of a revival of David Garrick's *Jubilee* at Drury Lane in the 1785–6 season. Reynolds's painting encapsulates Siddons's blend of Classical and Gothic-Romantic. She seems to have thrown herself into a chair, and somehow has ended up in a decorously languid posture. The fact that Siddons begged Reynolds not to add more colour to her complexion associates her with both statuary (as Joseph Roach argues) and with the melancholy whiteness of the Romantic Agony. On stage, she would look stark, her dark eyes and hair set off by her skin.

This mask-like quality is rather crudely rendered by the painter George Romney in his three-faced portrait of her, *Siddonian Recollections* (1785–90). He represents her as if he were trying to sell us a box set of Sarah Siddons tragedy masks. He misses the point of her paleness, which was that it was readable not only as classical but brooding gothic melancholy. It was a kind of Georgian English equivalent of 'heroin chic', designed to make a woman look pale and interesting. In the background of Reynolds's painting, Pity and Terror are glimpsed as dark, vague, mysterious, emotionally overwrought ghosts – the face of Terror perhaps being modelled by Reynolds on himself. Siddons's own face, seen in profile, is ambiguous, perhaps hovering between different passions, or even a composite of emotions, such as Le Brun had offered models of in his booklet. As Frederick Burwick writes, 'The shift from emotional reserve to emotional excess in her performances was a significant source of Siddons's power. The more stoic strength and reserve she exhibited, the more affecting were her scenes of emotional crisis' (in Asleson 2003: 129).

Three apocryphal stories arose of how the painting came to be composed. Differing as they do in their details, they nonetheless all draw upon the Romantic idea of spontaneous creation, of the individual genius and 'the myth of artistic creation as inspired accident' at the same time as 'discounting the collaborative nature and performative aspects of portrait painting entailed by the act of posing' (ibid.: 410). Frequently, Siddons would talk about acting as if she were possessed by it. She would 'get into character' and remain so for the entire performance, including when she was offstage. During those periods, she would be intently listening to the performance continuing in her absence. 'In short,' as she wrote about herself, 'the spirit of the whole drama took possession of my mind and frame, by my attention being incessantly riveted to the passing scenes' (in Cole and Chinoy 1995: 141). A significant part of the Siddons mystique – or 'Siddonmania' as it was known – was the belief that her acting cost her personally. She would go home in tears after a show, and cry for hours, we are told. Or she would appear to be in a trance, still under the demonic spell of Lady Macbeth long after she had finished playing the role onstage. Many of her admirers, too, appeared to have been possessed through a kind of emotional contagion in her presence, and behaved in suitably ecstatic ways, weeping, fainting, madly applauding her every move, and so on.

Boaden picked up on an innovative syncopation in her acting:

> The amazing self-possession of Mrs. Siddons rendered distance only the means of displaying a system of graceful and considerate dignity, or weighty and lingering affliction, as the case might demand. In the hurry of distraction, she could stop, and in some frenzied attitude speak wonders to the eye, till a second rush forward brought her to the proper ground on which her utterance might be trusted. (Boaden 1827: 333)

Like Garrick, Siddons was expert in such rapid emotional transitions and surprising changes of rhythm. For example, during Macbeth's short speech beginning 'We will proceed no further in this business', her reaction changed from 'animated hope and surprise to disappointment, depression, contempt, and rekindling resentment' (G. J. Bell in Fleeming Jenkin 1915: 46). On the challenging lines a few moments later in which she claims that she would be prepared to murder her baby to achieve her ambition, she had been 'at a distant part of the stage. She now comes close to him – an entire change of manner, looks for some time in his face, and speaks' (ibid.: 47). On 'We fail' she showed not 'surprise' but gave the words a 'strong downward inflection, bowing with her hands down, the palm upward' (ibid.: 48) – the ambiguous hand gesture perhaps recalling Eve's *Profero* to Adam. In the murder of Duncan scene, she performed 'Alack, I am afraid they have awaked' with, according to the critic Bell, the 'finest agony; tossing of the arms' (ibid.: 52). On Macbeth's 'There's one did laugh in's sleep, and one cried, "Murder!"' she performed a self-touching ('adaptor') gesture: 'As if her inhuman strength of spirit overcome by the contagion of his remorse and terror. Her arms about her neck and bosom, shuddering' (ibid.: 53).

What was new here was her capacity to counterpoint body and voice in an ingeniously suggestive manner. The demarcation line between posture and gesture – a boundary visually articulated in the bodies of earlier eighteenth-century actresses who wore conical stays that discouraged bending from the waist – was now fully merged into a forceful physical image, then combined with a voice that, while ranging through a large gamut of tragic effects, held fast to a conception of voice as elocution. Her voice signalled her affiliation to the classical tradition of restraint and decorum even as her body seemed hardly able to suppress its symptoms of melancholy and trauma. The blend was irresistible to her hordes of fans: her body was intense, and her voice classy. By choosing to combine her passionate gestures with a dignified eloquence, she suggested a mind moving beyond the confines of the given stage action. She did this not by presenting a unified impression of a single passion with body and voice but by driving a wedge between them. She embodied a contradiction: she was classical and Romantic at the same time.

Her performance of Lady Macbeth appears, if Boaden is to be believed, to have been calculated to silence critical voices that were suggesting she was only capable of embodying pure virtue. Her first scene with Macbeth certainly seems to have presented a magnificently varied display of dominance behaviour:

> His lady, bending steadily to her purpose, is equal to all occasions, and now breaks in upon her husband's fearful rumination ... She assails him with sophistry, and contempt, and female resolution, seemingly superior to all manly daring ... There was no *qualifying* with our humanity in the tone or gesture. This really beautiful and interesting actress did not at all shrink from standing before us the true and perfect image of the greatest of all natural and moral deprivations a *fiend-like woman*. (Boaden 1827: 258–9)

She dominated the audience too, it seems, and it paid off in terms of audience reaction:

> 'Give ME the daggers,' excited a general start from those around me. Upon her return from the chamber of slaughter, after gilding the faces of the grooms, from the peculiar character of her lip she gave an expression of *contempt* more striking than any she had hitherto displayed. (ibid.: 259)

As she exited with the daggers, 'stealing out she turns towards him stooping, and with the finger pointed to him with malignant energy says, "If he do bleed," &c.' (Bell in Fleeming Jenkin 1915: 55). And, as in her previous scene with Macbeth, she asserted her authority over him on the exit; clapping him on the shoulder in congratulation at having regained his manhood in the earlier scene, here she strikes him 'on the shoulder, pulls him from his fixed posture, forces him away, he talking as he goes' (ibid.: 57). In the banquet scene, after 'rapidly cutting down the question from Rosse – "What sights, my lord?"... [her] address displayed here drew down a thunder of applause' (Boaden 1827: 261). She deviated from convention by dominating Macbeth onstage until the text no longer gave her the opportunity to take an active role.

Sarah Siddons portrayed herself as a modest respectable married woman in her private life, but onstage her physical dominance of the stage, as well as of her male scene partners, was enthralling. It is arguable that it was Siddons who largely created the paradigmatic image of Lady Macbeth that has become a measure of performances since. 'The character of Lady Macbeth,' wrote Boaden, 'became a sort of exclusive possession of Mrs Siddons. There was a mystery about it, which she alone seemed to have penetrated' (Boaden 1827: 264–5).

It was perhaps her sleepwalking scene that most powerfully displayed her originality. Boaden wrote that before her performance, actresses would tend to glide around the stage during this scene, and came across as feebler than when awake (ibid.: 262). In all likelihood, he was thinking of Hannah Pritchard, who partnered David Garrick in the play. By contrast:

> Mrs Siddons seemed to conceive the fancy as having equal power over the whole frame, and all her actions had the wakeful vigour; she ladled the water from her imaginary ewer over her hands – bent her body to listen to the sounds presented by her fancy, and hurried to resume the taper where she had left it, that she might with all speed drag her pallid husband to the chamber. (ibid.)

To the modern reader this perhaps sounds quite familiar. If it does seem like a familiar reading of the character, then that is because Sarah Siddons made it so, just as Garrick permanently altered the image of Hamlet confronting his father's ghost.

Even her biggest fan G. J. Bell expressed a qualm about her flouting of convention in the scene: 'I should like her to enter less suddenly.

A slower and more interrupted step more natural. She advances rapidly to the table, sets down the light and rubs her hand, making the action of lifting up water in one hand at intervals' (in Fleeming Jenkin 1915: 66–7). Boaden answered the criticism that she put down her candle shortly after entering: 'People cant about originality, and yet dote upon precedent' (Boaden 1827: 262). The criticism seems to have been that Siddons put down the candle for practical reasons – she needed her hands free to perform her gesture of washing. Again, the hidden agenda here was to compare Siddons favourably with her predecessor Hannah Pritchard, who held onto her candle during the scene. Boaden countered that a real somnambulist would simply put the candle down quite mechanically (ibid.).

His account of Siddons as Lady Macbeth was far from impartial. It is interesting to see how he framed his comparison of her performance with predecessors in terms of how they presented the passions – anger, indignation, contempt, astonishment, dismay, terror. It is also significant that he referred the reader to a mezzotint of David Garrick and Hannah Pritchard with the daggers. His objection to the image was that it showed the actors in fashionable modern clothes; for Boaden the problem was not that the image is unhistorical, but that it is 'unpicturesque' (ibid.: 263). What he meant is that it lacks atmosphere: it does not produce the feelings of awe and dread that were associated with the sublime, feelings that he thought we ought to have in the presence of the Macbeths.

In an important essay on the Graeco-Roman sculpture of *Laocoon* written in 1766, Gotthold Lessing described the 'frozen moment' when the movement of the figure is just at the point of climax – the apex – so that the viewer can see the 'before and after, the inception and consequence of a depicted action' (Burwick in Asleson 2003: 141). The gesture is held in suspension – at the boundary of the movement segment – as in Siddons's gesture of reproach as Queen Katharine in *Henry VIII*, preserved in an illustration by her son Henry (Siddons 1807/1822: Plate 51). This gesture seems to have been a favourite of hers – one hand across the bosom, the other raised to Heaven with the index finger pointing. It was enormously influential: it was still being imitated at the end of the nineteenth century by Ellen Terry. As well as indicating sincerity, the hand across the bosom may sometimes have been practically motivated, since she is pictured holding up folds of her copious skirt in Thomas Cook's *Mrs. Siddons in the Character of the Tragic Muse* (1783), in a posture that recalls Cicero's advice to orators on using the left hand to hold up the toga.

Her left arm position may also have referred for some to the idealized image of her private life as a caring mother. The gesture was used by George Henry Harlow in his painting *The Court for the Trial of Queen Katharine*, a painting that features several of the Kembles in action. It is possible that Harlow saw the Siddons/Kemble 1806 production, although the painting was made 11 years later. The gesture is one of the few that is mentioned by G. J. Bell in his notes on her performance: 'When Campeius comes to her she turns from him impatiently; then makes a sweet bow of apology, but dignified. Then to Wolsey, turned and looking *from* him, with her hand pointing back at him, in a voice of thunder, "to *you* I speak"' (in Fleeming Jenkin 1915: 89).

Henry Siddons published plates of his mother in the role performing supplication (Siddons 1822: Plate 52) and sickness (Siddons 1822: Plate 54). Here again, especially in the gesture of supplication, can be observed a visual correlative for Lessing's idea of the 'before and after', as Burwick shows (in Asleson 2003: 143–5). The key is in this feeling of suspension, crucial to the sense of smoothness and thus to the perception of dominant status. That seems to have been exactly the impression that Siddons was capable of conveying in gesture.

Sarah Siddons played Hamlet numerous times over three decades until the age of 50. By so doing, she opened up a new possibility for Shakespearean performance – and for the art of impression management, since roleplaying as the opposite sex usually serves to intensify 'the uncanny allure of It' (Roach 2007: 11). By 'It', Roach is referring to 'presence' or charisma, which in Chapter 2 I associate with *sprezzatura*.

Perhaps out of a sense of rivalry with Dorothy Jordan, who was famous for her breeches roles, Siddons chose not to wear breeches for the part. Instead, she wore the kind of loose, swirling neoclassical coverings that lent her a more mysterious air of androgyny. Mary Sackville Hamilton, a fan, created watercolour illustrations of her in various costumes and performing a range of gestures from the play. Interestingly, she omits Siddons's face from the pictures and represents the hands only crudely. Instead, she depicts 'in careful and even affectionate detail the fall of fabric folds, the effect of a darker fabric seen through lace, and the lines and angles formed by fingers, arms, and hems' (Woo 2007: 579). Hamilton does attempt to record specific moments from the performance, such as Siddons folding her arms in defiance of Gertrude on 'Aye, madam, it is common' (1.2.74). But the illustrations, while offering a few instances of postures and gestures, communicate more about her costume than they do about Siddons herself.

True and false gestures

Sarah Siddons's eldest son Henry compiled his *Practical Illustrations of Rhetorical Gesture and Action* in 1807. While the book bears a clear relation to antecedent gesture manuals of the eighteenth century, at the same time it seems to point towards something new. The book was actually an adapted translation of Johann Jakob Engel's 1785 *Ideen zu einer Mimik*. Engel's text is a justification of a system for universalizing gestural expressions. Engel showed some appreciation of cultural differences, and argued that the actor must study the variations 'as they operate in various climates' (in Siddons 1822: 10). But he was attempting to root out 'the truly natural and essential part of the sentiment' (ibid.: 7), the prototypical form of movement that remained after the variations in cultural expression were taken into account. Engel gave the example of how people express pride and shame, asserting that he knows no single person on earth who expresses the feeling of shame by lifting up the head and straightening the back – if they did so, we would instinctively realize that the person was masking feelings of shame by a physical display of pride or contempt (ibid.). The book describes 35 passions or 'sentiments'. Where Engel had taken his examples from the performances of the German actors August Wilhelm Iffland and Friedrich Ludwig Schröder, Henry Siddons's text contains 69 engravings of his mother and her brother posing in costumes showing the current fashions in London theatres. His text moves from 'picturesque' (i.e. representational) gestures to 'expressive' gestures, which are divided into 'analogous' (having both pragmatic and representational functions) and 'physiological' (basically adaptors and affect displays). In his taxonomy, Engel does not especially distinguish his ideas from his predecessors.

However, in his introduction to the second edition of his book in 1822, Siddons also acknowledges the influence of a lecture called 'An Essay on Gesture' given at the Norwich branch of the Philosophical Society by the painter Michael William Sharp two years earlier. Sharp was known for his executions of theatrical group portraits featuring performers of the day, including of Sarah Siddons's younger rival Eliza O'Neill as Queen Constance in *King John* (1819). As Frederick Burwick writes, Sharp's lecture 'makes the case that gestures not only reveal emotions, they reveal even those emotions that a person might strive to conceal' (in Asleson 2003: 130).

Here then is a notion that is not found in previous manuals: that a gesture may signal not only an individual's conscious intention but something else that the individual did not mean to signal. Sharp's suggestion links in with a basic distinction made by Engel between true and false gestures. The first Engel calls 'expression' and the second 'painting'. True gestures are spontaneous, he claims, while false gestures are composed performances intended to deceive. Engel objected to so-called pantomimic acting because what is being modelled by the hands appears to be the word itself rather than the character's thoughts and feelings. Gestures that depicted features of an object were felt by Engel to be an unnecessary addition to poetic drama, since linguistic metaphor already carried this representational function.

Of great interest to Engel is mimetic representation – the character's bodily responses to external stimuli. Most important, though, is what he calls *mimismetic* representation. The term signifies the effort to put the moment of cognitive realization into flesh. It is manifested in the pace and style of the walk. The play of the hands

> is modified in the same manner as the walk – it is free, unconstrained, easy, and mobile, while the ideas develop themselves without any difficulty, and follow each other in a natural succession: It is inquiet and irregular, the hands are agitated, and move themselves without design, now towards the bosom, now towards the head, the arms fold and loosen, as the thought is arrested during his walk, or hurried into uncertain or strange tracks. (In Siddons 1822: 60)

The example given is Hamlet transitioning from doubt to apprehension. In the accompanying illustration (Plate X), Hamlet stands facing the audience in ballet third position, his left leg forward, his left arm across his waist holding a book, while his right arm, with bent elbow, points to his mind – or is it heaven? – with his index finger. This marks the 'change of sentiment' when 'the unhappy Prince has discovered the reasons which make self destruction so criminal a step – he exclaims, "ay, there's the rub," and at the same moment should give the *exterior* sign of that which his *interior* penetration alone has enabled him to discover' (ibid.: 60–1).

In Engel's original text, the index finger does not point upwards to heaven, or towards the brain, but instead 'forward, as if his eye has perceived without, what his intellect told him within' (in Barnett 1987: 308). In both cases, the problem is the same: to make a change of thought visible, the actor has to place it outside, or on the surface of, the body, and articulate it by a change of physical rhythm. The change of rhythm in Kemble's performance of Hamlet cannot be gleaned from the picture or the text alone but, according to James Boaden, he 'prolonged the word dream meditatingly' (Boaden 1827: 80), perhaps in that way giving a feeling of suspension before launching the gesture. Kemble was described as an academic or philosophical actor, inclined to a reflective approach, and Boaden among others drew attention to his pauses as the key signal to the audience of his thoughtfulness.

Sharp's lecture and Engel's mimismetic gestures are signposts towards a new emphasis in acting upon how the body reveals what the mind is incapable of concealing: what later would come to be codified under the theatrical rubric of 'subtext', the psychological rubric of 'non-verbal behaviour' and the aesthetic rubric of 'realism'. Here again, it is possible to discern how Shakespearean performance paralleled the movement of social morality away from the concern with one's sense of obligation to a higher purpose and towards an agenda of individual self-fulfilment.

Edmund Kean

No one exemplified the shock of the new at this time better than Edmund Kean. On the eve of battle, his Richard III 'stood fixed, drawing figures on the sand with the point of his sword, before retiring to his tent, and his sudden recovery of himself with a "Good night"' (Leigh Hunt quoted in Hawkins 1869: 165). Always conscious of his own celebrity and of his relationship to his predecessors, Kean toyed with the audience at such moments, and (when it worked, as here) he was rewarded with 'earnest applause' followed by 'uncontrollable enthusiasm' (ibid.: 166–7). Those who described his acting, such as William Hazlitt, drew upon metaphors from the new science of electromagnetism to describe his style – not always flatteringly, since to witness a performance that illuminated Shakespeare in lightning flashes would be to miss a lot when it was dark. But this was to belie the preparation Kean underwent for each role, as he said himself to Garrick's widow:

> These people don't understand their business; they give me credit where I don't deserve it, and pass over passages on which I have bestowed the utmost care and attention. Because my style is easy and natural they think I don't study, and talk about the 'sudden impulse of genius'. There is no such thing as impulsive acting; all is premeditated and studied beforehand. (Cole and Chinoy 1970/1995: 327–8)

His protest hardly made a dent in the public perception of him as impetuous. Keats, an admirer of his acting, wrote that he 'delivers himself up to the instant feeling without a shadow of a thought about anything else. He feels his being as deeply as Wordsworth' (quoted by Jackson in Marshall 2012: 151).

Kean was seen as an upstart and an outsider. Jeffrey Kahan writes of how high society barred its doors to this sordid, flamboyant provincial actor even when he had found fame. 'Embarrassed by this turn of events, the actor created a heroic narrative in which he turned his back on the nobility' (Kahan 2006: 80). William Robson said of him, 'Kean's person was mean' and added, 'no man, on the stage, was more ungraceful' (quoted in ibid.: 67). In a politically volatile era, his performances, onstage and off, took on something of the quality of class warfare against the Tory aristocracy. He moved in fits and starts, unexpectedly, like a disturbed reptile. Like a reptile, his Hamlet crawled across the floor in a highly indecorous manner:

> [Kean] forgot that inalienable delicacy, which should eternally characterize a gentleman in his deportment before the ladies, that he not only exposed his *derrière* to his mistress, but positively crawled upon his belly towards the King like a wounded snake in a meadow, rather than a Prince. ('The London Herald' quoted in Mills 1985: 83)

Twenty-two years later, William Macready was painted preparing himself for exactly the same belly crawl across the stage by Daniel Maclise in *The Play-scene in Hamlet*. Macready was in essence domesticated Kean.

Another example is among Kean's most famous *points*. The audience was expecting the usual ranting and raving in Hamlet's closet scene with Ophelia. Instead, he played the scene quietly and sombrely, then screamed 'To a nunnery, go' before rushing to the edge of the stage, stopping, turning, and returning 'with an almost gliding step', bending down gently and pressing his lips to her hand (Ludwig Tieck in Mills 1985: 81–2). This was then imitated by Victorian actors, including Herbert Beerbohm-Tree in 1892 who returned to kiss Ophelia's hair after she had collapsed in grief on a couch (Dawson 1995: 47).

'Betterton', an American critic for the Philadelphia National Gazette, wrote at length on Kean in 1821. He recognized that English critics (especially the 'cockney critics' like Hazlitt and Leigh Hunt) had observed a certain lack of elegance in Kean's style while at the same time forgiving him because he offered them instead 'masterstrokes of art and nature, and the energies of passion and action' (Cole and Chinoy 1995: 331). For this critic, the masterstrokes were few and far between, however, and, while it is appropriate in his opinion that Shylock should lack physical grace, 'in Richard and Othello, you find unremittingly an utter want of physical adaptation and patrician demeanor' (ibid.). He went further in a paragraph that in its disapproval sheds light on Kean's gestural style:

> Mr. Kean would seem to apply literally to his art, the lesson of Demosthenes with regard to oratory – action, action, action. His limbs have no repose or steadiness in scenes of agitated feeling; his hands are kept in unremitting and the most rapid convulsive movement; seeking, as it were, a resting place in some part of his upper dress, and occasionally pressed together on the crown of his head ... Quick and irregular motion, vehement and perturbed gesture, are occasionally apposite; but there is a discipline and temperament even for disorder, whether as to action or to utterance, on the stage ... It has been said that dignity has no arms ... The energetic use of the limbs spoils the true and effectual expression. (ibid.)

Kean spoke and moved fast. He made frequent use of self-adaptor gestures, touching his own body, his crown, his neck, his face as if highly agitated. His pauses were unnaturally long, and he strained his voice to hoarseness by alternating between low monotones and sudden outbursts. As the exemplary Romantic actor, he was deeply self-conscious to the point of self-loathing. Richard Sennett notes that in the nineteenth century, while the individual's class status was steadily being subjected to democratic beliefs about sameness, the personality was judged in terms of uniqueness. It is as though, in devaluing the conventional categories that made up one's 'natural character', a new approach to the problem of describing the person had to be found. It was found in the notion that 'people with different appearances are different persons' (Sennett 1977: 152). This aligns the period with the increasingly dominant social morality of individual self-fulfilment that had gained significant momentum from the American and French Revolutions. One manifestation of it in the wider culture was in the revival of physiognomy and the invention of phrenology, which purported to reveal personality from the bumps on the skull. Variations in personality, linked to the physical appearance of the individual, reflect the very instability of the idea of personality itself. Kean epitomized this new conception of personality. 'Betterton' wrote: 'His studied play of physiognomy borders on grimace; his animation of manner becomes incoherent bustle; what is spirited savours of turbulence; what is passionate, of frenzy' (Cole and Chinoy 1995: 330).

Kean's physical style smacked of resentful, low-status pathological attempts at dominance behaviour. He seemed obliged to no social code, which was why he was so well-suited to play destructive outsiders like Richard, Iago and Shylock and sadistic villains in the popular melodrama. Unlike with Sarah Siddons, there was no coherent blend of opposites in his acting: what you saw was what you got, and he bullied you into submission by administering one shock after the next. Only in his drawn-out moments of silence were the spectators invited to fill out in their own imaginations what he was really thinking.

Sennett argues that 'freedom of feeling at a given moment seems like a violation of 'normal' conventional feeling' (Sennett 1977: 152). This is important because it suggests how actors like Kean created a boundary line between themselves and the public. More than ever, the performer was separated from the spectator, who looked on in occasionally horrified fascination. The relationship between the two has very little to do with the polite ideals of a civil society such as the early eighteenth century had promoted. The needs of the group had, until this point, still been prioritized over the autonomy of the individual, whose impulse to design her or his own personal life would have been seen as threatening to the social fabric: 'civilizations arise when culture willingly serves society, when artists, artisans and warriors willingly subject themselves to a social and political order' (Jaeger 1985: 271).

Kean was 'sensational' not only in his rapid success, but also in the startling intensity of focus he placed upon the present moment of sensation itself. Furthermore, he was sensational in impetuously overturning the audience's prior expectations of a role – in upsetting the apple cart of classical decorum. He was only able to maintain this kind of reputation management in fits and starts, and quickly burned himself out through alcoholism. In this, as well as in his reckless sexual behaviour and his pugnacious self-aggrandizement masking a deep anxiety about his legitimacy, he feels quite like a modern celebrity. As C. Stephen Jaeger puts it:

> The role of the artist in romanticism generally is not a civilizing one; just the opposite. It is to emancipate the Promethean, and the subversion of a tyrannical or perverse or outdated political order can appear as a devout goal. (ibid.)

Kean's revisions of the acting paradigms of Richard, Shylock, Hamlet and Iago exerted a stranglehold over the next generation – of male actors, at least.

Victorian actors inherited the system of attitudinal points that showed one's relationship to the acting tradition. This was encouraged also by the rehearsal method, in which one tended to do most of the preparation work on one's role alone. The resulting style was further supported by inherited staging conventions such as the use of discovery scenes revealed by mobile flats that could be opened and closed in front of an acting space, and the bringing down of the curtain at the end of the act, both of which devices lent themselves to the creation of attitudinal tableaux.

For actresses, there was an added inducement to pose in idealized attitudes. Gail Marshall writes, 'The links between stage and sculpture are cemented in the late-eighteenth and early-nineteenth centuries in acting manuals and in a range of Classical motifs on the popular English stage ... the specific type of statuary which is consistently invoked is that from the Greek Classical Era and the Hellenistic period, and their Roman copies' (Marshall 1998: 5). Classical sculpture was seen as timeless, so, by association, when an actress posed like a statue she became timeless Woman. She was a symbol of both the Fall and the state of innocence, 'any sign of modesty ... both an admission and a forestalling of knowledge' (ibid.: 11) as when the Medici Venus (which was installed in the British Museum in 1886) shields her genitals from view.

Henry Irving's Darwinism

And yet the tide was beginning to turn away from both classicism and Romanticism towards something more akin to behaviourism. As I indicated in Chapter 2, the key figure in the transition to a new acting paradigm was not an actor but a scientist: Charles Darwin. His influence can be seen very clearly in the performances of Henry Irving, who along with his partner Ellen Terry was the most celebrated of English Shakespearean actors in the late nineteenth century. Henry Irving's style reveals how Darwin's core ideas throw light on the impression management tactics of actors, in particular the way that some actors (another was Richard Mansfield who toured for decades as Dr. Jekyll and Mr. Hyde) exploited the then fashionable idea that beneath the civilized masks of bourgeois society lurked a seething mass of bestial impulses.

Physical challenges to gaining audience acceptance proved an initial spur and an ultimate advantage. In childhood Irving had suffered an accident that had left him with a dragging leg when he walked. In addition, he developed a speech defect, which may have been partly due to separation from his mother during formative years. In later life, despite his dandyish outward demeanour and his circle of cronies, he cultivated an idea of himself as an essentially private soul. As he wrote himself *contra* Diderot, 'Every actor has his secret' (Pollock 1883: xix).

Irving's relationship with Bram Stoker is equally complex. Irving dismissed *Dracula*, whose hero uncannily brings to mind a number of associations – Jack the Ripper being one, and Irving's Macbeth another. Critics have observed how Stoker's description of the vampire tallies with Irving's facial characteristics in the role of Macbeth, in particular the hairiness of the face right down to the lambchop whiskers. Irving cultivated in his acting 'a repertoire of physical behaviours that were always suggestive of a barely submerged savagery' (Goodall 2002: 173). Even towards the end of his career, after having received the stamp of social approval in 1895 with a knighthood (an honour that he originally declined when Gladstone offered him it in 1883), he never quite lost this aura: an image of his Lear sitting on his throne surrounded by antiquarian objects hints at a dangerous wild man.

Irving's style exemplified Darwin's refusal to sever thought from feeling. In this he gives the lie to Diderot, who could not fathom how it is that an actor can recreate emotional spontaneity a second time. An emotional response has both a voluntary and an involuntary aspect. An actor might simulate the external signs of an emotional reaction such as sadness. In doing so, the very simulation itself may begin to draw upon involuntary responses. As Jane R. Goodall says, the process 'is not a smooth ride' (ibid.: 175). Irving seems to have been a specialist in such emotional border crossing, where his projection of himself as both an intellectual actor (he wore spectacles, he wrote prefaces to Diderot and Talma's writings on acting, he was obsessively detailed in his preparatory research) and as a kind of bestial throwback would present themselves as alternative readings. The idea that an actor either organically feels the moment or must mechanically reproduce that feeling is a kind of crude logic chopping, and fails to account for a performer like Irving.

Spectators had vigorously applauded Kean's points. But Irving began a procedure whereby points would give way to smaller, fussier, more obscure details of stage business – markers of Irving's individuality, his capacity to rethink tradition, as well as of the decline in a style of presentational acting in favour of the strategies of naturalism. Clement Scott, who saw Irving's first outing as Hamlet in 1874, wrote, 'Those who have seen other Hamlets are aghast. Mr. Irving is missing his points, he is neglecting his opportunities' (Scott 1900: 62). Irving did not stand under the footlights and address the audience during his soliloquies.

'His eyes are fixed apparently on nothing ... He gazes on vacancy and communes with his conscience' (ibid.: 63–4).

As so often happens in theatre history, the apparent innovation was viewed as more lifelike. 'He is not acting,' declares Scott, 'he is not splitting the ears of the groundlings; he is an artist concealing his art: he is talking to himself; he is thinking aloud' (ibid.: 65). It was not entirely innovative, though: both Garrick and Kean were supposed to have avoided making eye contact with their audiences at moments of aloneness on stage. Here, as I will clarify in the next chapter, naturalism can be seen to rely in part for its effect upon an idea of hypnotic possession.

Irving came to be identified with claustrophobically sentimental English values. But his appeal to the populace was in large part down to how successfully his Shakespearean performances drew upon a hunger for sensation. Tiffany Watt-Smith notes how it had become quite normal for Victorian actors to bend their knees and display *starts*. Irving received rounds of applause almost every time he appeared to flinch on stage (Watt-Smith 2014: 62). The technique of bending the knees and starting was of course standard procedure by the end of Garrick's era. But Irving's initial attempts to graft Shakespeare onto the popular melodramatic imagination were sufficiently novel to secure his reputation. He annoyed critics by his perverse accenting of the text. He stressed pronouns like 'you' instead of laying emphasis on the clarifying parts of speech like nouns: 'I have heard of *your* paintings well enough ... *You* jig and amble and nickname God's creatures and make *your* wantonness your ignorance' (quoted in West 1955: 416). There was nothing new in the nit-picking: Garrick's pronunciation was also subjected to detailed feedback from his educated audience. What was new was the motive. Garrick wanted his public to imagine he was one of them; Irving wanted to be seen as inimitably private.

Irving's gestural behaviour offers examples of how he tried to prise open a gap between word and movement, a gap that could then be read as inner life. The two pictures of the old king Hamlet and Claudius had always presented a staging conundrum. In Rowe's 1709 illustration, they are pictures on the wall, although it seems that from the Restoration onwards the usual practice was for Hamlet to produce two miniatures from his pocket. Kean's innovation was to find Claudius's miniature on a chain around Gertrude's neck. Irving dispensed with pictures altogether, instead gesturing deictically into thin air: 'Look here on this picture, and on this!' (3.4.53).

The business of writing in his commonplace book before 'So, uncle, there you are' after his first encounter with the ghost (1.5.110) was echoed in a cliffhanging moment at the end of 2.2: 'The play's the thing/Wherein I'll catch the conscience of the king'. As the curtain fell, Irving 'scrawled his notes with an excited up-and-down movement which must have formed letters quite twelve inches high', according to Edward R. Russell, although that did not stop the audience from bursting into applause at the novelty (in West 1955: 416).

The more tastefully Romantic Edwin Booth (1880) at this moment had made a metaphoric gesture 'as if encompassing his victim with a net' (Hapgood 1999: 174). Irving's gesture seems more obviously designed for effect, but it is Booth's Power Grip gesture that would seem self-consciously theatrical with the arrival of fourth-wall staging, electric lighting and darkened auditoria. The difference between Booth's and Irving's gestures signals a shift away from movements aimed squarely at the spectator, towards self- and object adaptors that hint at hidden motives and conflicts. Gesture became a matter of manipulating the real objects in the environment so as to suggest an authentic (i.e. mimetic) reality to the fictive world, and to hint at the movement of thought within a character.

Not everyone agreed that Irving's gestural business was warranted, although all agreed it was frequently novel. Dutton Cook objected to his messing around with some candlesticks in the chamber scene with Gertrude, while much was made of his playing with Ophelia's peacock-feather fan during the 'Mousetrap' sequence. After Claudius's exit, he leapt onto the now vacant throne with the fan before throwing it away on 'A very, very – peacock' (3.2.286). There is precedent for this: Garrick would at this moment flourish his pocket handkerchief over his head, while Fechter (who is considered to have brought from France to England a more credibly conversational style of delivery) tore pages from his playbook and scattered them, before holding his own throat as if choking on 'Ah ha!' (3.2.293). But Irving moved byplay to a whole new level, insisting on its right to exist.

Disapproval of his fussy insistence on physical detail surfaced in the reaction to his Iago – although that performance was certainly seen as an improvement on his Othello:

> There is peril of the player being subordinated to the 'properties' he makes play with. Mr. Irving sat or lolled upon a variety of chairs and tables, toyed with a pen, with his swordbelt and trappings, used a poniard as a toothpick, rumpled his hair incessantly, waved a red cloak about him bull-fighter fashion, and otherwise occupied himself, naturally enough, no doubt, yet often superfluously. (Dutton Cook, in West 1955: 417)

Most of the gestures mentioned in Cook's criticism are either self- or object adaptors. They are in essence stylized indicators of psychic turbulence. Irving's restless behaviour was a kind of ticking time-bomb, a self-conscious psychologizing of what previous actors had presented as choleric symptoms. Sometimes the bomb would go off in a display of ranting and raving. The behaviour ties his acting style not only to Darwin but to the Charcot–Freud diagnosis of hysteria, a diagnosis applied usually to heavily corseted Victorian women who had trouble with their breathing. After his American tour, Irving's 1885 Hamlet pared down the behavioural eccentricities. Ten years earlier, it must have seemed at times to his audiences that Irving was in the throes of a nervous breakdown. But it was really the art of acting itself that was in crisis. Eccentric and grand though it still was, Irving's style can be seen as prophetic of film acting.

Although this chapter has inevitably been rather selective, the given illustrations suggest ways in which the transformations of gesture in Shakespearean performance paralleled the gradual transformation from a social morality of publicly declared obligation towards higher purposes to a morality centred upon the rights and claims of the individual. The gestural style of Irving, for example, reveals how the combination of Darwin and Freud would prove irresistible to the acting profession in its search for a model of credible behaviour that would appeal to a new cosmopolitan audience driven by a morality of self-fulfilment. The next chapter will pursue this theme through the work of modernist and postmodernist Shakespeareans.

6
Modern and Postmodern Gestures

In 1884 William James published a paper called 'What is an Emotion?' The essence of James's idea is that an emotion is no more than bodily changes in response to an external stimulus. A year later the related ideas of Carl Lange were published, leading to what became known as the James–Lange theory. From around this time onwards, personality would usually come to be seen in terms of either inheritance from one's parents or influences from the environment. The conception of the individual as subject to uncontrollable forces reached an apogee in the theory and practice of naturalism. Underpinning naturalism is a conception of the wellsprings of behaviour that reflects a dominant social morality of self-fulfilment in an inverted way. If individual happiness through meaningful experiences is the goal of your life's journey, inheritance and social forces may well impede your chances – the sins of the fathers are passed onto the sons, a tragic fact for which the sons cannot be held responsible. This idea of personality was expressed forcefully in the character of Oswald in Ibsen's *Ghosts* (1889), whose syphilitic father has passed the disease onto him. While the cultural work of naturalism was in the main based on new writing, though, the debate about the bodily basis of emotion, as I have indicated in the example of Irving, carried over into the Shakespearean theatre world.

This chapter explores what happened to Shakespearean performance in the eras of modernism and postmodernism. Beginning with Konstantin Stanislavski, whose work on *Othello* crystallizes a central issue within acting of the relation between emotion and technique, I move on to consider how the Ukrainian director Les Kurbas's *Macbeth* illustrates key non-verbal tropes of modernist performance. What connects many of the modernist Shakespearean innovators is sometimes referred to as a 'turn to the East', and I contextualize that turn with reference to how some practitioners recovered and relabelled the precepts of the Noh Theatre master Zeami Motokiyo. Finally, I explore the use of gesture in some more recent productions of Shakespeare by companies like The Wooster Group and dreamthinkspeak, whose work can be seen to reflect a postmodern aesthetic.

Stanislavski's Othello

No part reveals more clearly how Shakespeare's theatre relied upon a series of emotional shock effects than Othello. Julie Hankey, writing on the play, argues that 'the indications are that both in acting and in nature, feelings or "the affections" could be thought of as separate and autonomous qualities that arrived, took possession, and departed more or less mysteriously' (Hankey 1987: 9). In some strange way, the actor was not responsible for these effects, but rather was subject to them as if in a trance.

The Russian actor and director Stanislavski saw the Italian actor Tommaso Salvini play Othello in 1882. Salvini's performance displayed uncontrollable emotionality on an operatic scale. Salvini seemed to offer to the young Stanislavski an experiential model of acting. In fact it was a single gesture of Salvini's that unlocked Stanislavski's imagination:

> Salvini approached the platform of the doges, thought a little while, concentrated himself and, unnoticed by any of us, took the entire audience of the Great Theatre into his hands. It seemed that he did this with a single gesture – that he stretched his hand without looking into the public, grasped all of us in his palm, and held us there as if we were ants or flies. He closed his fist, and we felt the breath of death; he opened it, and we knew the warmth of bliss. We were in his power, and we will remain in it all our lives, forever. (Stanislavski 1956: 266)

The gesture is reminiscent of Booth's Power Grip as Hamlet, although performed without looking directly at the spectators. Salvini performed in Italian, a language unfamiliar to Stanislavski. As a result, Stanislavski's description of the performance focused on the non-verbal details; in the event, it was critical to Stanislavski's development that he reimagined the non-verbal.

At the same time, the play is unusual in its realism – there are no supernatural events or characters, no epic battles that would have to be staged using theatrical shorthand, and so on. For Stanislavski, the challenge of playing a character who in no way resembled him, yet who could be made to exist in a realistic world, must have been mouth-watering. If he could persuade his audience he 'was' Othello, then his reputation as a creator of believable characters was secured.

It is peculiar to the character of Othello that it would have prompted Stanislavski to restlessness regarding technique and emotional sponta-neity. As Lois Potter writes, 'the history of playing Othello is the history of a desire for a degree of identification between hero and role that might almost be seen to rule out the need to act at all' (Potter 2002: 1). According to Potter, what critics remembered about Salvini's Othello were his 'moments of strength and violence', which Potter does not find surprising since 'these are things that cannot be faked' (ibid.: 44). This seems a rather strange assertion to make to me. If the actor does not fake such things, for instance because she or he is aiming at authentic-ity, she or he incurs risks, not least the potential for physical harm. It bugged Stanislavski greatly that, in his dress rehearsal, he cut his Iago's hand with a dagger, so that the action had to stop while a doctor was sent for. But what really bothered him was not that he had injured his fellow actor: 'what hurt me most was that notwithstanding the deadli-ness of my play the audience remained completely cold' (Stanislavski 1956: 284). He knew that it would do his reputation good to be thought of as having an unrestrained temperament, but the truth was he had wounded his Iago in a moment of cool restraint. He assumed that because he did not really care, the spectators did not care either. He could not yet see how smoothness of movement can function as a guar-antee that gives the spectator permission to feel.

A key battleground in Stanislavski's struggle was gesture. In *An Actor Prepares* he attempted to clear a space for inspiration by separating it from the 'rubber stamp' procedures he associated with mechanical act-ing. Tradition, he wrote, taught the actor to spread the hand over the heart in order to express love, to show the teeth and roll the whites of the eyes when jealous (a display that he himself tried when rehears-ing his Othello), to cover the face with the hands when weeping, to tear the hair when feeling desperate. Some gestures were inherited from great actors, as rubbing the brow with the back of the hand in moments of tragedy, a movement he noted in the performances of Vera Komissarzhevskaya (Stanislavski 1936/1989: 24–5).

Stanislavski's pursuit of authenticity had led him to the affective psy-chiatry of Ribot. It was Ribot who had proposed that forgotten events left traces that could later be recovered by the memory. This would seem on the surface to be a promising approach to 'becoming' a character like Othello. In practice, however, Stanislavski had been left dismayed by his failure to feel more truthfully using this procedure. In reaction, he would resort to ideas of immobility, of stripping away what he saw as 'the coarse strain of muscles which tears the threads of emotion', a strain that the aristocrat Stanislavski associated with manual labour (Stanislavski 1956: 544). When immobility too appeared to fail, he made a breakthrough discovery through his work directing opera, a discovery he was to define as *tempo-rhythm*. (ibid.: 562).

Stanislavski sought to establish an authentic feeling of inner life. At the same time, influenced by his encounter with Tolstoy, he recognized a contradictory need for transparency – if you really feel something, but cannot reliably *show* that you do, there is no benefit in terms of your reputation. The contradiction was solved in his mind by the conception of a compositional score for the actor, in which the actor would establish an external tempo for a segment of movement while attempting to sustain the feeling of an internal rhythm. The unity of the performance would then be a function of both tempo and rhythm together. An example might be the behaviour of a waiter in a busy restaurant, who may have to work fast but who seeks to maintain an air of composure. In other words, the waiter deploys the principle of *festina lente*.

Stanislavski's second encounter with *Othello* was in 1930. It seems that the play once again forced him to question his procedures. He reversed his usual approach of moving from detailed work on the text and character psychology to creation of a physical form for the performance, and, after a read through of the play, plunged into physical improvisation before undertaking any further textual work.

In the last five years of his life he began to elucidate a new Method of Physical Actions. The essence of his new approach was that the actor's attention should be focused on the precise, uninflected carrying out of physical actions, rather than on accessing some inner core of remembered feelings. Crucially, each action would have its own essential rhythm. As Jean Benedetti explains, playing an emotion then became a matter of creating a story through physical actions (Benedetti 2008: 93) rather than attempting to conjure up states of feeling. Stanislavski had come to believe that appropriate emotions would be released in spite of (or because of) the fact that the actor is *not* concentrating on them.

The model he worked towards, now known as 'psychophysical' acting, is beginning to displace the received idea of Stanislavski as the proponent of 'truth-through-emotion-memory' in actor training regimes in the UK. One reason for this is that it aligns with current thinking about cognition as an *embodied* activity. Stanislavski's model here can be seen to link with the work of a number of practitioners, including Dalcroze, Laban, Meyerhold, Copeau and Lecoq, who found a common ground in the concern with essentializing movement.

Modernism and the East

One origin of this essentializing impulse within modernism can be traced to the influence of the Japanese theatrical forms of Noh and Kabuki. Zeami Motokiyo, the fifteenth-century Noh Master, wrote that the highest ideal of perfection for the performer is *yugen* – grace, a virtue that 'the actor must never separate himself from' (Zeami 1984: 93). This is most clearly shown in the nobility:

> ... whose deportment is of such a high quality ... their dignified and mild appearance represents the essence of Grace. Therefore, the stage appearance of Grace is best indicated by their refined and elegant carriage ... when presenting a role of fearsome appearance, a demon's role for example, even should the actor use a rough manner to a certain extent, he must not forget to preserve a graceful appearance, and he must remember the principles of 'what is felt in the heart is ten,' and 'violent body movements, gentle foot movements,' so that his stage appearance will remain elegant. Thus he may manifest the Grace of a demon's role. (ibid.)

Zeami taught that the actor should 'feel ten and play seven'. This idea nicely captures Hamlet's principle of smoothness, of controlling energy by holding it in potential. It finds a parallel in the work of Meyerhold, who stressed the need to always apply *tormoz* – 'the brake' – upon one's movement. Similarly, Laban attempted to articulate an idea of 'flow' that separated into two aspects he called 'free flow' and 'bound flow'; the second, which expresses the notion that the performer is always able to stop the movement once it is begun, can be seen as still another elaboration of the Renaissance humanist ideal of *festina lente* (see Davies 2006: 48). Again, for Brecht, *leichtigkeit* – translated as 'lightness and ease' – was an essential antidote to emotional hysteria (Brecht 1964/1984: 174–5). Lecoq too demanded that his students perform with a feeling of *élan* – a suspension in the body achieved in part through conscious manipulation of the centre of mass (Lecoq 2002: 70–1). All these practitioners were influenced by the stylizations of Far Eastern theatre; and all four shared a commitment to the principle of smooth movement. Zeami also extended the concept of *jo-ha-kyu*, originally applied in the eighth century to the rhythmic structure of the *bugaku* court dance, to movement, in which a preparation phase (introduction) leads to an acceleration (scattering) and finally to a climax (rushing) that nonetheless ends in a deceleration. This is a surprisingly accurate biomechanical description of intentional human movements like gestures. Its modernist expression can be found in Meyerhold's basic compositional structure: *otkaz* (the refusal – a preparatory counter-movement to gather energy), *posil* (the sending – the commitment to the action) and *tochka* (a point) or *stoika* (a stance) (Meyerhold's vocabulary is described by Marianne Kubik in Potter 2002: 8–9).

The thrilling novelty of the encounter with Japanese theatre is caught by Grigori Kozintsev in his diary of the making of his film of *King Lear*. In 1928 the young Kozintsev went to see the Kabuki Theatre, who were touring Russia, several times with his friend Sergei Eisenstein. 'Synthetic art, which was so much talked about in the first years of the revolution, was before our very eyes', he wrote later. 'The cascades of movements executed by Sadanji Ichikawa were broken by static poses, gesture was followed by sound, sound turned into colour, song into dance. Everything was metaphorical and had a particular significance which was far removed from its apparent likeness' (Kozintsev 1977: 5). He was even more amazed by the Noh Theatre, and considered it to be 'the true presentation of tragedy'. Above all, what registered with Kozintsev in the Noh performance was its 'peace, extreme restraint and complete clarity' (ibid.: 7). In his diary, he acknowledges how the story he watched reminded him at the time of *King Lear*.

The modernism of Les Kurbas

Modernist performance was intensely concerned with stylization; if there is one word that can be said to sum it up, that word would be *montage*. The idea can be turned to use in different contexts, but its essential feature is rhythmical contrast. It is exemplified in the work of the Ukrainian director Les Kurbas, whose experiments seem to have left their mark on many Soviet theatre artists at the time. Kurbas drilled his actors in 'mimo-dramas' – short, mimed sequences on quotidian topics to be created by the individual actor, who was required to 'fix' and 'objectify' gestures and movements and then repeat them again and again at will (Makaryk 2004: 72). The capacity to repeat the exact form of the gesture was for Kurbas evidence of the actor's skill. The resemblance of this technical work to the biomechanical études of Meyerhold is striking, except that where Meyerhold circumscribed in exact detail the exercises the actor should undertake, Kurbas invited the actor to perform pretty much anything, 'even a sentence from an encyclopedia' (ibid.). The mimo-dramas were to be carried out without allowing personal mood or attitude to interfere with the precise execution of the movement. At the same time, it was understood that the actor would endow the movement with an internal dramatic justification.

Kurbas's great originality shows through in his modernist approach to the Shakespeare text, which he saw as a resource for theatre-making rather than a literary object. In a sense there is nothing new in this idea; indeed, the overall number of productions of Shakespeare's plays that treat the text as sacrosanct has probably always been rather small compared to the number that cut and adapt the material. Kurbas's insight, expressed in an article he wrote in 1923, was that modern productions of Shakespeare must grapple with the key issue of rhythm. Marx and Engels in *The Communist Manifesto* had declared the annihilation of time and space under capitalism (Marx and Engels 1948/2007: 12). The experience of life in the twentieth century appeared to be getting quicker and more spatially compressed. Kurbas saw how a Shakespearean soliloquy seemed to work in the opposite direction, slowing down time so that the full implications of an ethical dilemma could be considered. Somehow the Shakespearean text, with (as he saw it) its pausing rhythms, had to be made to function within a modern rhythmic structure; only then would it matter to a new age.

Kurbas made four attempts at *Macbeth*. By the time he set to work on the fourth version in 1923, he was ready to dismantle the painterly illusionism that he saw as the untheatrical legacy of the Enlightenment. His rehearsals involved tapping out a rhythm with his hand while groups of actors made their way through the play without words. The rhythmicity of the performer was placed within the greater rhythms established by the composition of the production itself. The geometrical angularity of the actors' bodily and facial gestures were probably derived in part from the full-body gesturing of silent film actors (Kurbas was a cinephile with a taste for D.W. Griffith) and in part from dancers such as Isadora Duncan, who the company saw in performance in Kiev two months before the first night of their *Macbeth* and whose work they compared favourably with their own mimo-dramas (Makaryk 2004: 72). Duncan had a similar effect on Stanislavski, prompting him to rethink his approach to the non-verbal.

The style of Kurbas's *Macbeth* comes across like a checklist of modernist tropes, as if Kurbas had in one blow invented, and at the same time exhausted, the forms of avant-garde theatre for the modern age. The audience faced a brick wall; the stage was black. Perspectival illusions of depth were eschewed in favour of a relatively flat horizontal space. This rejection of traditional mimetic techniques was further strengthened by the use of stylized make-up, drawing attention to the actor's face as a painted object or a flat mask rather than a surface that is given 3-D texture by the play of light and shadow. Gigantic moving placard screens were deployed like cinema title-cards, naming the space as 'Castle', 'Precipice', etc. The actors wore simple work clothes or military costumes with geometric designs suggestive of both medievalism and the latest styles of Futurism and constructivism. The Porter was reimagined as a grotesque Fool figure whose bulbous nose lit up (it was electrically wired, as were the costumes of the Witches). Actors doubled and tripled their roles. And, in perhaps the riskiest move, the actors would enter, assume their character, and then, when they had finished the scene, would drop the character before leaving the stage. Kurbas had been working with this principle, known to the company as 'turning on and off', for some time, and in performance the effect was utterly disconcerting, as this account reveals:

> When, after the first scene, the screen with its title raced up to the flies in full view of the audience, and the actresses-witches walked out into the wings using their normal walk (as normal actresses, no longer as witches) Ludmyla Mykhailivna terrifiedly exclaimed, 'Oh God!', and I felt that she must have crossed herself. (Quoted in ibid.: 82)

Ludmyla was a member of the intelligentsia, who were delighted and scandalized in equal measure by the production. During the sleepwalking scene, Lady Macbeth (played by Liubov Hakkebush) crossed to the centre of the stage:

> where she placed her candle, took off her mantle, shook her head until her long dark hair tumbled around her shoulders, and only then proceeded emotionally to 'Out, damned spot!' Completing her work as the sleepwalking Lady Macbeth, she then left the stage as 'herself'. (Makaryk in Makaryk and Tkacz 2010: 445)

There is a curious parallel here with Sarah Siddons, whose decision to put the candle down in this scene was equally scandalizing to some of her audience.

Kurbas drew upon the formalist critic Viktor Shlovski's concept of 'defamiliarization' but, unlike with Brecht's transposition of the concept into *verfremdung*, Kurbas held onto an essentially expressionist sense of the spiritual and miraculous revealed through this estrangement effect – the word Kurbas used was *ochudnennia* meaning 'making or endowing with the marvellous'. The Brechtian *gestus* is a tricky idea to clarify, but its antecedents in the theatres of the Far East and in Soviet-Ukrainian modernism are clear enough. It also seems to reach back further still, into popular forms of the Middle Ages, to that combined meaning of *gest* as both an exemplary deed (as in the *Gesta Romanorum*) and an anti-authoritarian joke (as in the word 'jest').

Cinematic gestures

A number of critics have fastened on a perceived relationship between the concept of bodily economy and the demand for an efficient work-force under industrial capitalism (see for example Pitches 2003: 33). It is true that both Meyerhold and Laban justified their interest in human movement in part by appealing to ideas of productive effort that bear some relation to the 'time and motion' studies of Frederick Taylor, con-ducted between 1878 and 1911. But a greater influence upon modern acting came from the *cinema*.

The camera amplified those small details of behaviour that would not come across vividly on a large stage, especially the details of face acting. Henry Irving had struggled with this problem. He felt that byplay with objects, as he called it, was essential to an artist-actor like himself. Yet in large auditoria his movements had to be scaled up, so that to some it seemed absurd that his Hamlet would pretend to write enormous let-ters in his commonplace book. It may not have seemed absurd to the people sitting in the gods. And Irving knew that such moments would be constituted as psychological clues that an audience could be trained through repetition to look out for.

On smaller stages, and on screen, self- and object adaptors are a preferred method of conveying subtext, partly because they are a kind of low-key, therefore supposedly subtle, percussive comment upon speech. They often come across like visual punctuation marks to the words they accompany. In addition, they communicate an idea of spontaneous emotion, because in everyday life they are involuntary. Performance, though, is characterized by a high signal-to-noise ratio. Unwanted background distortion, such as fidgeting or attempts to repair one's speech errors, are usually minimized or eliminated. So if such things are introduced into the performance, we take it that the actor is sending a purposeful message about (say) the anxiety levels of the character.

I say 'supposedly subtle' because it is not correct to assume that in acting 'small' is the same as 'subtle'. In the theatre, size of gesture usually relates to matters of visibility – in other words, size of auditorium, and size and position of audience. 'Subtle' should be defined in terms of the quality of the idea one wishes to communicate, rather than how big or small one's gestures happen to be. This point continues to bedevil discussions of acting, in which, typically, acting in the theatre is assumed to be closer to faking and acting for the camera is assumed to be closer to the truth.

This confusion sometimes reveals how the British theatre continues to privilege a concept of disembodied voice. Having tested the newly constructed thrust stage at the Royal Shakespeare Theatre in Stratford-upon-Avon, the actor Nick Asbury tells us, 'I came in booming. I found I had to drop it down. You can, finally, be subtle. Not something I've ever been accused of before' ('RSC shows off its £112m revamp', *The Guardian*, 23 November 2010). A peculiarly British obsession with 'text-as-voice', and an idea of stage movement as little more than 'blocking', has marked Royal Shakespeare Company (RSC) policy since the days of Peter Hall (for a defence of Hall's practice see Holland, 'Peter Hall' in Brown 2008: 140–59).

Now, though, the RSC has begun to include within its doors performers who have trained in non-conventional ways such as the Lecoq system, for example Kathryn Hunter and Marcello Magni (originally of Theatre de Complicite), Paul Hunter (of Told By An Idiot), and Christine Entwisle and Richard Katz (who both appeared in Hunter's 2010 production of *The Comedy of Errors*). As a result of such shifting within the profession in the UK, Lecoq's philosophy of training has become normalized, with all that that suggests, in British actor training, as a generation who trained with him in the 1980s and 1990s have grown up, as it were, and joined the mainstream.

One of the master themes of Shakespearean performance over the last hundred years or so has been acts of translation. It often seems to me that the most ambitious and imaginative treatments of the plays have emerged out of cultural contexts that stand in a dialogic relation to English culture. The so-called 'physical theatre' tradition – a convenient label at best – draws upon a set of practices and principles, shared between and passed down by practitioners, and this tradition as it is perceived has had no small part to play in the translation of Shakespeare's writing into a decidedly modern set of performance styles.

Postmodernist gestures

Lecoq himself remained at heart a modernist in his outlook; it is indicative of his idea of performance that he drew a distinction between quotidian behavioural gestures and gestures expressive of a poetic and theatrical imagination. It is characteristic of postmodernist performance, by contrast, that it attempts to break down such hierarchical distinctions between what is and is not thought of as 'performance'. With respect to gesture on stage, this is the key point to be noted and, as the following examples will show, in seeking to blur the edges of performance and everyday life, postmodern Shakespearean performance tends to undermine ideas of the authenticity of the body as a site of meaning. Instead, bodily gestures become unreliable codes or pastiches of codes, their truth claims hollowed out, often leaving little more than the fleshy materiality of bodily experience itself.

Robert Lepage

The Canadian actor-director Robert Lepage's Shakespearean work has focused on a particular set of plays: *A Midsummer Night's Dream* (four times), *Macbeth* (four times), *The Tempest* (four times), *Romeo and Juliet* (once), *Coriolanus* (once) and *Richard III* (once). *Hamlet* he used as a resource for creative adaptation in *Polygraph* and *Elsinore*. For *Elsinore* he used only Shakespeare's words – at least in the English version. In fact, critics of this production brought attention to how he had managed in some aspects to stick quite close to his source material, even though the piece was a one-man performance. The shape of the story was still recognizable, as were the characters he (or his English stand-in Peter Darling) played.

Lepage's Québecois background has drawn a considerable amount of comment, as with his 'tradaptations' for the 1993 Shakespeare Cycle. His *auteurist* approach to the plays – which he seems to see as resources to be mined rather than as texts to be faithfully presented – has been interpreted as an act of rebellion against a colonial father. A frequent move in this process of harnessing Shakespeare to his own purposes is that the text is translated into another language. For Lepage the work of making theatre involves creating a first-level story that echoes a second, bigger story – the 'what's behind it'. He will either zero in on a small gesture, almost invisible within a symphony of movement yet nonetheless of great significance, or he will drive towards the large-scale action, the equivalent of an aria. He tries to achieve this in voice as well as in movement. Both are subjected to an essentially musical treatment with the focus on achieving an effect of visual and aural counterpoint from moment to moment, sequence to sequence, where the small and the large are echoes of each other.

His intention is to cross-fertilize the text with other available materials to create a work that speaks as much of his own obsessions as it does of (what we imagine to be) Shakespeare's. For his English production of *A Midsummer Night's Dream* at the Royal National Theatre (1992), a non-textual resource was prioritized over the written play: the dream-life of the acting company. It was only after their remembered dreams had been offered up in drawings, and elaborated upon in improvisations, that Lepage turned with the actors to the script. It was essential to Lepage that the imagistic resources deployed in the production would emerge not only from the text but also from the imaginations of the acting company.

The opening of the play – arguably the most startling and memorable moment of the entire production – featured Puck, played by contortionist Angela Laurier, crossing the stage before the audience (who were presumably expecting the house lights to go down) had fully settled into their seats, then passing through a pool of muddy water (real dirty water!) to reach up and switch off a lightbulb hanging down centre stage, 'the counter-intuitive gesture of a light being extinguished rather than being turned on' (Fricker 2008: 240). The association of Puck with an animal like a crab from the beginning of the performance, achieved by an uncanny contortion of the actor's limbs during a lateral glide across the stage, was immediately troubling. Isn't Puck meant to be just a naughty little hobgoblin? This Puck wasn't even going to be human. What is the status of this character's agency? What is it like to be a crab – or, to borrow a famous question from the philosopher Thomas Nagel, a bat, as Sally Dexter (Titania) at one point appeared to become, dangling upside down from the hanging light? In her bizarre opening move, Angela Laurier seemed literally to sidestep the essential question of intentionality, and thus of responsibility for her actions.

We were taken, in a dreamy way, from that moment into a fictive world of murk and muck. The critical response at the time noted that Lepage was carving a space for himself as a major international artist in opposition to Peter Brook. Brook's legendary *Dream* had been a pure white box, with actors behaving like figures from the old days of music hall variety shows. Of course, we were reminded, the verse was spoken well, so that could always be used to excuse the antics on stage. Lepage's *Dream* came across to many critics as the diametric opposite: dark,

sleazy and, worst of all, poorly spoken. Lepage, though, is acutely sensi-
tive to how the same text will function differently according to how it
is sounded in a particular language and cultural milieu. He knows that
the actor in pursuit of realness will stress words and phrases that have a
certain quotidian flavour to them. As a result, other ideas, other perhaps
stranger resonances, will become muffled. For Lepage, authenticity is
not to be found in an identification with the world of the play, but in a
recognition of its distance from us. In such an interpretive environment
the gestures of an actor like Angela Laurier can appear like messages
from another planet. Yet, since she was playing a non-human character,
her contorted behaviour could still be justified on dramatic grounds.
Thus Lepage remains committed to the idea that a play like this one can
speak to a contemporary audience even if its voice is strange.

The Wooster Group: *Troilus and Cressida*

The same may not always be said of the experiments carried out by The
Wooster Group. In their work, it is possible to see one outcome of a social
morality of individual self-fulfilment taken to extremes, where gestural
behaviour threatens to break with communally held understanding
altogether and become a self-mocking form indicating either a private
sense or no sense at all. But closer inspection reveals that the company
in performance displays a common gestural language, thus suggesting
the possibility of a residue of shareable meaning in their work.

Nowhere was this more evident than in their collaboration with the
RSC on *Troilus and Cressida* (2012). The Greek characters were rehearsed
in London by RSC actors under the director Mark Ravenhill, who took
over the job when Rupert Goold departed; the Trojans, performed by
members of The Wooster Group, rehearsed separately in New York with
the company director Elizabeth LeCompte.

Scott Handy, who played Ulysses, was singled out by *The Guardian*
critic Michael Billington in an otherwise damning review. He wrote,
'Only Scott Handy as a scholarly Ulysses delivers the verse with a kind
of witty intelligence that we used to take for granted at the RSC' (*The
Guardian*, 9 August 2012). Handy seemed somehow at odds with the
production. He created an impression that he was more civilized than
everyone else in the play, not just by speaking in that restrained voice
that Billington prefers (he was not the only actor to do that) but more
through his gestural style. He made frequent use of open hand prone
and vertical palm gestures that associate with discreet rejection, or holding something at a distance – the something in this case possibly being

the situation he felt obliged to operate within. Pronated gestures are usually made by individuals who are not feeling very open to negotiation or suggestion. He used a particular feature of the vertical palm gesture in a rather subtle manner. Its associations rely partly on its distal projection: held away from the body, the gesture gives priority to the receiver ('You must stop'), a little closer to the body to the shared space ('We must stop'). He never used it close to his own body (as in 'I must stop').

The British RSC actors deliberately over-invested in a display of machismo. By contrast, the American actors performing as Trojans were obliged to seek out a collective behavioural style that accommodated a painful self-consciousness. This seemed to be in the service of an idea that the Trojans were suffering an identity crisis; they were played as white Americans pretending to be Native American Indians. They then had to try during numerous scenes to imitate the gestures of Eskimos represented on TV screens high up all around them. Perhaps the characters on TV were meant to be an ironic equivalent of the Trojan gods. A similar approach was taken by the company in their version of *Hamlet*, where the actors mimicked a video of John Gielgud's legendary Broadway production of 1964 starring Richard Burton. The idea of a paralysing burden of debt to tradition was enforced by their headdresses, which made visual allusions to classical statues.

Many of the gestures of the Trojans were abstractions of American Indian clichés, like holding spears or drinking 'firewater'. These iconic gestures were performed without conviction or dexterity, as if technical skill were inherently suspect as a value. Thus, we witnessed a clash of styles in which one side (Trojan) under-performed the text while the other (Greek) over-performed it.

Is *Troilus and Cressida* incoherent? The production seemed to suggest the play promulgates an idea of life as being full of irreconcilable contradictions. Yet, in their desire to present the contradictions that perhaps lie at its heart, they mistakenly assumed that no character in the play is capable of meaning what they say. Human beings, though, have an extraordinary capacity for meaning what they say. That includes the capacity for believing their own lies, for remembering events that never happened to them, for defending their irrational opinions in the face of attack, for justifying the most inexcusable selfishness and hypocrisy as natural and inevitable. They use gestures to help them manage the process of making meaning so that they can both believe and appear to believe what they say. Postmodern culture has done nothing to alter this facet of human behaviour – it has simply diverted its expression into new technological modes such as Facebook and Twitter. Shakespeare, trained and accomplished in the rhetorical arts, exposes exactly such hypocrisy in *Troilus and Cressida*.

Dreamthinkspeak: *The Rest is Silence*

The radicalism of the gestural styles of both Lepage and The Wooster Group, rooted in a group sense of the text's larger meanings rather than in individual character, is nevertheless predicated upon a spectacle separated from the audience; in that respect, their work has remained conventional. Meanwhile, a new wave of theatre practitioners has attempted to break down that separation. In the summer of 2012 dreamthinkspeak's version of *Hamlet* – called *The Rest is Silence* – was performed in Newcastle Playhouse. But the company did not, in a sense, actually perform in the playhouse; rather, they hijacked the playhouse in order to perform their work inside a large box situated on the stage of the studio theatre. The audience made its way into the centre of this box and waited for the performance to start. There were no seats; the audience stood about inside the box. The performance took place around us. The walls of the box, it transpired, were large Perspex windows, beyond which were rooms that recalled the Scandinavian minimalism of a corporate hotel, office environment or contemporary apartment. As the performance progressed in a fluent choreography from room to room, in a technique that recalled cinematic cutting, the audience was tacitly invited to wander around the box to get a vantage point for viewing the unfolding action. This feeling of apparent freedom for the spectator was illusory, however. As the director Tristan Sharps put it in an interview, 'the audience are completely locked within a world, immersed, and I use that as a verb, within a world that we are creating around them' (in Machon 2013: 269).

   The production on other occasions deployed large video projections onto the walls and ceiling of the box – as when we looked up to find ourselves apparently sharing a coffin with Ophelia, while a video showed mourners peering down and scattering soil over the lens. The production, centrally concerned as it was with our status as spectators, offered numerous similar perspectival tropes. The actor Richard Clews, who played Polonius, told me afterwards that when the lights were switched off in a particular part of the set, the actors were able to see the audience through that window, whereas when we the audience could see the actors in a lit space, they could not see us. We were never acknowledged by the actors until the play was finished, and were free to move about as we pleased inside the box. The alienating effect of wandering around witnessing scenes through windows was enhanced by the use of amplification for the voices. Just as the spatial relationship to the audience was in a sense de-authorized, so the language of the play itself was de-authorized by microphone technology.

At the same time, the performances aimed for a reality effect through mundane behavioural gestures, many of which were adaptors and muted illusionistic – in fact, televisual – acting. Even when attempts were made to draw our attention to the gestures on display, this was always situated within a behavioural frame, as when Claudius tried out various gestures in front of the bathroom mirror in preparation for his first big speech as the king. The presence of a video camera for the king's speech – which was filmed as if in a corporate conference room to an absent audience – reinforced the feeling that the production wanted the audience to imagine the play as being akin to a classy Danish television drama about political corruption.

There was a curious blandness in the characterization, most of all in Edward Hogg's portrayal of Hamlet; the actor's introverted persona required the close-up of film to register with any real impact. This effect was perhaps intensified by the extent to which the text had been cut down for performance. At times the political force of the characters was reduced. For example, Polonius, Rosencrantz and Guildenstern were presented as self-regarding idiots who amused only themselves. This was manifested in the gestural behaviour of Richard Clews as Polonius, whose interactional gestures, extending out from his bent torso to the edge of his peripersonal space, seemed at odds with the show's low-key behavioural style.

For Michael Billington, the production's intention to convey a 'disjunction between private and public faces' was evident when Ruth Lass's Gertrude 'at one point prays silently in her dressing room while Michael Bryher and Stewart Heffernan as Rosencrantz and Guildenstern quietly cackle in their closet over Hamlet's carefully recorded utterances' (*The Guardian*, 7 May 2012). Yet we were given little access to either private or public faces behind the fishtank windows. The notion that an actor might want to share her or his performance with the public was treated here as if it were suspect.

One possible future for Shakespeare is suggested by dreamthinkspeak's *The Rest is Silence*. It was an immersive experience in the sense outlined by Josephine Machon in her book *Immersive Theatres*. Site-specific and participatory theatre until recently occupied a rather confined niche of the theatre-going public's activity. It is now becoming increasingly normal for the digital generation. Machon shows how the hunger for involvement as well as for new sensations has benefited a raft of emerging companies such as Punchdrunk – whose *Sleep No More* (2011) translated *Macbeth* into a kind of dance-art installation in which the spectators, wearing masks, wandered through a number of meticulously arranged rooms conjuring up *noirish* atmospheres of seedy hotels, mental asylums, children's bedrooms and so on.

In Punchdrunk's production, Shakespeare's words were not featured; in fact, the actors hardly spoke at all. Instead, as the *New Yorker* review had it, 'We can only watch as the performers reduce theatre to its rudiments: bodies moving in space' (*New Yorker*, 2 May 2011). Thus, for all its striking attention to detail and skilful manipulation of the spectator's sense of dread, the production was premised upon an entirely conventional assumption of the priority of the body as the guarantor of authenticity. Meanwhile, the text was deployed as no more than one among a number of resources (another one being the films of Alfred Hitchcock) for an event aimed at creating mood – in contrast to *The Rest is Silence*, which offered an edit of Shakespeare's script that for much of the time retained at least a linear coherence. What, to my mind, both of these Shakespearean events have in common though is a certain air of melancholy produced by the uncanny feeling that, despite being publicly staged, they are in some way not *communal* experiences, but rather represent a theatrical summation of the social morality of self-fulfilment. They do not, in that respect, signal a radical departure from the decision to darken the auditorium that began with the Victorians, but rather its existential end point. In a similar way, the privatization (or personalization) of gesture that Henry Irving innovated in his *Hamlet* reached a certain *cul-de-sac*. In spite of the literal closeness of the performer to the audience at times, the kind of contact achieved through gesture that was so celebrated by the admirers of Garrick, Siddons and by Stanislavski in the presence of Salvini, seems strangely out of reach in these experiments in immersive staging.

Gamification of gesture

Where does an embodied Shakespeare go from here? Much has been written concerning the ever-increasing dominance of the digital image in Western culture. One rapidly growing phenomenon has been called the *gamification* of reality. This refers to the application of game techniques and mechanics in contexts other than computer games. So far interest has largely been centred upon consumer products and the training of workers; one such product is the 'Shakespeare's Globe 360' app, which offers a virtual and augmented reality tour of the London theatre.

There is as well, though, a momentum in the direction of greater complexity within the gaming industry, and it is this industry that is leading the charge into the digital future for commercial reasons. At the time of writing, *Grand Theft Auto V* is the most profitable computer game in history. It cost $260 million to produce and made $1 billion within three days – beating the three largest movie launches by 16 days. In part that is down to the blending together of game mechanics with cinematic values of visual storytelling: much of the praise for this game focused on its eye-catching graphics. Indeed, the environments of the game are 'open world', meaning that they can be explored by the user outside of the gameplay itself. In this, it bears comparison with Punchdrunk's *Sleep No More*.

The drive for further sophistication of game architecture is impacting on performance as well. As the technology of motion capture allows for ever more detailed representations of movement qualities, so the development of a character's body movement within games will become more refined. The alternative descriptor *performance capture* speaks of an attempt to reconfigure the boundaries of art – an attempt driven as so often by technological innovation. And, as so often, the attempt is premised upon recognition of skill in a field where evaluation of quality is ambiguous; after all, who is actually controlling the avatar, the actor or the software operator?

A recent article in *The Observer* hints at what may be to come. Game author David Cage's *Beyond: Two Souls* is a narrative-driven game in which the performances of actors Ellen Page and Willem Dafoe were captured in rich detail. Seventy motion capture cameras recorded the actors from many angles. Without the assistance of illusionistic settings, the actors had to produce a gamut of emotional reactions – four or five variations of a single scene were the norm in this game. Both performers in interview referred to the acting process in such an environment as being somehow purer or more essential than acting in more conventional situations:

> I would respond, take a beat, give the other response, take a beat, another response. It's difficult just for the basicness of memorising the dialogue and having to constantly emotionally pivot. You're doing multiple versions, and that is like some sort of sadistic acting boot camp! (Ellen Page, in *The Observer*, 13 October 2013)

This approach to acting makes a demand upon the performer that recalls a similar demand made upon Shakespeare's company. The actor must use her or his imagination to fill out the details missing in the immediate working environment, because from the point of view of resources for stimulation that environment is poor. In fact, poorer than the Globe: there is no real set or character costume to work with, and the props may be only vaguely similar to the objects depicted in the game. That said, live performance capture data can nowadays be streamed directly into animation software packages, so that an actor can perform an animated character against a backdrop that the actor can see in real time. This may have some interesting possibilities with respect to, for instance, non-human characters like Oberon, Titania, Puck, Ariel and Caliban. Indeed, at the time of writing the RSC's artistic director Gregory Doran is preparing a production of *The Tempest* that updates old-fashioned magic tricks like 'Pepper's Ghost' through combining 3-D holographic projection with (offstage) performance capture.

The agenda of performance capture is usually to achieve a visual hyper-realism. In practice, what it tends to produce in the actor is to some degree an abstraction – a reaching for a significant form. The actor is very aware that his or her movements are being recorded as data for further attention. One corollary of this is that when the actor produces behavioural gestures such as small pacifying (adaptor) movements, the effect upon the onscreen avatar is curiously comical, as if small moments of embarrassment have been amplified. Adaptors – fidgeting, weight-shifting from foot to foot and so on – are routinely deployed within game worlds to suggest a reference point of normal behaviour, a phenomenon known in the gaming world as the avatar in 'idle' mode.

In other words, even the minutiae of behaviour are abstracted, and I think performers who are exposed to performance capture environments will adapt their style accordingly. It is as though the actor takes on something of the quality of an animated figure. At a recent conference, where I spoke on the subject, a delegate expressed dismay that, if I am right, the art of acting will be reduced to cartoonish exaggeration. Yet the *line of action* – a principle taught to animators since at least Walt Disney – has its origin in the classical line of beauty that was described by William Hogarth, and that was crucial to actors like David Garrick in the management of their reputation as sophisticated artists. In this respect, the stylizations produced by performance capture are nothing new. But what it does suggest to me is that the current debate, centred as it usually is upon how the technology is progressing towards a hyper-realism, is the wrong way up. In performance capture, the technology does not try to capture the impulses behind the performance: it is the performance that tries to capture the imperatives of the technology.

Perhaps one way to carry things forward may be through engagement with those very technologies that could be seen as threatening to Shakespeare's survival – such as gaming. In certain ways Shakespearean performance cannot compete with *Grand Theft Auto*. But Shakespeare's success over the last 400 years has hinged not only on the power of his writing but on its translatability. I have suggested that this is one key feature of his work that has guaranteed its survival. One can imagine an event in a synthetic 3-D world, in which it is not your real body that goes to a real building to watch a real performance of *Hamlet*, but your avatar that visits a virtual auditorium to watch other avatars performing Shakespeare. If that experience still seems too passive for you, you might prefer to perform your own *Hamlet* within a world that you have yourself constructed. In that sense, Garrick's ghost would return in the machine: your Hamlet would not only be like you – your Hamlet would really *be* you.

7
The Use of Video in the Study of Gesture

In this book I have advanced a concept, borrowed from both *Hamlet* and movement science, called *smoothness*. And I have identified it by some of the other names it has been given in performance histories – *yugen, sprezzatura, tormoz, leichtigkeit, élan*. I have asserted that the concept is inherent in social cognition, because it directly influences the way in which people perceive other people's behaviour and form intuitive judgements about them; hence, smoothness is a moral category as well as an aesthetic one.

Such an assertion can hardly be disputed when one looks into the (often depressing) history of how people who struggled to 'move well' have been treated. But I take the optimistic view in seeing that, as the social morality of self-fulfilment continues to make inroads into Western culture, definitions of what we mean by moving well are opening up, in the interests of freedom of expression, to include bodily shapes and movement paradigms previously held to be ungraceful. That story is not for this book. Instead, I have explored smoothness as an aesthetic concept, seeing it as a basic component of an effective performance. I would argue it is probably the single most important one. There is a risk here that I am simply making a selective argument for the type of acting I happen to prefer. So I should like here to offer a method of research that could provide evidence for such a claim.

As Judith Hall Koivumaki wrote, 'There is no single, correct methodology for studying nonverbal communication' (Koivumaki 1975: 26). Nevertheless, there are methodologies, one such being micro-analysis using video. Here I want to offer an example of a comparative microanalysis. For illustration, I choose two English actors working within

136

mainstream theatre organizations, the first in a performance adapted for filming, the second in an archive recording of a live performance. I have chosen a soliloquy from Iago for analysis, to show how the same material is handled by two different actors. I have transcribed the actor's speech as it is spoken by them in *italics* and have indicated terms drawn from psycholinguistics and gesture studies in **bold**. The <u>underlined</u> words indicate the **stroke** phase of the gesture, i.e. its most significant accent.

Ian McKellen

In 1989 Ian McKellen played Iago for the Royal Shakespeare Company in a production directed by Trevor Nunn. His performance was celebrated as an especially brilliant interpretation of the character. Here, I want to use the video recording that was made of the production in 1990 and I take for analysis his performance of Iago's soliloquy in Act 1 Scene 3 (381–402).

In the recorded version, which is almost exactly two minutes long, Iago has just bid farewell to Roderigo (Michael Grandage), who exits camera right. Iago, wearing the uniform of an American Civil War officer, stands side on to camera in front of a small table lit from above by a hanging lamp. His right hand is in his waist pocket of his jacket as he begins with his face to camera.

> *Thus do I ever make my fool my purse:*
> *For I mine own gained knowledge should profane*
> *If I would time expend with such a snipe*
> *But for my sport and profit.*

He sits down at the table facing forward (left side to camera) and places his hands on the table in a clenched position, right hand over left with the left thumb up. This is a **frustration gesture**, and the height of the hands normally correlates to the force of the attitude. The thumb moves down as:

> *I <u>hate</u> the Moor …*

He draws a little away from the table and looks down with eyes closed in a low-power (hunched) attitude. This is an **affect display** of rage. He looks to camera.

> *And it is thought abroad that 'twixt my sheets*
> *He's done my office. I know not if't be true,*

But I for mere suspicion in that kind
Will do as if for surety.

During the above section his left thumb rubs the top of his right wrist in a **self-adaptor** gesture that often signals the speaker is seeking reassurance. Peter Holland notes how McKellen felt the character's sexual suspicions were an acceptable foundational motive on which to base the portrayal, in contrast to Coleridge's idea of Iago's 'motiveless malignity' (in Brown 2012: 148).

... He holds me well,
The better shall my purpose work on him.

A slight readjustment of his hands in a self-adaptor gesture that also cues a preparation for change of topic. His eye gaze moves to camera right on:

Cassio's a proper man.

The look offscreen here towards the door is an ocular **deictic**. It implies the use of what David McNeill calls an *origo* – an assumed shared horizon with the viewer. He continues to knead his fingers.

... let's see now

He makes a tiny arm movement as if in preparation for the next gesture:

To get his place, and to make up my will

His right hand travels up to his head and he places an index finger on his right temple. This is a negative ruminating or **evaluating** gesture.

Hmm

He points with the same index finger off camera right to the imagined Cassio planted earlier.

A double knavery

He taps his temple with his index finger twice while the middle finger rests on his upper lip. This is another **evaluation gesture**. The closed hand resting on the cheek with one finger on the mouth and index finger pointing up to temple suggests critical or negative evaluation.

How? How?

He strokes his chin with three fingers of the right hand in a further extension of the evaluation gesture cluster. The **chin-stroke** – which Darwin described as a meditation gesture, and which is mentioned in Henry Siddons as the gesture of a wise man making a judgement – begins a process of softening the critical or negative connotations of the evaluation gesture cluster.

Let's see

He taps his lip three times with the middle finger. His face now changes to register surprise, as if an idea has struck him.

After some time to abuse Othello's ear

He holds his hand in an upside-down three jaw chuck **Precision Grip** gesture. This signals specificity of thought.

That he is too familiar with his wife.

He now lays his right hand palm down across the left lower arm on the table.

He hath a person and a smooth dispose

The first two fingers and thumb of the left hand now rub together or pick at each other in a **self-adaptor** reassurance gesture.

To be suspected, framed to make women false.

He clenches and unclenches a fist with his left hand, a **Power Grip** gesture showing stress or frustration.

The Moor is of a <u>free</u> and open nature

The right hand reaches forward to take a cigar box from the table. The left hand clutches the box from underneath.

That thinks men <u>honest</u>

The right hand opens the box while the left hand tips it over. He takes out three cigars from the box.

   ... that but seem to be so

He shuts the box and puts it back on the table with the left hand.

   And will as <u>tenderly be led</u> by th' nose

The right hand puts the cigars in his breast pocket while the left hand holds the pocket open. The left hand reaches forward to collect his cap as the right hand finishes putting the cigars away.

   As asses are.

He collects the cap and puts it on his head, straightening the peak with both hands as he does. Both hands are brought down to the table.

   I have't, it is ...

The left hand is brought up to the left temple where the index finger revolves in a small circular motion. This is a **metaphoric gesture** in which the completion of an idea is imaged as the turn of a wheel. The stroke is landed just before:

   ... engendered.

He stands up. His left hand touches the left waist pocket of the jacket as he looks up at the lamp. He looks to camera in a return to the opening position, but with his upper body posture now more open to the viewer.

   Hell and night
   Must bring this monstrous birth to the world's light.

The scene cuts on his gaze to camera.

   Although a full appreciation of the soliloquy would depend on situating the gestural display within his overall execution of the role, it is clear that McKellen makes extensive use of *adaptors* here to signal the character's repression of his negative emotions. The aggressive impulse is shown explicitly on 'I hate the Moor'. As the speech moves towards evaluation and planning mode, the gestures complement this shift by focusing his temples and his mouth in a sequence of revolving **self-touching** motions. These gestures are apparently not for the viewer's benefit, while the culminating metaphoric gesture on 'it is engendered', accompanied as it is by a look to camera, gives the idea that Iago wants us to be impressed by his Machiavellian intelligence. He appeals to our search for signals of *competence* as one of the two primary components of social cognition.

The use of the cigars (he associates the character with smoking throughout, in a naturalistic variation on a theme of Iago as fiery devil) was part of how McKellen sought to position his acting style within the overall context of the production, which was 'defined by a kind of hyper-realism' (Holland in Brown 2012: 149) that loaded the stage with objects. The gestures had to fit in with this contextualization and thus were grounded in the quotidian. In this, the performance is an illustration of the influence of the cinema upon gesture in Shakespearean performance. This version of Iago could not have been performed on the stage of Shakespeare's Globe without sacrificing the impact of its behavioural repertoire. McKellen, by scaling his constantly busy, fussy, yet meticulous performance for the camera, is able to solve the acting problem that had exercised Henry Irving. Here too smoothness can be detected even at the height of his rage. His body conveys a sense of lightness, of suspension punctuated by precise fixed points, throughout. It lends the performance a curious air of vulnerability, fragility even – a regular feature of McKellen's performances.

Tim McInnerny

Wilson Milam's production of the play for the London Globe Theatre in 2007 featured a well-received performance of Iago from Tim McInnerny. In contrast to Trevor Nunn's version, this production was given a Jacobean setting (with some particularly gorgeous costumes).

In the scene, Roderigo shouts his exit line 'I'll sell all my land' from beyond the upstage door. McInnerny, standing downstage centre, chuckles to himself, looking half behind at the door with his torso facing front, then quickly turns to face front, dropping his expression.

Thus do I ever make my <u>fool</u> my purse

He makes a **pointing gesture** behind him at the door with the left arm, his fingers giving a little contemptuous flick as if brushing away an insect. He crosses stage left.

For I mine own gained <u>knowledge</u>

Addressing the audience still, he holds out his arms to chest height as he walks in an **openness** gesture.

... should profane
If I would time expend with such a snipe
But for my <u>sport</u> and profit.

The arms lower to waist height, brings them into his body, then his right hand takes hold of his sword hilt in termination of the idea and preparation for:

I hate the Moor

His head (seen in close-up on the video) moves as if his neck is uncomfortable. He takes a few steps to the right. At the same time the volume of his voice drops and moves to a higher register to signal self-pity on:

And it is thought abroad that 'twixt my sheets
He's done my office.

He purses his lips as if swallowing his feelings. This movement is exaggerated by the half-beard he is sporting. He looks down, shifting his weight from one foot to the other and putting on a defensive smile to mask his misery.

I know not if't be <u>true</u>

The left hand comes up to cover and rub the mouth in a **self-adaptor** gesture of anxiety. It may be that holding the hand to the mouth is also a signal that he is lying (it is a gesture that children often make when they tell fibs) – if so, it would indicate that he thinks that it *is* true, but feels too humiliated to fully admit it. He pulls at his nose quickly before the left hand moves forward and the index finger points at the audience on:

But <u>I</u> for mere <u>suspicion</u> in that kind

He looks to stage right while the **pointing** finger draws back slightly to partly indicate his left temple.

Will do as if for surety.

He draws a line down the front of the upper torso with the pointing finger on:

He holds me well

The left hand now makes a **closed fist** thumbs up gesture towards himself.

The better shall my purpose work on him.

He takes one step forward putting his weight onto the right foot with an inbreath, as the left hand returns to rest by his side, and the right hand comes up with index finger directed to audience:

Cassio's a proper man.

Holding up the finger as the head comes up with a bitter smile to look at the upper tiers of the audience.

Huh, let me see now

The right hand comes down on:

To get his place

Both arms spread out to make an **openness** gesture which is held on:

… and to plume up my will.

The arms come down again.

A double knavery. How, how?

The head is tilted up as if ruminating.

Let's see.

The eyeline moves down to the middle distance.

After some time

The left hand comes up to the left side of the face and is held suspended in a **vertical palm** gesture signalling that he is working out his idea.

to abuse Othello's ear

He turns his gaze and torso towards stage left as the left hand moves into a gesture with the **palm addressed** to the audience.

That he is too familiar with his wife.

The hands are now at waist height with some discreet movement of the torso.

He hath a person and a smooth dispose
To be suspected, framed to make women false.

Now there is a quick movement as the left hand comes up to make a gesture that moves from a **deictic** on:

The Moor

… to an **open palm vertical beat** gesture on:

… is of a free and open nature
That thinks men honest

The hand has been lowered by now to waist height again. The head and body are turned to stage right and looking slightly down.

… that but seem to be so

The left hand rises up again in palm prone position to make a **metaphoric** gesture of an undulating path on:

And will as tenderly be led by th' nose

The gesture ripples another time as he pauses, then is held for:

As asses are.

A slight laugh of satisfaction as the left hand is lowered. He looks up to the upper seating area.

I have't, it is engendered.

He leans back and opens out his arms once more as if addressing God, taking one step back onto his weight-bearing left leg.

Hell and night
Must bring this monstrous birth to the world's light.

The sound of a thunderclap offstage as he stares at the sky.

Here, the choice to use quite flat-handed open palm gestures signals a certain crudeness of manner without resorting to animal pantomimes. These gestures attempt to communicate *warmth* as a primary component of social cognition, in contrast with McKellen's precise, highly controlled but frigid signals of *competence*. But these feelings are undercut by McInnerney's repeated use of deictics partly as if looking to apportion blame, including at the audience, and partly to bolster his own ego when self-pointing. He also uses self-adaptors to signal anxiety. This accords with the fact that he shifts his weight constantly from foot to foot as if unable to get stable or comfortable. You could read into this that he is already suffering from an internal sense of being eaten up by resentment or that he has a kind of restless choleric humour – burning up from within, as it were, an impression reinforced by his effortful, bellows-like breathing pattern. He comes across as coarser, heavier, less meticulous, less smooth but more vulnerable in his humiliation than McKellen. This is a film of a live event rather than a staged video recording, though, which would account for some of its rougher edges. It is possible that McInnerney did not follow the exact gestural pattern he produces in the archived version every time he performed the role, although it was probably quite consistent over time. The speech is a soliloquy, so he would no doubt have felt that he had more freedom to produce whatever gestures came through in the moment of performance.

Comparison between the two performances suggests that McKellen's work is the more carefully prepared. This could be in line with his conception of the character; it is just as likely a result of the fact that he was making a film.

8
Interviews and Closing Thoughts

I have sought out connections between a performance history of Shakespeare and a theory of gesture. Here, I want to look for these connections through a comparison of the work of the choreographer Siân Williams and the gesture scholar David McNeill. My aim is not to recruit my interviewees to support my ideas, but to allow their own words to suggest resonances.

Siân Williams

On 17 August 2014 I met Siân Williams in a café in Hammersmith. A dancer and choreographer since 1982, Siân was in West London to work on the movement for a concert performance given at Hammersmith Apollo by the singer Kate Bush. Numerous thoughts emerge from the interview that resonate with the general themes of this book. She talks of the basis of the actor's power in the effortful practice of bodily disciplines like dance. She puts forward the ideas of research as something done 'on your feet' and of non-verbal expressiveness as the basis of theatrical storytelling. She pays homage to collaborators who approach the problem of making theatre in unusual ways; she notes the importance of an embodied knowledge of how costume shapes bodily practice, and she thinks deeply about the essential musicality of human movement both onstage and off. In the following edited transcript, 'SW' refers to Siân and 'DT' to me.

DT: You trained at the London College of Dance and Drama. What was that like?

SW: I'd done a lot of ballet from the age of 11 to 18 with a wonderful teacher at a convent, where they thought it was important for deportment to do dance. We had to do it for three years compulsorily, once a week, and it was the best thing that could have happened. Ann Collier, my teacher, helped several of us who all wanted to train, and we auditioned for all the usual places and I got into London College. I really liked the place because we did an incredible range of techniques: jazz, tap, folk dancing, ballroom dancing – which was a real challenge for the teacher; she used to marvel at our inability to walk in a parallel line. In theatre, although I've not done masses of that face-to-face partner dancing, when I do I love it because I have no fear of that.

DT: One of things you do nowadays at the Globe is historical dancing – did you do any of that at college?

SW: We had an amazing teacher called Belinda Quirey who was an authority on period dance. We'd have it once a week throughout the year for the three years, so I got a great grounding in terms of her opinion on the quality of movement. When I started to work at the Globe, I had to do it on my feet and do research. They've got a fantastic research department there. And I had books from college, which have remained my cornerstones, and I always go back to them. I read the same things over and over again, because you have to remind yourself of a period which seems similar to another block of a hundred years, but there were lots of subtle changes in them. I love interpreting the music of that period, but I'd have my own take on it for the purposes of what the director wants, I like to introduce things that are not conflicting with that period but I don't want to play an archive version of it.

DT: Was that where you met the person you founded The Kosh with?

SW: I got a job with Ludus Dance Company. Ludus did physical, narrative dance-theatre, with social issues for young people. They were intentionally non-verbal, pursuing communication only through the physical. We worked collaboratively, and that's where I met Michael Merwitzer. We were both interested in starting a company with that amalgamation drawing in song, dance, movement, anything we felt served the story. We were most interested in playing with expressive forms of human emotion. We wanted to take theatre to places that didn't necessarily get it. And we were telling a story in innovative ways to do with unexplored forms, like acrobatics. Johnny Hutch had come to see a show I'd done with Ludus. Emil Wolk, who was a wonderful performer from the People Show, had brought him. We loved the idea of working with Johnny, this veteran acrobat from the tail-end of the music hall. Not only did he have knowledge of his own specialist area, he loved soaking up things other people did. He was a mine of information and was eager to have it passed on to the next generation. Our work was right up Johnny's street, so we'd have sessions together, try things out, and we'd say 'Oh, that's like dancing, only it's tumbling – let's use it!' So we put all these different forms together. It was like physics for Johnny. He'd look at somebody, and see the fulcrum, 'there's my bearer, and there's my two balances,' that's what he'd done all his life and it was in him, to understand the way two bodies can move together, the pivot points to help you balance and make incredible things happen. We'd think, 'Is that humanly possible?' and then, 'That's the perfect image for somebody saying something about what is threatening, or risky.' We were also working with people that were not necessarily highly trained dancers. They were actors who were very good movers. So we had to find a common ground in terms of the physicality we wanted to use, and work to people's strengths and also challenge ourselves.

DT: How did the Globe Theatre thing happen? I'm jumping now from the '80s to the late '90s.

SW: I'd worked with Greg Doran at the RSC [Royal Shakespeare Company] for a few years. That was a really big leap working with a big company, and Helena Kaut-Howson I'd done some work with, so I was starting to do some different theatre work. I met Mark Rylance and Claire van Kampen who ran the Globe because Claire had been brought to see a show by Sue Parrish, who ran the Women's Theatre Group. A few years went by then they were running the Globe. And Tim Carroll, who was an Associate at the Globe, had seen our production of *A Matter of Chance*, had really liked the form and was working with an actor who'd been in that show. So it was those connections with seeing work by The Kosh, and I worked with Tim on *Two Noble Kinsmen* at the Globe. I hadn't been to the Globe before. And I've been lucky enough never to look back – 15 years later, and I've had this amazing opportunity of working there every season. When Dominic Dromgoole came in, my familiarity with the place was recognized in a positive way. With your own company, you form your own language and way of communicating. In some ways that's irreplaceable. I think if

I can do this work well it's because of The Kosh, of the way I was able to take risks, make something happen that was a crazy mixture of ideas from all places –

DT: It's a sort of proving ground.

SW: Yeah, where you think, 'We're going to make this work and it's really strange, we don't quite know what this form is but that's where we're going with it.' In some of these larger companies they can't afford to take those risks so it would be ridiculous to try. With my background I can think there is something exciting about the avenues you can go down. And you can appreciate the mind of the director – 'There's something bubbling away here that I want to try and make happen for them'. There isn't a conflict, because I'd always worked in that collaborative way with Michael, I'd always have to understand what he was thinking before I could start choreographing. The shift was quite an easy one.

DT: I'm interested in what it's like for you with actors when you go into the room.

SW: If you ask them, they'd probably say, 'Oh, she expects me to be able to do the impossible!' And you have to almost demystify it, to say, 'This isn't any more than you can already do, it's not a dance step, it's walking with a particular kind of quality to it'.

DT: It's often a choric thing.

SW: I love watching unison in movement but I also love seeing that there are individuals doing it, and the Globe has given me that sense that it doesn't have to be so tightly, regimentally drilled. It can have a feeling that it belongs to those real people who come together to make a dance happen. As I understand it, language was a very valuable currency at that time. So people really needed to get on the dance floor, however comfortable or uncomfortable they might have felt with it. They had to be there, so they could network, and they had to execute the pavanne, and it had a really important social function. I love the notion that it's an essential requirement even among the non-court classes. The dances are simple in many ways, so you could all join in without having to work something out, and be part of one rhythm. There was an Elizabethan sensibility about symmetry, the harmony of moving together. Not that we can't do it. We're just bouncing up and down to that bass beat, but we're finding a common thread with each other. That's always a delight for us. But it had a lovely refinement, moving one way then another, there's something really beautiful about that. In a lot of the dances that come at the end of the play in the Globe, they sometimes have that very pure form, but with a little bit of chaos within it as well, because it suits the release that comes at the end of the story, and then it suddenly falls back into order. That's been a lovely choreographic theme we've found a few times. You highlight the purity of partnering somebody in a graceful fusion because you've jostled it about a little bit.

There's a woman who works at the Globe called Glynn MacDonald, who's an Alexander specialist, and she's got a wonderful sense of physical presence that she advises on. She does these sessions with the company that's just about feeling yourself in the space and your use of the upper body. She has these images like the sternum is like a dagger pointing the way, to enable you to have that bearing that reflects what they wore. The style of clothing has such a command and show, and that's something you've got to pull off. We are so far away from that in our mode of carrying ourselves and our display of clothing. We almost like to play down the things we're wearing. But you'd have to hold your arms slightly away from your body because you had these massive sleeves. There's a lovely kind of spatial awareness that you needed to spiral around each other, because the woman wears voluminous folds of skirt so she has to make her way in figures of eight. That's a courtly thing, because their clothing was so much more ostentatious. You realize that all these clothes were held together with pins. You didn't just crumple up, because you'd risk stabbing yourself. If they sat down, it was perching. And it clearly seemed to matter, that there were very precise ways of conducting yourself and it would be frowned upon if you didn't observe some of those things.

DT: Say you're working on a sequence. How does it begin for you – with steps, with a rhythm?

SW: It very often starts with the music because it's the known thing, and I'm often presented with that. Someone like Claire [van Kampen] has a very good sense of what can be danced to. I love listening to the music, and I make my own framing of it. I read music, and I always write out the music for my 'dancer' thinking. I hear it in a timing of movement rather than notes on an instrument. I hear a complete phrase and I can imagine a shape that would fit with that phrase, and that's how I get each of the sections logged. Then I see the overall picture of the music, and if I see that it's roughly the right length, I start to divide that up into little sections of events in my head: 'It would be lovely if these characters came together at this point, then if they departed and danced with other people'. So in that sense I like to think of patterning that lends itself to people meeting other people on the dance floor. Sometimes it's being presented to a world out there, and sometimes it's a more intimate thing with each other. I have little 'x's on the page and little stick people drawings and shapes, lines of things, and I work on it in that way. Then there's the unknown which is the people themselves, and what they produce sometimes in interpreting that is really lovely. So sometimes it goes off on a slightly different path because of what they're producing. With a play we're reviving at the Globe – *A Midsummer Night's Dream* – Dominic wanted Titania and Oberon to come together with their entourage, and he wanted two chaotic, excited bands of fairies moving through the forest who suddenly come together in an aggressive face-off. So to do that I want them leaping and catching each other and maybe some lifts, but I can only make that happen with the people, so as we're recreating that I see one person, 'Oh, you're quite small, you could easily be lifted by that great big person, and that's the kind of energy we need.' I wouldn't have planned anything before I saw them. So it's always a bit of a mixture of responding to the people you have and the direction you want to go in.

DT: There's a visual music, one phrase leading to another phrase, repetitions of things –

SW: Very much. And contrast, building to something. And having done a lot of this work at the Globe, it's interesting to see how it moves into other areas of your work.

DT: Looking at the behaviour of these people here in the café, do you see patterns?

SW: Yes. It's to do with, say, are they for each other in their body language, the way they're positioned in the space in relation to the people around them. You start to pick up on their mannerisms with each other. It's always fascinating to be asked about that, because I don't know how I do it. I just see things, as I'm sure lots of people do. In our last Kosh production, we did a piece called *Café Chaos*, we had these little vignettes of people coming into a café. It's really to do with the architecture of the space. There was a limited number of tables and chairs, but because it was an abstraction of a café, you had to have a certain number of tables for it to be a café in your mind. And how I felt people should be positioned, then lifting off from that, taking things to extremes. We had them moving on top of the tables, extending what was happening to them. I like seeing people and not superimposing anything on them until they tell me something. And so in life I look at someone and think, 'Why does that particular person make me have a magnetic draw to them?'

DT: I was learning 'neutral mask' with Simon McBurney, and he said that stage presence is something you can work on. It's about rhythm and variety and contrast. Your charisma is something you can build, you cut out the noise, find out who you are, and you can work on the rhythm of that. Would you say that's true?

SW: I take that in terms of the task I've had of convincing some actors they can dance, in that way of thinking: 'Of course you can, it's yours for the taking'. They may not be comfortable with applying their movement to a given parameter of a phrase of music, and you saying, 'It has to finish by the time I say eight!' But they can always move, sometimes really beautifully. Sometimes they feel they don't own that ability. I see people at the beginning of a rehearsal process having a scepticism about their own ability to achieve certain things, and by the end of it being really confident, suddenly realizing, 'Of course that's me, *I'm* doing this, not somebody laying that on me'. I've seen it happen, people flourishing in an area of performing that they felt they had not got the command of as well as others. It's not that long ago I started working on a form of improvising. This was a door opening for me in the sense of anything is possible, and this thing that's always talked about of being in the moment and thinking 'I hope I can achieve that'. It's to do with focusing on the things around you, and not planning, not being so worked out, and when something doesn't fall into place, you don't think, 'Oh, it hasn't gone the way I wanted it to, so I'll steer it back to that', but flow with the new thing. All of that is amazing to watch when you see it onstage and you think, 'These two actors are working off each other rather than presenting at right angles to what each other is saying'. I think there are lots of techniques that open doors for development of a performance, even when you think you've done it all, and sometimes the ones you resist are really exciting. He won't mind me saying this, but Tim Carroll's rigorous way of approaching Shakespearean poetry is really hard on some – they feel they're being intimidated by the language before they come out the other side and think, 'What a revelation'. I've been on the receiving end of some of his exercises and think, 'If I ever get out of this room in one piece!' but it's endlessly rewarding.

DT: There's no freedom without rules. What are the rules of the Globe as a space?

SW: It's to do with welcoming into the shared space. You acknowledge that you're on a stage that's sort of floating on this sea of people. And because they're right there with you, they don't need any delay or halting of the storytelling, they're almost as present as you are on the stage, so the pace of things is acutely balanced. When you're in a darkened space and you have to pull this imaginary audience into you, that's another process. You're still communicating, but it's just that at the Globe you're literally making eye contact when you're telling them your thoughts. Spatially, that theatre welcomes things like being on the move when you're thinking. If it's a slightly heightened thing, you go for a walk as you're thinking to yourself. Or if you're listening to someone, you position yourself ready to respond to them, but only in the sense that, like when you're washing the dishes, without you even being aware of it, you're listening to the person who's giving you their thoughts. And you move, and when you finally decide to say something, that's going to be the moment when you stop. It's very like life in that way, it's just slightly expanded. That's why I like those moments when you work with the actors in the scene in conjunction with the director, and there's a heightening of what's happening. That's always really fascinating.

The next interview moves from a compelling theory of human gesture in general towards the work of the actor on Shakespeare.

David McNeill

At a few points in this book I have acknowledged the influence of Professor David McNeill, co-founder with Susan Duncan of the Gesture Lab at the University of Chicago. It is McNeill's basic psycholinguistic model of gesture that has gained much currency over the past 30 years, supported by experimental data from cognitive psychology. Although McNeill is not a scholar of performance, he has in recent times shown an interest in the subject from the perspective of the actor's gestures.

What follows is an edited transcription of an email correspondence I had with Professor McNeill (DM) between August 2014 and February 2015. In his responses, it is noteworthy that he stresses that gestural styles are personal to the speaker, a thought that resonates with the idea developed in the book regarding the increasing dominance of the social morality of individual self-fulfilment: recall that an actor like David Garrick may have been familiar with the canons of gesture outlined in the manuals of oratory, but his impact depended upon his particular style of movement. My insistence that gesture is how the actor thinks with her or his body is partly McNeill's theory of co-speech gesture – what he elaborates on here as 'communicative dynamism', expressed in a simple phrase. Of interest also is how McNeill relates gesture in performance to intentionality (see the paragraph below on 'old' and 'new' actions) – in Stanislavskian terms, to 'the objective'.

> **DT:** If it's OK with you, I'd like to begin the conversation by asking you to talk a little bit about your background – what led you to the field of gesture studies?

> **DM:** Of course. A good way to start. My interest in gesture goes way back (as do I). I can identify the landmarks fairly precisely. The first was in the early 1960s, at the Harvard Center for Cognitive Studies. I had just arrived fresh out of grad school (Berkeley) and found myself surrounded by the greatest luminaries of the then new field of cognitive studies. Two of the bright lights, Volney Stefflre and Roger Brown, I saw in constant dialogue. Physically they were very different, Stefflre a chunky muscular man, Brown tall and elegant, but what caught my eye was their contrasting gesture styles. This was the first time I had paid attention to gesture. I had no idea then that gesture and speech formed a unity or that language was involved at all. That realization came few years later; I've described the event – my seeing in mid-sentence that language and gesture were one 'thing'– in the preface of *Gesture and Thought*, 2005. But before then I saw S and B sculpting imaginary materials, S hammering some blocky stuff, I imagined marble, clenched fists banging on it; B weaving something delicate, I imagined spider webs. So this was my first awareness of gesture – they occur, they differ with the person, and they are imaginary sculpting.

DT: Your description of the gestural styles of Volney Stefflre and Roger Brown remind me of John Napier's elaboration of the Power Grip and the Precision Grip.

DM: This works well for Brown. His spider-web gestures did include the Precision Grip, but not so for Stefflre – his fists were closed as he pressed against the open, constantly changing space in front of him. What unites their two gesture depictions is a metaphoric use of space. Both were presenting meaning as spatial arrangements modified as meaning changes. They differed physically rather than metaphorically, Brown pinches, Steffler pushes, but agreed in depicting meaning as something like a structure in space.

DT: One of the reasons why I find your work interesting is that there has in recent decades been something of a change in British acting. In the 1980s and 90s a number of companies began to create work that drew upon what were felt to be continental traditions of theatre-making, the most famous example being Theatre de Complicite. Often, it was just a matter of British actors learning how to work with non-British collaborators. Over time, many of the performers associated with these companies found themselves working in the mainstream – that's to say, in institutions like the Royal Shakespeare Company – and they brought with them a way of working that was more (to use the cliché) 'physical'. That is, they would tend to refuse the traditional prioritization of voice over body in the creation of theatre, and they would see verbal acts as embodied. I count myself among these artists, having trained and worked in both the 'physical theatre' world (there really isn't a good term for it) and companies like the RSC; part of my motive for this book is to build the bridge between text- or voice-based drama and movement- or gesture-based performance. I think your concept of *communicative dynamism* is helpful in this regard. I wonder if you could just outline what communicative dynamism means to you?

DM: I've given a lot of thought to communicative dynamism (or 'CD'), but I can't claim it. It comes out of the Prague School of linguistics, Jan Firbas in particular, who introduced the concept as part of a movement they had launched called functional sentence perspective. CD is the communicative 'push' or 'weight' the word has in a sentence for advancing meaning. I've found this inherently dynamic idea to be enormously powerful in explaining how gesture and speech combine in English or any other language (not just free word order ones). The more the CD, the more elaborate the gesture; the less the less, even to the point of the gesture vanishing beneath the surface. I think all this bears on your bridge. It is a concept in which the two halves, text and action, converge. Another concept that bears on the bridge is the psychological predicate; I borrow this from Vygotsky. The psychological predicate is the point of newsworthiness in the immediate context of speaking. Putting CD and the psychological predicate together, we get the idea that the push in discourse comes from differentiating newsworthiness in the immediate context; and the more the departure from expectation, the greater the newsworthiness, the more the push and the CD, and the more elaborate the gesture. This conception of language automatically takes us beyond the sentence, the limit of most linguistic analysis. I can imagine actors must know all this already intuitively. And in gesture–speech unity, there is again the bridge. I wonder how far this goes in thinking about performance? Can entire scenes, all the dialogue, stage setting, actors' movements, etc. etc. be comprehended in terms of CD and psychological predicates?

Here is another idea (not borrowed for once). In speaking, the speaker shapes context to make the differentiation of a psychological predicate with the right significance possible. Part of the bridge in this natural setting is this shaping, a self-creation of context for one's own psychological predicate. One meaning is two things – the context and the psychological predicate, and is irreducible to two single meanings. The speaker manages both at once. Is this anything like a performance, including in it the author of the speech? What does an actor do that self-shapes the context? (I guess many things.) You can see how the performance triangle comes from these sorts of considerations.

DT: I just want to clarify a few things to make sure I've got you right. In performance, stylization is always at work to some degree. You recognize this in your paper on speech–gesture mimicry in performance when you refer to 'extremes of conceptualization' and to exaggeration. But your interest is not in consciously stylized gestures. You see gesture as the enactment of imagery that is fundamental to the process of speaking itself. The gesture conveys imagery and that is its most important feature. The physical embodiment of the gesture is in fact not strictly necessary – it's possible, as it were, to gesture without actually physically gesturing. Absent the physical movement, the speech is as you say already orchestrated by a gestural impulse.

DM: All this is right on. I am interested in how stylized gestures, as one performs them, seem to the actor. I have a pet distinction between 'new' gesture-actions and 'old' action-actions. The adjectives refer to phylogenesis (and ontogenesis), 'new' in human evolution, 'old' in primate action. The distinction is fundamentally whether the action has a goal; goal-direction defines the 'old' but the 'new' gesture-actions do not have goals; one intends to communicate something, this is a goal; and the gesture and the speech it unites with is part of the realization of this goal; but there is no goal of the gesture itself. It orchestrates the speech (changing it from vegetative action, with goals, into speech) but this is not a goal of making the gesture. The gesture arises as part of speaking. These terms refer to the actions themselves, and to how they are organized, qua actions. Now, taking all this into consideration, it may be that an actor's gestures do have goals, qua actions. The actor is thinking of the gesture as a part of the performance itself? Does this seem to be so? Then the gesture is really an action-action, and relates to speech in a fundamentally different way from a gesture-action. Of course, an actor may have both at once, which is quite interesting in its potential for interactions of the two modes.

DT: I have tried this exercise in rehearsals and classes lots of times: take a phrase of text – usually something that can be spoken in something like three seconds, that seems like a self-contained statement. As you speak, make a gesture of some kind. Keep trying different gestures until what emerges feels completely connected to the words: an image of them. Now take away the physical movement, but speak with exactly the same prosody, exactly the same energy as you did when you moved. Imagine yourself making the physical gesture as you speak. Now, it's interesting that what first tends to happen is that the actor's voice changes when they stop making the gesture – their prosody changes. I then have to insist that the text should sound precisely as it did when they moved their body while speaking. When that is finally achieved, it doesn't matter if they move or not – it feels like they have caught the movement of the text in their voice. In the performance, they may decide to make the physical gesture or they may not. One corollary of this is that the actor finds it easier to remember her or his lines.

DM: This is close to what I would hope! I have the idea gesture merges with speech by 'orchestrating' it, as I mentioned – we form speech around it. Even non-grammatical speech chunks this way. Your students seem to be following this path. The initial prosody changes are most telling. Gesture and prosody are so alike, and the gesture would orchestrate it most directly. Then, at last, they move into a mode of secure performance where the gesture seems to have dropped out (though I suspect it is present internally).

DT: Similarly, Michael Chekhov, whose work is being explored by Tom Cornford in relation to Shakespeare at the moment, would talk of an inner gesture, a 'Psychological Gesture'. This is private – it's only for the actor, not shown to the audience in the final performance.

DM: I know Cornford, indeed, and something of his conception of inner gestures. I think he called them phantom gestures as well (unless they are for some other conception he is interested in). Inner gestures may be unmixed gesture-actions, so clues the audience or other actors detect would be untainted by goals, this creating an impression of reality.

DT: When did you start to become interested in performance, and what prompted your interest?

DM: I had worked out a novel idea of how language came to exist, in us as a species, and wrote about it in the *How Language Began* book [2012]. As I thought about it, I kept seeing areas of life where this origin, if it had occurred, would change things. One was the idea that written prose contains hidden gestures. What we sense as good form is actually a gesture, placed there by the author. I cited passages from *Pride and Prejudice* as examples – saying that we touch gestures placed in them by Jane Austen 200 years ago. This then brought the theatre to mind. If we can do this with *Pride and Prejudice*, actors can do it with Shakespeare ... I met two theatre people, Tom Cornford and Ofer Ravid, and read some books addressed to actors (like Chekhov and Lecoq), and from this developed a great respect for actors' art and self-discipline.

I've also been thinking about 'physical' approaches to performance. Does the following have any relevance? One aspect of gesture is that it frames or, as I say, 'orchestrates' speech. Speech is built around it (the reverse of the popular view). I wonder if there is an equivalent orchestration of performance by the actor's movements? Both spoken lines and movements are meaningful, but gesture/movement is fundamental. Is this anything like a physical approach?

There are numerous points of interest here. But perhaps the most important one for my purposes can be teased out of his final proposition: that if, contrary to what is usually believed, speech is built around gesture, then perhaps a Shakespearean performance is built, first of all, not around the text but around the gestures of the actors.

Conclusion

This book has been premised upon three ideas:

1. Gesture and speech are not separable systems, but are intertwined because all thought is embodied.
2. In order to gain social acceptance, actors had to learn and display a principle of smoothness because people associate smoothness with high status.
3. The cultural developments in gestural behaviour among influential Shakespearean actors parallel historical developments in social morality.

In a recent newspaper article, John Sutherland argued that Shakespeare's words are dying for us, and that soon we will barely be able to understand his language at all (*The Guardian*, 11 October 2013). The case is open to debate, but nonetheless it seems clear to me that those who wish to produce Shakespeare for new audiences must pay renewed attention to the actor's body. In particular, practitioners and theorists need to reflect upon how gesture and speech are a single system, so that neither gesture nor speech is prioritized as more authentic. It is impossible to say what the results of such reflection might be. The futures for Shakespeare in practice that I have suggested are only a handful of possibilities, and they may turn out to be irrelevant. History is not a deterministic process; it is an unpredictable mix of forces and accidents, and Shakespearean practice is no exception.

Further Reading

The following can inevitably be no more than a general guide to further research and exploration into what is a vast and complex subject. The reader is encouraged to use my indications as encouragements towards the discovery of her or his own patterns and connections.

For gesture theory the reader is urged to consult David McNeill (1992/1995), Adam Kendon (1988, 2004), and Paul Ekman and Wallace Friesen (1969).

For a cultural history of gesture see Bremmer and Roodenburg (1991). Elaine Fantham (1982, 2002, 2006) is a valuable guide to Roman rhetoric in performance, while Corbeill, (2004), Aldrete (1999) and Brilliant (1963) all produced important works on the topic. Anglo-Saxon and medieval gesture is treated in varying ways by Dodwell (2000), Barasch (1987/1990, 2003) and Schmitt (1991). For Renaissance gesture and its relation to courtesy, see the monumental work of Norbert Elias (1939/1994) as well as Bryson (1998), Burke (1995/2007) and Becker (1988). For Renaissance uses of rhetoric see Plett (2004), Mack (2011) and Enterline (2012). For Reformation culture and its influence on theatre see Degenhardt and Williamson (2011), Pettegree (2005) and King (1982).

For questions of acting relating to Shakespearean and other Renaissance practitioners, some useful material is found in Astington (2010), Stern (2004, 2009), Gurr and Ichikawa (2000), Dessen (1986) and Styan (1967). Peter Thomson (2000) takes the long view and is a witty and sensible guide. In the Introduction I refer to some of the major players in the central debate on Elizabethan acting – the reader is invited to consult those works also. For the subject of the passions and humours on Shakespeare's stage, see Escolme (2013) and Paster (2004).

For gesture in acting from 1650 to 1850, the essential (though also contestable) text is Barnett (1987), but see also Woo (2008), West (1991) and Woods (1984). See also Hughes (1987), Pullen (2005), Asleson (2003) and Howe (1992) on actresses, Cunningham (2008), Benedetti (2001) on Garrick and Kahan (2006) on Kean. Of interest also is Roach (1985).

For Victorian actresses, see Marshall (1998). On Irving and Darwinism, see Goodall (2002). Of interest for the period is Schoch (2006). Paul Ekman's edition of Darwin's work on emotion (1872/1998) is essential reading.

Stanislavski's *Othello* is discussed in Stanislavski (1936/1989), Hankey (1987) and Potter (2002). The Modernism of Les Kurbas is covered in Makaryk and Tkacz

(2010) and Makaryk (2004). Material on Laban is found in Davies (2006) as well as in his own works (especially 1988/2001). Other influential movement practitioners such as Lecoq are discussed in Evans (2009). For Lepage, see Dundjerovic (2009) and Fricker (2008). Useful material on dreamthinkspeak is found in Machon (2013).

Bibliography

Unless otherwise stated, all Shakespeare quotations are from:
Proudfoot, Richard, Thompson, Ann and Scott Kastan, David, eds (2011). *The Arden Shakespeare: Complete Works*. Revised edition. London: Methuen.

Other editions consulted:
Bate, Jonathan, ed. (1995). *Titus Andronicus*. London: The Arden Shakespeare.

Brooke, Nicholas, ed. (1994). *Macbeth*. Oxford: Oxford University Press.

Hapgood, Robert, ed. (1999). *Shakespeare in Production: Hamlet*. Cambridge: Cambridge University Press.

DVD recordings:
Shakespeare, William (1990/2003). *Othello*. Directed by Trevor Nunn. From the Royal Shakespeare Company production (1989). Released by Metrodome.

Shakespeare, William (2007). *Othello*. Directed by Wilson Milam. Shakespeare's Globe Theatre Production. Released by New Heritage/NHK Enterprises Video Production.

Other works consulted:
Aldrete, Gregory S. (1999). *Gestures and Acclamations in Ancient Rome*. Baltimore, MD and London: The Johns Hopkins University Press.

Ashelford, Jane (1983). *A Visual History of Costume: The Sixteenth Century*. London: Batsford.

Asleson, Robyn, ed. (2003). *Notorious Muse: The Actress in British Art and Culture 1776–1812*. New Haven, CT and London: Yale University Press.

Astington, John H. (2004). '"Language in their very gesture": Shakespeare's Actors and the Body'. Paper delivered University of Toronto 7 May 2004. Accessed at www.semioticon.com/virtuals/gestures/astingtongesture.pdf on 16 May 2016.

Astington, John H. (2010). *Actors and Acting in Shakespeare's Time: The Art of Stage-Playing*. Cambridge: Cambridge University Press.

Austin, Gilbert (1806/1966). *Chironomia, or a Treatise on Rhetorical Delivery*. Ed. Mary Margaret Robb and Lester Thonssen. Carbondale, IL: Southern Illinois UP.

Bachrach, A.G.H. (1949). 'The Great Chain of Acting', *Neophilologus 33*, pp.160–72.

Bacon, Francis (1670). *Sylva Sylvarum, or, A Natural History, in Ten Centuries. Published by W. Rawley after the Author's Death*. London: W. Lee.

Barasch, Moshe (1987/1990). *Giotto and the Language of Gesture*. Cambridge: Cambridge University Press.

Barasch, Moshe (2003). *'Elevatio*: The Depiction of a Ritual Gesture', *Artibus et Historiae 24:48*, pp.43–56.

Barish, Jonas (1981/1985). *The Antitheatrical Prejudice*. Berkeley, CA and London: University of California Press.

Barkan, Leonard (1995). 'Making Pictures Speak: Renaissance Art, Elizabethan Literature, Modern Scholarship', *Renaissance Quarterly 48:2*, pp.326–51.

Barnett, Dene (1987). *The Art of Gesture: The Practices and Principles of 18th Century Acting*. With the assistance of Jeanette Massy-Westropp. Heidelberg: Carl Winter Universitätsverlag.

Barry, Jonathan and Brooks, Christopher, eds (1994). *The Middling Sort of People: Culture, Society and Politics in England, 1550–1800*. New York: St Martin's Press.

Becker, Marvin (1988). *Civility and Society in Western Europe 1300–1600*. Bloomington: Indiana University Press.

Beckerman, Bernard (1962). *Shakespeare at the Globe: 1599–1609*. New York: Macmillan.

Belsey, Catherine (1985). *The Subject of Tragedy: Identity and Difference in Renaissance Drama*. London and New York: Methuen.

Benedetti, Jean (2001). *David Garrick and the Birth of Modern Theatre*. London: Methuen.

Benedetti, Jean (2008). *Stanislavski: An Introduction*. 4th revised edition. London: Methuen.

Bertelsen, Lance (1978). 'David Garrick and English Painting', *Eighteenth-Century Studies 11:3*, pp.308–24.

Betteridge, Thomas and Walker, Greg, eds (2012). *The Oxford Handbook of Tudor Drama*. Oxford: Oxford University Press.

Bevington, David M. (1984). *Action is Eloquence: Shakespeare's Language of Gesture*. Cambridge, MA and London: Harvard University Press.

Boaden, James (1827). *Memoirs of Mrs Siddons. Interspersed with Ancedotes of Authors and Actors*. Philadelphia, PA: H.C. Carey and I. Lea and E. Littell.

Bouwsma, William J. (2000). *The Waning of the Renaissance 1550–1640*. New Haven, CT and London: Yale University Press.

Bowers, Robert H. (1948). 'Gesticulation in Elizabethan Acting', *Southern Folklore Quarterly XII*, pp.267–77.

Brambilla, Marco and Leach, Colin Wayne (2014). 'On the Importance of Being Moral: The Distinctive Role of Morality in Social Judgment', *Social Cognition 32:4*, pp.397–408.

Braun, Edward, ed. (1998). *Meyerhold on Theatre*. Revised edition. London: Methuen.

Brecht, Bertolt (1964/1984). *Brecht on Theatre: The Development of an Aesthetic*. Edited and translated by John Willett. London: Methuen.

Bremmer, Jan (1991). 'Walking, Standing, and Sitting in Ancient Greek Culture', in Bremmer, Jan and Roodenburg, Herman, eds, *A Cultural History of Gesture: From Antiquity to the Present Day*, pp.15–35. Cambridge: Polity Press.

Bremmer, Jan and Roodenburg, Herman, eds (1991), *A Cultural History of Gesture: From Antiquity to the Present Day.* Cambridge: Polity Press.

Brewer, John (1997). *The Pleasures of the Imagination: English Culture in the Eighteenth Century.* London: HarperCollins.

Brilliant, Richard (1963). *Gesture and Rank in Roman Art: The Use of Gestures to Denote Status in Roman Sculpture and Coinage.* New Haven, CT: The Connecticut Academy of Arts and Sciences.

Bristol, Michael and McLuskie, Kathleen with Holmes, Christopher, eds (2001). *Shakespeare and Modern Theatre: The Performance of Modernity.* London and New York: Routledge.

Brockbank, Philip, ed. (1988). *Players of Shakespeare 1: Essays in Shakespearean Performance by Twelve Players with the Royal Shakespeare Company.* Cambridge: Cambridge University Press.

Brown, John Russell (1953). 'On the Acting of Shakespeare's Plays', *Quarterly Journal of Speech 39*, pp. 477–84.

Brown, John Russell (1999). *New Sites for Shakespeare: Theatre, the Audience and Asia.* London and New York: Routledge.

Brown, John Russell, ed. (2008). *The Routledge Companion to Directors' Shakespeare.* Abingdon and New York: Routledge.

Brown, John Russell, ed. (2012). *The Routledge Companion to Actors' Shakespeare.* Abingdon and New York: Routledge.

Brown, Peter (1983). 'The Saint as Exemplar in Late Antiquity', *Representations 2*, pp.1–25.

Bryson, Anna (1998). *From Courtesy to Civility: Changing Codes of Conduct in Early Modern England.* Oxford: Clarendon Press.

Bulwer, John (1644). *Chirologia: or the Naturall Language of the Hand. Composed of the Speaking Motions, and Discoursing Gestures thereof. Whereunto is added Chironomia: or the Art of Manuall Rhetoricke. Consisting of the naturall expressions, digested by art in the hand, as the chiefest instrument of eloquence.* London: Thomas Harper.

Bulwer, John (1648). *Philocopus: Or the Deaf and Dumb Man's Friend … by J.B., Sirnamed by Chirosopher (John Bulwer).* London: Humphrey Moseley.

Burke, Peter (1995/2007). *The Fortunes of the Courtier: The European Reception of Castiglione's Cortegiano.* Cambridge: Polity Press.

Campbell, Thomas (1834). *Life of Mrs. Siddons.* 2 vols. London: Effingham Wilson.

Carney, Dana R., Cuddy, Amy J.C. and Yap, Andy J. (2010). 'Power Posing: Brief Nonverbal Displays Affect Neuroendocrine Levels and Risk Tolerance', *Psychological Science 21*, pp.1363–68.

Castiglione, Baldassare (1974). *The Book of the Courtier.* Translated by Sir Thomas Hoby with an introduction by J.H. Whitfield. London: J.M. Dent and Sons.

Cavanaugh, William T. (2001). 'Eucharistic Sacrifice and the Social Imagination in Early Modern Europe', *Journal of Medieval and Early Modern Studies 31:3*, pp.585–605.

Chambers, Edmund K. (1923). *The Elizabethan Stage.* 4 vols. Oxford: Clarendon Press.

Churchland, Patricia S. (2011). *Braintrust: What Neuroscience Tells Us about Morality*. Princeton, NJ and Oxford: Princeton University Press.

Cibber, Colley (1739/2000). *An Apology for the Life of Colley Cibber. With an Historical View of the Stage during his own Time*. Edited by B.R.S. Fone. Mineola, New York: Courier Dover Publications.

Cicero, Marcus Tullius. *Brutus, De Finibus Bonorum et Malorum, De Oratore*. Accessed at: www.loebclassics.com on 16 May 2016.

Cleary, James W. (1959). 'John Bulwer, Renaissance Communicationist', *Quarterly Journal of Speech 45*, pp.391–8.

Clune, Michael W. (2013). *Writing Against Time*. Stanford, CA: Stanford University Press.

Coldewey, John C. (2004). 'From Roman to Renaissance in Drama and Theatre'. In Milling, Jane and Thomson, Peter (eds). *The Cambridge History of British Theatre Volume 1*, pp.3–69. Cambridge: Cambridge University Press.

Cole, Toby and Chinoy, Helen Krich (1970/1995). *Actors on Acting: The Theories, Techniques and Practices of the World's Great Actors, Told in Their Own Words*. New York: Three Rivers Press.

Cook, Amy (2010). *Shakespearean Neuroplay: Reinvigorating the Study of Dramatic Texts and Performance through Cognitive Science*. Basingstoke and New York: Palgrave Macmillan.

Corbeill, Anthony (2004). *Nature Embodied: Gesture in Ancient Rome*. Princeton, NJ and Oxford: Princeton University Press.

Cunningham, Vanessa (2008). *Shakespeare and Garrick*. Cambridge: Cambridge University Press.

Darwin, Charles (1871/1981). *The Descent of Man, and Selection in Relation to Sex*. With an introduction by John Tyler Bonner and Robert M. May. Princeton, NJ: Princeton University Press.

Darwin, Charles (1872/1998). *The Expression of the Emotions in Man and Animals*. With Introduction, Afterword and Commentaries by Paul Ekman. Chicago: University of Chicago Press.

Davidson, Jenny (2004). *Hypocrisy and the Politics of Politeness: Manners and Morals from Locke to Austen*. Cambridge: Cambridge University Press.

Davies, Eden (2006). *Beyond Dance: Laban's Legacy of Movement Analysis*. New York and Abingdon: Routledge.

Davies, Glenys (2010). 'Togate statues and petrified orators', in Berry, D.H. and Erskine, Andrew (eds). *Form and Function in Roman Oratory*, pp.51–73. Cambridge: Cambridge University Press.

Davies, Thomas (1818). *Memoirs of the Life of David Garrick*. Boston: Wells and Lily.

Davis, Tracy C. (1991). *Actresses as Working Women: Their Social Identity in Victorian Culture*. London: Routledge.

Dawson, Anthony B. (1995). *Shakespeare in Performance: Hamlet*. Manchester and New York: Manchester University Press.

Degenhardt, Jane Hwang and Williamson, Elizabeth (2011). *Religion and Drama in Early Modern England: The Performance of Religion on the Renaissance Stage*. Aldershot: Ashgate.

Della Porta, Giambattista (1586). *De Humana Physiognomia*. Vico Equense: Apud Iosephum Cacchium.

Dessen, Alan C. (1986). *Elizabethan Stage Conventions and Modern Interpreters*. Cambridge: Cambridge University Press.

Dodwell, Charles R. (2000). *Anglo-Saxon Gestures and the Roman Stage*. Cambridge: Cambridge University Press.

Donohue Jr., Joseph W. (1970/2015). *Dramatic Character in the English Romantic Age*. Princeton, NJ: Princeton University Press.

Downer, Alan S. (1943). 'Nature to Advantage Dressed: Eighteenth Century Acting', *PMLA 58:4*, pp.1002–37.

Downer, Alan S. (1946). 'Players and Painted Stage: Nineteenth Century Acting', *PMLA 61:2*, pp.522–76.

Dundjerovic, Aleksander (2009). *Robert Lepage*. London and New York: Routledge.

Dutsch, Dorota (2002). 'Towards a Grammar of Gesture: A Comparison of the Types of Hand Movements of the Orator and the Actor in Quintilian's *Institutio Oratoria* 11.3.85–184', *Gesture 2:2*, pp.265–87.

Ehrstine, Glenn (2001). *Theater, Culture and Community in Reformation Bern, 1523–1555*. Leiden, Boston and Köln: Brill.

Ekman, Paul and Friesen, Wallace V. (1969). 'The Repertoire of Nonverbal Behavior: Categories, Origins, Usage and Coding', *Semiotica 1:1*, pp.49–98.

Elias, Norbert (1939/1994). *The Civilizing Process*. Oxford: Blackwell.

Elliott, John R., Jr. (1976). 'The Shakespeare Berlioz Saw', *Music & Letters 57:3*, pp.292–308.

Enterline, Lynn (2012). *Shakespeare's Schoolroom: Rhetoric, Discipline, Emotion*. Philadelphia: University of Pennsylvania Press.

Escolme, Bridget (2005). *Talking to the Audience: Shakespeare, Performance, Self*. London and New York: Routledge.

Escolme, Bridget (2013). *Emotional Excess on the Shakespearean Stage: Passion's Slaves*. London and New York: A&C Black.

Evans, Elizabeth C. (1969). 'Physiognomics in the Ancient World', *Transactions of the American Philosophical Society, New Series 59:5*, pp.3–101.

Evans, Mark (2009). *Movement Training for the Modern Actor*. New York and Abingdon: Routledge.

Fantham, Elaine (1982). 'Quintilian on Performance: Traditional and Personal Elements in "Institutio" 11.3', *Phoenix 36:3*, pp.243–63.

Fantham, Elaine (2002). 'Orator and/et Actor', in Easterling, Pat and Hall, Edith, eds, *Greek and Roman Actors: Aspects of an Ancient Profession*, pp.363–94. Cambridge: Cambridge University Press.

Fantham, Elaine (2006). *The Roman World of Cicero's De Oratore*. Oxford: Oxford University Press.

Feinberg, Matthew and Willer, Rob (2015). 'From Gulf to Bridge: When do Moral Arguments Facilitate Political Influence?', *Personality and Social Psychology Bulletin 41:12*, pp.1665–81.

Fiske, Susan T., Cuddy, Amy J.C. and Glick, Peter (2006). 'Universal dimensions of social cognition: warmth and competence', *Trends in Cognitive Sciences 11:2*, pp.77–83.

Fitgerald, Percy (1893). *Henry Irving: A Record of Twenty Years at the Lyceum*. London: Chapman and Hall.

Fleeming Jenkin, Henry Charles (1915). *Papers on Acting III: Mrs Siddons as Lady Macbeth and as Queen Katharine*. New York: Dramatic Museum of Columbia University.

Foakes, R.A. (1954) 'The Player's Passion: Some Notes on Elizabethan Psychology and Acting', *Essays and Studies*, pp.62–77.

Fögen, Thorsten (2009). '*Sermo corporis*: Ancient Reflections on *gestus*, *vultus* and *vox*', in Fögen, Thorsten and Lee, Mireille M., eds, *Bodies and Boundaries in Graeco-Roman Antiquity*, pp.15–43. Berlin: Walter de Gruyter.

Fraisse, P., Pichot, P. and Clairouin, G. (1949). 'Les aptitudes rythmiques. Etude comparée des oligophrènes et des enfants normaux', *Journal de Psychologie Normale et Pathologique 42*, pp.309–30.

Fraisse, Paul (1984). 'Perception and Estimation of Time', *Annual Review of Psychology 35*, pp.1–36.

Fricker, Karen (2008). 'Robert Lepage', in Brown, John Russell, ed., *The Routledge Companion to Directors' Shakespeare*, pp.233–50. Abingdon and New York: Routledge.

Frijhoff, Willem (1991). 'The Kiss Sacred and Profane: Reflections on a Cross-cultural Confrontation', in Bremmer, Jan and Roodenburg, Herman, eds, *A Cultural History of Gesture: From Antiquity to the Present Day*, pp.210–36. Cambridge: Polity Press.

Frisch, Harold (1987). 'Shakespeare and the Language of Gesture', *Shakespeare Studies 19*, pp.239–51.

Fudge, Erica (2011). 'The Human Face of Early Modern England', *Angelaki: Journal of the Theoretical Humanities 16:1*, pp.97–110.

Geen, Thomas R. and Tassinary, Louis. G. (2002). 'The Mechanization of Emotional Expression in John Bulwer's *Pathomyotomia* (1649)', *American Journal of Psychology 115:2*, pp.275–99.

Genest, John (1832). *Some Account of the English Stage, From the Restoration in 1660 to 1830*. 10 vols. Bath: H.E. Carrington.

Gibbs, Raymond W. Jr. (2005). *Embodiment and Cognitive Science*. Cambridge: Cambridge University Press.

Gildon, Charles (1710). *The Life of Mr. Thomas Betterton, The Late Eminent Tragedian*. London: printed for Robert Gosling.

Gleason, Maud W. (1999). 'Elite Male Identity in the Roman Empire', in Potter, D.S. and Mattingly, D.J., eds, *Life, Death, and Entertainment in the Roman Empire*, pp.67–84. Ann Arbor, MI: The University of Michigan Press.

Goffman, Erving (1959/1990). *The Presentation of Self in Everyday Life*. London: Penguin.

Golding, Alfred S. (1984). *Classicistic Acting: Two Centuries of a Performance Tradition at the Amsterdam Schouwburg to Which Is Appended an Annotated*

Translation of the Lessons on the Principles of Gesticulation and Mimic Expression of Johannes Jelgerhuis, Rz. New York and London: Lanhem.

Goldman, Ellen (1994). *As Others See Us: Body Movement and the Art of Successful Communication.* New York and London: Routledge.

Goodall, Jane R. (2002). *Performance and Evolution in the Age of Darwin: Out of the Natural Order.* London and New York: Routledge.

Goring, Paul (2005). *The Rhetoric of Sensibility in Eighteenth-Century Culture.* Cambridge: Cambridge University Press.

Gould, John (1973). 'Hiketeia', *The Journal of Hellenic Studies 93*, pp.74–103.

Gowland, Angus (2006). 'The Problem of Early Modern Melancholy', *Past and Present 191*, pp.77–120.

Graf, Fritz (1991). 'Gestures and Conventions: The Gestures of Roman Actors and Orators', in Bremmer, Jan and Roodenburg, Herman, eds, *A Cultural History of Gesture: From Antiquity to the Present Day*, pp.36–58. Cambridge: Polity Press.

Green, Douglas E. (1989). 'Interpreting "her martyr'd signs": Gender and Tragedy in *Titus Andronicus*', *Shakespeare Quarterly 40:3*, pp.317–26.

Greenblatt, Stephen (1980). *Renaissance Self-Fashioning from More to Shakespeare.* Chicago and London: University of Chicago Press.

Griffith, R. Drew (1998). 'Corporality in the Ancient Greek Theatre', *Phoenix 52:3/4*, pp.230–56.

Gurr, Andrew and Ichikawa, Mariko (2000). *Staging in Shakespeare's Theatres.* Oxford and New York: Oxford University Press.

Hall, Jon (2004). 'Cicero and Quintilian on the Oratorical Use of Hand Gestures', *Classical Quarterly 54:1*, pp.143–60.

Hampton-Reeves, Stuart and Escolme, Bridget, eds (2012). *Shakespeare and the Making of Theatre.* Basingstoke and New York: Palgrave Macmillan.

Hankey, Julie, ed. (1987). *Plays in Performance: Othello.* Bristol: Bristol Classical Press.

Harbage, Alfred (1939). 'Elizabethan Acting', *PMLA 54:3*, pp.685–708.

Hardison, O.B., Jr. (1965) *Christian Rite and Christian Drama in the Middle Ages: Essays in the Origin and Early History of Modern Drama.* Westport, CT: Greenwood Press.

Harrison, Peter (1998). *The Bible, Protestantism and the Rise of Natural Science.* Cambridge: Cambridge University Press.

Harrison, Peter (2007). *The Fall of Man and the Foundations of Science.* Cambridge: Cambridge University Press.

Harvie, Jen and Hurley, Erin (1999). 'States of Play: Locating Québec in the Performances of Robert Lepage, Ex Machina and the Cirque du Soleil', *Theatre Journal 51*, pp.299–315.

Hawkins, Frederick William (1869). *The Life of Edmund Kean.* London: Tinsley Brothers.

Heninger, S.K., Jr. (1984). 'Speaking Pictures: Sidney's Rapprochement between Poetry and Painting', in Waller, Gary F. and Moore, Michael D., eds, *Sir Philip*

Sidney and the Interpretation of Renaissance Culture: A Collection of Critical and Scholarly Essays, pp.3–16. London and Sydney: Croom Helm.

Hewes, Gordon (1957). 'The Anthropology of Posture', *Scientific American 196:2*, pp.122–32.

Heywood, Thomas (1612/1841). *An Apology for Actors. In Three Books. From the Edition of 1612, compared with that of W. Cartwright.* London: Reprinted for the Shakespeare Society.

Hogan, Neville and Flash, Tamar (1987). 'Moving Gracefully: Quantitative Theories of Motor Coordination', *Trends in Neurosciences 10:4*, pp.170–4.

Hogarth, William (1753/1997). *The Analysis of Beauty.* Edited by Ronald Paulson. New Haven, CT and London: Yale University Press.

Honan, Park (1998). *Shakespeare: A Life.* Oxford: Oxford University Press.

Howe, Elizabeth (1992). *The First English Actresses: Women and Drama 1660–1700.* Cambridge: Cambridge University Press.

Hughes, Alan (1987). 'Art and Eighteenth-Century Acting Style', *Theatre Notebook 41: 1–3.* Part 1: 'Aesthetics', pp.24–31; Part 2: 'Attitudes', pp.79–89; Part 3: 'The Passions', pp.128–39.

Hurstfield, Joel and Smith, Alan G.R., eds (1972). *Elizabethan People: State and Society.* London: Edward Arnold.

Jaeger, C. Stephen (1985). *The Origins of Courtliness: Civilizing Trends and the Formation of Courtly Ideals 939–1210.* University of Pennsylvania Press.

James, William (1884). 'What is an Emotion?', *Mind 9:34*, pp.188–205.

Jelgerhuis, Johannes (1827). *Theoretische lessen over de gesticulae en mimiek gegeven.* Amsterdam.

Johnson, Mark (1987). *The Body in the Mind: The Bodily Basis of Meaning, Imagination and Reason.* Chicago: University of Chicago Press.

Johnson, Mark (2007). '"The stone that was cast out shall become the corner-stone": The Bodily Aesthetics of Human Meaning', *Journal of Visual Art Practice 6:2*, pp.89–103.

Joseph, Bertram L. (1959). *The Tragic Actor.* London: Routledge and Kegan Paul.

Joseph, Bertram L. (1960). *Acting Shakespeare.* London: Routledge and Kegan Paul.

Joseph, Bertram L. (1964). *Elizabethan Acting.* Oxford: Oxford University Press.

Joseph, Bertram L. (1971). *Shakespeare's Eden: The Commonwealth of England 1558–1629.* London: Blandford Press.

Kahan, Jeffrey (2006). *The Cult of Kean.* Aldershot and Burlington, VT: Ashgate.

Kalavrezou, Ioli (1997/2004). 'Helping Hands for the Empire: Imperial Ceremonies and the Cult of Relics at the Byzantine Court', in Maguire, Henry, ed., *Byzantine Court Culture from 829–1204*, pp.53–79. Washington DC: Dumbarton Oaks.

Kendall, Gillian Murray (1989). '"Lend me thy hand": Metaphor and Mayhem in *Titus Andronicus'*, *Shakespeare Quarterly 40:3*, pp.299–316.

Kendon, Adam (1988). 'How Gestures Can Become Like Words', in Poyatos, F., ed., *Cross-cultural Perspectives in Nonverbal Communication*, pp.131–41. Toronto: Hogrefe.

Kendon, Adam (2004). *Gesture: Visible Action as Utterance*. Cambridge: Cambridge University Press.

Kennedy, Denis (2004). *Foreign Shakespeare: Contemporary Performance*. Manchester: Manchester University Press.

King, John N. (1982). *English Reformation Literature: The Tudor Origins of the Protestant Tradition*. Princeton, NJ: Princeton University Press.

King, Ros (2007). 'Reading Beyond Words: Sound and Gesture in *The Winter's Tale*', *Pedagogy 7:3*, pp.385–400.

Knowlson, James R. (1965). 'The Idea of Gesture as a Universal Language in the XVIIth and XVIIIth Centuries', *Journal of the History of Ideas 26:4*, pp.495–508.

Knox, Dilwyn (1996). 'Giovanni Bonifacio's *L'arte de' cenni* and Renaissance Ideas of Gesture', in Tavoni, M., ed., *Italia ed Europa nella Linguistica del Rinascimento: Confronti e Relazioni, Atti del Convegno internazionale, Ferrara, 20–24 Marzo 1991*, pp.379–400. Ferrara: Franco Cosimo Panini.

Koivumaki, Judith Hall (1975). 'Body Language Taught Here', *Journal of Communication 25:1*, pp.26–30.

Kozintsev, Grigori (1977). *King Lear: The Space of Tragedy*. Translated by Mary Mackintosh. Berkeley and Los Angeles: University of California Press.

Laban, Rudolf (1988/2001). *The Mastery of Movement*. Originally published by Macdonald and Evans Ltd. in 1950 as *The Mastery of Movement on the Stage*. Fourth edition revised and enlarged by Lisa Ullmann. Tavistock: Northcote House.

Laban, Rudolf and Lawrence, F.C. (1947/1974). *Effort: Economy of Human Movement*. 2nd edition. London: Macdonald and Evans Ltd.

Lakoff, George (2012). 'Explaining Embodied Cognition Results', *Topics in Cognitive Science 4:4*, pp.773–85.

Lakoff, George and Johnson, Mark (1980). *Metaphors We Live By*. Chicago and London: The University of Chicago Press.

Lamb, Warren and Watson, Elizabeth (1979). *Body Code: The Meaning in Movement*. London, Boston and Henley: Routledge & Kegan Paul.

Lateiner, Donald (1992). 'Affect Displays in the Epic Poetry of Homer, Vergil and Ovid', in Poyatos, Fernando, ed., *Advances in Non-verbal Communication: Sociocultural, Clinical, Esthetic and Literary Perspectives*, pp.255–70. Amsterdam and Philadelphia: John Benjamins Publishing.

Lecoq, Jacques (2002). *The Moving Body: Teaching Creative Theatre*. In collaboration with Jean-Gabriel Carasso and Jean-Claude Lallias. Translated by David Bradby. London and New York: Bloomsbury.

Lefebvre, Henri (1991). *The Production of Space*. Translated by Donald Nicholson-Smith. Oxford: Basil Blackwell.

Lefkowitz, Mary R. (1991). *Heroines and Hysterics*. New York: Duckworth.

Levin, Richard (2002). 'The Longleat Manuscript and *Titus Andronicus*', *Shakespeare Quarterly 53:3*, 323–40.

Lichtenberg, Georg Christoph (1938). *Lichtenberg's Visits to England as Described in his Letters and Diaries*. Translated and edited by Margaret L. Mare and W.H. Quarrell. Oxford: The Clarendon Press.

Lieberman, Matthew D. (2007). 'Social Cognitive Neuroscience: A Review of Core Processes', *Annual Review of Psychology 58*, pp.259–89.

Lieberman, Matthew D. (2013). *Social: Why Our Brains Are Wired to Connect.* Oxford: Oxford University Press.

Little, David M. and Kahrl, George M., eds (1963). *The Letters of David Garrick.* 3 vols. Boston: Belknap Press of Harvard University Press.

Lyne, Raphael (2013). 'The Shakespearean Grasp', *Cambridge Quarterly 42:1*, pp.38–61.

Machon, Josephine (2013). *Immersive Theatres: Intimacy and Immediacy in Contemporary Performance.* Basingstoke and New York: Palgrave Macmillan.

Mack, Peter (2011). *A History of Renaissance Rhetoric 1320–1620.* Oxford: Oxford University Press.

Makaryk, Irena R. (2004). *Shakespeare in the Undiscovered Bourn: Les Kurbas, Ukrainian Modernism, and Early Soviet Cultural Politics.* Toronto: University of Toronto Press.

Makaryk, Irena and Tkacz, Virlana (2010). *Modernism in Kyiv: Jubilant Experimentation.* Toronto: University of Toronto Press.

Manvell, Roger (1971). *Sarah Siddons: Portrait of an Actress.* New York: Putnam's Sons.

Markus, R.A. (1957). 'St.Augustine on Signs', *Phronesis 2:1*, pp.60–83.

Marr, David and Vaina, Lucia (1982). 'Representation and Recognition of the Movements of Shapes', *Proceedings of the Royal Society of London. Series B, Biological Sciences 214:1197*, pp.501–24.

Marshall, Gail (1998). *Actresses on the Victorian Stage: Feminine Performance and the Galatea Myth.* Cambridge: Cambridge University Press.

Marshall, Gail (2009). *Shakespeare and Victorian Women.* Cambridge: Cambridge University Press.

Marshall, Gail, ed. (2012). *Shakespeare in the Nineteenth Century.* Cambridge: Cambridge University Press.

Martin, John (1997). 'Inventing Sincerity, Refashioning Prudence: The Discovery of the Individual in Renaissance Europe', *The American Historical Review 102:5*, pp.1309–42.

Marx, Karl and Engels, Friedrich (1948/2007). *The Communist Manifesto.* Authorized English translation. New York: International Publishers.

McConachie, Bruce and Hart, F. Elizabeth, eds (2006). *Performance and Cognition: Theatre Studies and the Cognitive Turn.* London and New York: Routledge.

McKenzie, Alan T. (1978). 'The Countenance You Show Me: Reading the Passions in the Eighteenth Century', *Georgia Review 32*, pp.758–73.

McNeill, David (1992/1995). *Hand and Mind: What Gestures Reveal About Thought.* Chicago and London: University of Chicago Press.

McNeill, David (2014a). 'The Emblem as Metaphor', in Seyfeddinipur, Mandana and Gullberg, Marianne, eds, *From Gesture in Conversation to Visible Action as Utterance*, pp.75–94. Amsterdam: John Benjamins.

McNeill, David (2014b). 'Speech-gesture Mimicry in Performance: An Actor→Audience, Author→Actor, Audience→Actor Triangle', *Journal for Cultural Research*. DOI: 10.1080/14797585.2014.920184.

McNeir, Waldo F. (1941). 'Gayton on Elizabethan Acting', *PMLA 56:2*, pp.579–83.

McPherson, Heather (2000a). 'Masculinity, Femininity, and the Tragic Sublime: Reinventing Lady Macbeth', *Studies in Eighteenth-Century Culture 29*, pp.299–333.

McPherson, Heather (2000b). 'Picturing Tragedy: Mrs. Siddons as the Tragic Muse Revisited', *Eighteenth-Century Studies 33:3*, pp.401–30.

Mills, John A. (1985). *Hamlet on Stage: The Great Tradition*. Westport, CT: Greenwood Press.

Mahood, Molly M. (1998). *Playing Bit Parts in Shakespeare*. London: Routledge.

Moore, Carol-Lynne and Yamamoto, Kaoru (1988). *Beyond Words: Movement Observation and Analysis*. London: Routledge.

Morse, Ruth, Cooper, Helen and Holland, Peter, eds (2013). *Medieval Shakespeare: Pasts and Presents*. Cambridge: Cambridge University Press.

Murphy, James J. (1974). *Rhetoric in the Middle Ages: A History of Rhetorical Theory from Augustine to the Renaissance*. Berkeley, LA and London: University of California Press.

Napier, John (1980/1993). *Hands*. Revised by Russell H. Tuttle. Princeton, NJ: Princeton University Press.

Newtson, Darren and Engquist, Gretchen (1976). 'The Perceptual Organization of Ongoing Behavior', *Journal of Experimental Social Psychology 12:5*, pp.436–50.

Nicholson, Watson (1920). *Anthony Aston, Stroller and Adventurer. To which is appended Aston's Brief Supplement to Colley Cibber's Lives; and a Sketch of the Life of Anthony Aston, written by Himself*. South Haven, MI: published by the author.

Nochlin, Linda (1991). *Style and Civilization: Realism*. London: Penguin.

Orgel, Stephen (1988). 'The Authentic Shakespeare', *Representations 21*, pp.1–25.

Palfrey, Simon (2011). *Doing Shakespeare*. Revised edition. London: Methuen.

Palmer, Scott (2013). *Light: Readings in Theatre Practice*. Basingstoke and New York: Palgrave Macmillan.

Parker, John (2004). 'What a Piece of Work Is Man: Shakespearean Drama as Marxian Fetish, the Fetish as Sacramental Sublime', *Journal of Medieval and Early Modern Studies 34:3*, pp.643–68.

Parker, Patricia and Hartman, Geoffrey, eds (1985). *Shakespeare and the Question of Theory*. New York and London: Methuen.

Parr, Anthony, ed. (1995). *Three Renaissance Travel Plays*. Manchester and New York: Manchester University Press.

Parry, Edward Abbott (1891). *Charles Macklin*. London: Kegan Paul, Trench, Trubner and co.

Paster, Gail Kern (1993). *The Body Embarrassed: Drama and the Disciplines of Shame in Early Modern England*. New York: Cornell University Press.

Paster, Gail Kern (2004). *Humoring the Body: Emotions and the Shakespearean Stage*. Chicago and London: University of Chicago Press.

Paulson, Ronald (1971). *Hogarth: His Life, Art and Times.* 2 vols. New Haven, CT: Yale University Press.

Pavis, Patrice (1981). 'Problems of a Semiology of Theatrical Gesture', *Poetics Today 2:3*, pp.65–93.

Pearson, Lu Emily Hess (1957). *Elizabethans at Home.* Stanford, CA: Stanford University Press.

Pettegree, Andrew (2005). *Reformation and the Culture of Persuasion.* Cambridge: Cambridge University Press.

Pitches, Jonathan (2003). *Vsevolod Meyerhold.* London and New York: Routledge.

Pittard, Joseph (1758). *Observations on Mr. Garrick's Acting: In a Letter to the Right Hon. The Earl of Chesterfield.* London: printed for J. Cooke and J. Coote.

Plett, Heinrich F. (2004). *Rhetoric and Renaissance Culture.* Berlin and New York: Walter de Gruyter.

Plett, Heinrich F. (2012). *Enargeia in Classical Antiquity and the Early Modern Age: The Aesthetics of Evidence.* Leiden and Boston: Brill.

Poll, Melissa (2012). 'Robert Lepage's Scenographic Dramaturgy: The Aesthetic Signature at Work', *Body, Space and Technology 11:2.* Accessed at: http://people. brunel.ac.uk/bst/vol1102/ on 16 May 2016.

Pollard, Tanya, ed. (2004). *Shakespeare's Theater: A Sourcebook.* Malden, MA, Oxford and Victoria: Blackwell.

Pollock, Walter Herries (1883). *The Paradox of Acting: Translated with Annotations from Diderot's 'Paradoxe sur le Comédien'. With a preface by Henry Irving.* London: Chatto and Windus.

Pöppel, Ernst (1989). 'The Measurement of Music and the Cerebral Clock: A New Theory', *Leonardo 22:1*, pp.83–9.

Pöppel, Ernst (1997). 'A Hierarchical Model of Temporal Perception', *Trends in Cognitive Sciences 1:2*, pp.56–61.

Pöppel, Ernst (2004). 'Lost in Time: A Historical Frame, Elementary Processing Units and the 3-second Window', *Acta Neurobiologiae Experimentalis 64*, pp.295–301.

Potter, Nicole, ed. (2002). *Movement for Actors.* New York: Allworth Press.

Potter, Lois (2002). *Shakespeare in Performance: Othello.* Manchester and New York: Manchester University Press.

Pratt, Kathryn (2007). 'Thomas Sheridan, Sarah Siddons, and the Eloquence of Theatrical Melancholia in Romantic Culture', *South Atlantic Review 72:2*, pp.46–69.

Pullen, Kirsten (2005). *Actresses and Whores on Stage and in Society.* Cambridge: Cambridge University Press.

Quintilian (1920). *Insititutio Oratoria.* Accessed at: www.loebclassics.com on 16 May 2016.

Ramage, Edwin R. (1963). '*Urbanitas*: Cicero and Quintilian, a Contrast in Attitudes', *The American Journal of Philology 84:4*, pp.390–414.

Richards, Jennifer (2001). 'Assumed Simplicity and the Critique of Nobility: Or, How Castiglione Read Cicero', *Renaissance Quarterly 54:2*, pp.460–86.

Ritchie, Fiona and Sabor, Peter, eds (2012). *Shakespeare in the Eighteenth Century*. Cambridge: Cambridge University Press.

Roach, Joseph R. (1982). 'Garrick, the Ghost and the Machine', *Theatre Journal 34:4*, pp.431–40.

Roach, Joseph R. (1985). *The Player's Passion: Studies in the Science of Acting*. Ann Arbor, MI: The University of Michigan Press.

Roach, Joseph R. (2007). *It*. Ann Arbor, MI: University of Michigan Press.

Roodenburg, Herman (1991). 'The "Hand of Friendship": Shaking Hands and Other Gestures in the Dutch Republic', in Bremmer, Jan and Roodenburg, Herman, eds, *A Cultural History of Gesture: From Antiquity to the Present Day*, pp.152–89. Cambridge: Polity Press.

Rosenberg, Marvin (1954). 'Elizabethan Actors: Men or Marionettes?', *PMLA 69:4*, pp.915–27.

Rubin, Edward L. (2015). *Soul, Self and Society: The New Morality & The Modern State*. Oxford: Oxford University Press.

Rubin, John M. and Richards, W.A. (1985). 'Boundaries of Visual Motion'. *MIT (CSAIL) Report, AI Memo 835*. Accessed at: ftp://publications.ai.mit.edu/ai-publi cations/pdf/AIM-835.pdf on 16 May 2016.

Ryrie, Alec (2013). *Being Protestant in Reformation Britain*. Oxford: Oxford University Press.

Scheflen, Albert E. (1974). *How Behavior Means*. New York: Anchor Books.

Schleidt, Margret (1988). 'A Universal Time Constant Operating in Human Short-term Behaviour Repetitions', *Ethology 77:1*, pp.67–75.

Schleidt, Margret and Kien, Jenny (1997). 'Segmentation in Behavior and What it Can Tell Us About Brain Function', *Human Nature 8:1*, pp.77–111.

Schmitt, Jean-Claude (1991). 'The Rationale of Gestures in the West: Third to Nineteenth Centuries', in Bremmer, Jan and Roodenburg, Herman, eds, *A Cultural History of Gesture: From Antiquity to the Present Day*, pp.59–70. Cambridge: Polity Press.

Schoch, Richard W. (2006). *Shakespeare's Victorian Stage: Performing History in the Theatre of Charles Kean*. Cambridge: Cambridge University Press.

Schofield, Mary Anne and Macheski, Cecilia, eds (1991). *Curtain Calls: British and American Women and the Theater 1660–1820*. Athens: Ohio University Press.

Scott, Clement (1900). *Some Notable Hamlets of the Present Time*. London: Greening & Co.

Scribner, Bob (1989). 'Popular Piety and Modes of Visual Perception in Late-Medieval and Reformation Germany', *The Journal of Religious History 15:4*, pp.448–69.

Sechelski, Denise S. (1996). 'Garrick's Body and the Labor of Art in Eighteenth-Century Theater', *Eighteenth-Century Studies 29:4*, pp.369–89.

Sennett, Richard (1977). *The Fall of Public Man*. London: Faber and Faber.

Shaughnessy, Robert (ed.) (2000). *Shakespeare in Performance: Contemporary Critical Essays*. Basingstoke and London: Macmillan.

Shaw, Teresa M. (1998). '*Askesis* and the Appearance of Holiness', *Journal of Early Christian Studies 6:3*, pp.485–99.

Shuger, Debora (1999). 'The "I" of the Beholder: Renaissance Mirrors and the Reflexive Mind', in Fumerton, Patricia, and Hunt, Simon, eds, *Renaissance Culture and the Everyday*, pp.21–41. Philadelphia: University of Pennsylvania Press.

Siddons, Henry (1807/1822). *Practical Illustrations of Rhetorical Gesture and Action; Adapted to the English Drama; from a work on the subject by M. Engel, Member of the Royal Academy of Berlin*. London: Sheerwood, Neely and Jones.

Sonkowsky, Robert P. (1959). 'An Aspect of Delivery in Ancient Rhetorical Theory', *Transactions and Proceedings of the American Philological Association 90*, pp.256–74.

Spicer, Joaneath (1991). 'The Renaissance Elbow', in Bremmer Jan, and Roodenburg, Herman, eds, *A Cultural History of Gesture: From Antiquity to the Present Day*, pp.84–128. Cambridge: Polity Press.

Stallybrass, Peter and White, Allon (1986). *The Politics and Poetics of Transgression*. London: Methuen.

Stanislavski, Constantin (1936/1989). *An Actor Prepares*. Translated by Elizabeth Reynolds Hapgood. New York: Routledge/Theatre Arts Books.

Stanislavski, Constantin (1956). *My Life in Art*. Translated by J.J. Robbins. New York: Meridian Books.

Stern, Tiffany (2004). *Making Shakespeare: From Stage to Page*. London: Routledge.

Stern, Tiffany (2009). *Documents of Performance in Early Modern England*. Cambridge: Cambridge University Press.

Stone, George Winchester Jr. and Kahrl, George M. (1979). *David Garrick: A Critical Biography*. Carbondale: Southern Illinois University Press.

Styan, J.L. (1967). *Shakespeare's Stagecraft*. Cambridge: Cambridge University Press.

Sullivan, Frances A. (1968). 'Tendere Manus: Gestures in the *Aeneid*', *The Classical Journal 63:8*, pp.358–62.

Swift, Daniel (2013). *Shakespeare's Common Prayers: The Book of Common Prayer and the Elizabethan Age*. Oxford: Oxford University Press.

Taylor, George (1989). *Players and Performances in the Victorian Theatre*. Manchester: Manchester University Press.

Thomas, Keith (2009). *The Ends of Life: Roads to Fulfilment in Early Modern England*. Oxford: Oxford University Press.

Thomson, Peter (1992). *Shakespeare's Theatre*. London: Routledge.

Thomson, Peter (2000). *On Actors and Acting*. Exeter: University of Exeter Press.

Tribble, Evelyn B. (2011). *Cognition in the Globe: Attention and Memory in Shakespeare's Theatre*. Basingstoke and New York: Palgrave Macmillan.

Tunstall, Darren (2012). 'Shakespeare and the Lecoq Tradition', *Shakespeare Bulletin 30:4*, pp.469–84.

Urkowitz, Steven (1986). '"I am not made of stone": Theatrical Revision of Gesture in Shakespeare's Plays', *Renaissance and Reformation 22:1*, pp.79–93.

Van Lennep, William, ed. (1942). *The Reminiscences of Sarah Kemble Siddons*. Cambridge: Widener Library.

Vickers, Brian (1988). *In Defence of Rhetoric*. Oxford: Clarendon Press.

Walker, John (1781). *Elements of Elocution*. 2 vols. London.

Walker, John (1789). *The Academic Speaker*. Dublin.

Ward, Alfred C., ed. (1945). *Specimens of English Dramatic Criticism XVII–XX Centuries*. London: Oxford University Press.

Watt-Smith, Tiffany (2014). *On Flinching: Theatricality and Scientific Looking from Darwin to Shell-Shock*. Oxford: Oxford University Press.

Webster, John (2007). *The Works of John Webster Volume Three*. Edited by David Gunby, David Carnegie and Macdonald P. Jackson. Cambridge: Cambridge University Press.

Wells, Stanley, ed. (1998). *Shakespeare Survey Volume 51: Shakespeare in the Eighteenth Century*. Cambridge: Cambridge University Press.

West, E.J. (1955). 'Irving in Shakespeare: Interpretation or Creation?', *Shakespeare Quarterly 6:4*, pp.415–22.

West, Shearer (1991). *The Image of the Actor: Verbal and Visual Representation in the Age of Garrick and Kemble*. New York: St. Martin's Press.

Wickham, Glynne, Berry, Herbert and Ingram, William, eds (2000). *English Professional Theatre, 1530–1660*. Cambridge: Cambridge University Press.

Wilkes, Thomas (1759). *A General View of the Stage*. London: J. Coote.

Wilson, Richard (2005). 'Dyed in Mummy: Othello and the Mulberries', in Rupp, Susanne and Dörring, Tobias, eds, *Performances of the Sacred in Late Medieval and Early Modern England*, pp.135–54. Amsterdam: Rodopi.

Wind, Edgar (1968). *Pagan Mysteries in the Renaissance*. New York: W.W. Norton.

Wollock, Jeffrey (1996). 'John Bulwer's (1606–1656) Place in the History of the Deaf', *Historiographia Linguistica 23*, pp.1–46.

Wollock, Jeffrey (2001). 'John Bulwer (1606–1656) and the Significance of Gesture in 17th Century Theories of Language and Cognition', *Gesture 2:2*, pp.227–58.

Wollock, Jeffrey (2010). 'John Bulwer and the Quest for a Universal Language', *Historiographia Linguistica 38:1–2*, pp.37–84.

Woo, Celestine (2007). 'Sarah Siddons's Performances as Hamlet: Breaching the Breeches Part', *European Romantic Review 18:5*, pp.573–95.

Woo, Celestine (2008). *Studies in Shakespeare Volume 16: Romantic Actors and Bardolatry: Performing Shakespeare from Garrick to Kean*. New York: Peter Lang.

Woods, Leigh (1984). *Garrick Claims the Stage: Acting as Social Emblem in Eighteenth-Century England*. Westport, CT and London: Greenwood Press.

Wright, Thomas (1601/1986). *The Passions of the Mind in General*. Edited by William Webster Newbold. New York and London: Garland.

Zeami, Motokiyo (1984). *On the Art of the Nō Drama*. Translated by J. Thomas Rimer and Yamazaki Masakazu. Princeton, NJ: Princeton University Press.

Index

184   *Index*

.

Printed in Great Britain
by Amazon

48089297R00115